T. Morgan Owen

A History of England and Wales

From the Roman to the Norman Conquest

T. Morgan Owen

A History of England and Wales
From the Roman to the Norman Conquest

ISBN/EAN: 9783337007133

Printed in Europe, USA, Canada, Australia, Japan

Cover: Foto ©ninafisch / pixelio.de

More available books at **www.hansebooks.com**

A FEW WORDS TO THE READER.

FIRST EDITION.

THE reader should bear in mind that the History of England and Wales from the Roman to the Norman Conquest is a mere record of the doings or sayings of a few individuals—such as Cæsar, Caradog, Boadicea, Agricola, in the time of the Roman occupation; of Augustine, Penda, Offa, before England became a kingdom; and afterwards, of Alfred, Hastings, Ethelfleda, Edmund the Ironside, Edric, Canute, Godwin, Griffith the Pendragon, William of Normandy, and Harold the King. These men and women were the human *whirlwinds* of their respective times, for they acted upon their contemporaries with the same concentrated force and intensity that the atmospheric whirlwinds influence the objects with which they come in contact. And yet they were but the representatives of the *people:* for we read that when Boadicea fought, she fought *"as one of the people;"*[1] *"every man"*[2] took an interest in the doings of Edmund the Ironside; and, it was the *humblest*[3] as well as the highest of the people who fought with Harold at Hastings. It should also be borne in mind that, in an age of *action*, it was

---

[1] The Annals of Tacitus.   [2] *Saxon Chronicle*, 1016.
[3] Described as "pueros" in the Bayeux Tapestry.

eloquence that swayed the masses; thus, before the Battle of the Grampians, the Caledonian chief and Agricola incited their forces with speeches; and so did Harold and William before the Battle of Hastings, and with such effect that the forces of the latter rushed upon the Saxons and left him speaking to himself![1] It will thus be seen that a Record of the words and doings of the *heads* of the people is a continuative Biography of the *people* themselves.

Before the Conquest the chroniclers were sparing of their words: the *Saxon Chronicle* records the last years of the reign of Alfred the Great, thus—"899. 900." And the Welsh chronicler described a battle that led to a change of rulers in North Wales, thus—"Gwaith Carno." Happily, the events preceding the Norman Conquest are fully described by contemporary and other writers; but here another difficulty arises, namely, to hold the balance between rival authorities, and to explain why the Saxon writer should call a man "*blessed*," and the Norman writer should characterize the same man[2] a "*dog*."

I have particularised the course of the Severn, as it is the historic river of Great Britain. I have given an ethnographical description of the Danes at Buttington, because Hastings was the forerunner of Rollo and Canute, and was the guiding principle of the spirit of unrest that menaced the thrones of England and France

---

[1] Henry of Huntingdon.   [2] Godwin, the earl.

towards the end of the ninth century. I have given a topographical description of one of Ethelfleda's exploits, and one of King Griffith's, because of the influence they had over the affairs of England and Wales. And I have given a full account of the Battle of Hastings, in order to show that the descendants of the contending forces may feel proud of such ancestors. I have also tried to show that the ancestors of the Welsh were not " robbers and assassins."[1]

I trust that the genealogical tables, which may aptly be termed the maps of history, will prove useful.

In conclusion, it gives me pleasure to acknowledge the benefits I have derived from the Lectures of Professors Barlow and Dowden, and from the kind advice of Professor Ingram, of the University of Dublin.

Dr. Lingard.

Bronwylfa, Rhyl,
　St. David's Day, 1882.

SECOND EDITION.

I have to express my thanks for the rapid sale of the first edition of this History, and for the kind and encouraging comments that have been expressed concerning it in the public Press, and in private circles.

The Second Edition differs in a few particulars from the first—as it contains an account of Agricola's Caledonian campaign, and a little additional information concerning Taliesin, Egbert, Ethelwulf, Alfred, Athelstan, Godwin, Welsh affairs, and Baldwin of Flanders. It has also the advantage of a marginal index, a list of leading events, &c.

Bronwylfa, Rhyl,
     1st August, 1882.

CONTENTS.

GENEALOGICAL TABLES.

A HISTORY

OF

ENGLAND AND WALES,

FROM THE

ROMAN TO THE NORMAN CONQUEST.

THE ROMAN CONQUEST.

CHAPTER I.

THE country in which we live, a little more than two thousand years ago, was inhabited by the Britons, or Celts, whose descendants are now called Welsh. About that time the Celts of Britain went over to France to help its people, who were of the same race as themselves, against the Romans under the famous Julius Cæsar. Cæsar, after he had conquered the Gauls of France, made up his mind to defeat the Celts also. So he sailed over to Britain, B.C. 55. The Celts were not afraid of him. And when they saw the Roman ships coming near their country they ran into the sea to meet and fight the Roman soldiers. A storm helped them. Cæsar came a second time into this country, and subdued part of it, B.C. 54. *Cæsar, B.C. 55.*

B.C. 51.

The chief tribes of England and Wales were the Iceni, occupying Norfolk and Suffolk, and the bordering counties: the Brigantes, in the North: the Silures, in South Wales and part of England: the Ordovices, to the north of the Silures: the Trinobantes, whose capital was London, lived in the vicinity of the Thames.

The Roman general Ostorius Scapula defeated the Iceni and the Brigantes. The Ordovices were also *Ostorius Scapula.*

A

overcome. But the Silures, who were naturally fierce,[1] determined to fight to the very last against the invaders of their country. The only Celt of those days whose name is worth remembering was Caradog, king
Caradog. of the Silures. Caradog is generally known by the name of Caractacus. He was a very brave man, and an able soldier and leader of men. He loved his country and his people very dearly, for he was a true prince. He was one of the noblest of patriots, and the most perfect of heroes. He fought against the Romans time after time. His fellow-countrymen fully believed in him, and after defeat they continued faithful to him. At last he determined to fight one great battle, and, if possible, to destroy the Roman soldiers under Ostorius. He took his stand with his brave subjects upon some lofty hills, which he protected with heaps of stones: in his front was a river.[1] Before the battle began Caradog encouraged his men to fight for freedom; and then each man took an oath that he would not shrink in the coming struggle.[2] The Romans crossed the river, rushed up the hills, and pulled down the walls of stones that protected the Britons. So far the Romans were at a disadvantage, for as they came up the hill they were killed by the darts and arrows of the enemy; but when they came to fight hand to hand, they were able to defeat Caradog's forces, as the Romans were protected by armour, while the limbs and breasts of the Britons had no protection from the swords, spears, and javelins of their assailants.[3] Caradog and his men fought long and bravely, but to no purpose; so they dispersed and fled.

---

[1] The Annals of Tacitus, book xii. chap. 33.   [2] Ibid, chap. 34.
[3] Ibid, chap. 35.

The brave King went to the Queen of the Brigantes, who was his mother-in-law. But she was afraid of the Romans, and, wishing to please them, she delivered Caradog in chains to Ostorius. The news of his capture was soon carried throughout the island and the neighbouring countries. His fame as a good general was known in many lands. For nine years he had defied the power of the Romans. Caradog.
A.D. 51.

Caradog was carried to Rome. When he saw that wonderful city, with its large and beautiful buildings, and its riches and greatness, he did not show any surprise or anxiety. Nor did the splendour that surrounded him cause him to forget that he was a king, although he was clothed in skins and coarse cloth. So he held up his head and looked about him in a very quiet and easy manner. The Emperor Claudius summoned the people to see the British captives, and all were eager to see the great Caradog. The Emperor Claudius sat upon one throne, and his fourth wife, the infamous Agrippina, mother of the Emperor Nero, sat upon another throne. But neither their presence nor that of the Roman legions and of thousands upon thousands of people affected Caradog, who neither by looks nor words sought pity.[1] The Emperor was so pleased with his brave appearance and calm dignity that he set him free, together with his wife and brothers. The Roman Senate delivered speeches on the capture of Caradog, and declared that his exposure to the Roman populace was as glorious as the display of any captive prince by any of their generals to the people of Rome.[2]

The capture of Caradog did not discourage the

[1] The Annals of Tacitus, book xii. chap. 36.

[2] Ibid, chap. 38.

Silures. They were enraged[1] because Ostorius had declared that their name ought to be blotted out. Again and again they attacked the Roman soldiers, and at last the Roman general was worn out[1] by his anxieties, and died in the year 51.

The Druids.

The Celts had a religion called Druidism. Their priests were very clever men, and very good speakers. Before a battle they always spoke to the soldiers, and encouraged them to fight well. Because of this the Romans under Suetonius Paulinus, the conqueror of the Moors of Africa, determined to kill the Druids. The Saxons afterwards followed their example, and killed the Welsh preachers and students. And the Danes followed the example of both Roman and Saxon, and killed as many priests as they could find, whether they belonged to the British or Romish Church. The island of Anglesey, then called Mona, was the chief abode of the Druids. So Suetonius Paulinus prepared to attack it with cavalry and infantry. The former swam[2] by the side of their horses, and the latter got across the Menai Straits by means of flat bottomed vessels. They were opposed by the British warriors, and also by their wives and priests. The women, dressed in black, with their hair all loose and with flaming brands in their hands, encouraged the men to fight ; whilst the Druids lifted up their hands to heaven and cursed the foe.[3] The Roman soldiers were terrified at such an extraordinary spectacle, and stood motionless for a time. But, urged on by their general, they rushed forward and overthrew the hapless throng of British men and women. Such as escaped their swords they put on fire

Suetonius Paulinus.

The Conquest of Anglesey. 61.

---

[1] The Annals of Tacitus, book xii. chap. 39.

[2] Ibid, book xiv. chap. 29. [3] Ibid, book xiv. chap. 30.

with their own brands.[1] They also cut down the woods in which the Druids performed their religious rites, and overthrew the altars over which human blood[1] was wont to flow. This took place in the year 61.

While these events were taking place in the west, terrible things were happening in the east. The King of the Iceni, before he died, left part of his kingdom to his daughters and part of it to the Emperor of Rome. He did this to gain the good-will of the Romans. But the latter beat his wife Boadicea, outraged his daugh- ters,[2] reduced his relations to slavery, and deprived the chief men of their estates. Boadicea, accompanied by her daughters, rode among her subjects in her war chariot, and called upon them to arise and drive the cruel and wicked Romans out of the land. She was obeyed, as the people burned to avenge the slaughter of their male relatives and the outrage of their female ones; they bore in mind that their children had been taken from them, and that the invaders held their lands. The Iceni were joined by their neighbours the Trinobantes.

Boadicea's Victory, 61.

The combined forces surrounded the Roman colony at Colchester,[3] which was unprotected. The town, with its temple dedicated to the Emperor Claudius, and its inhabitants, were destroyed. A Roman legion, except some cavalry, was utterly routed. London and St. Albans were laid waste. Suetonius retreated before the victorious Britons until he came upon a favourable position of defence, which was approached by a narrow defile. A plain was in his front, and a forest behind him.

---

[1] The Annals of Tacitus, book xiv. chap. 30.
[2] Ibid, book xiv. chap. 31. [3] The Romans called it **Camalodunum.**

Boadicea declared to her excited listeners that "as *one of the people* I avenge lost freedom, my scourged body, the outraged chastity of my daughters. Heaven is on the side of a righteous vengeance." Her exhortations were joyfully received. In the battle that followed the Britons were impeded by the waggons in which their wives had come to see the destruction of the Romans. The Britons fought well. Boadicea, with her long yellow hair floating in the breeze, encouraged her followers; but all in vain. Discipline prevailed over patriotism. This battle ranks among the decisive ones of the world. The victorious Romans revenged the seventy thousand killed by the British, by the indiscriminate slaughter of eighty thousand native men, women, and children.[1] Boadicea despaired of her country, and poisoned herself. After this battle the hostile tribes were ravaged with fire and sword. This unpardonable severity led to the recall of Suetonius.

Death of Boadicea, 61.

After Seutonius several Roman generals came to Britain, but it is not necessary to mention even their names. The best of them was Agricola. He was the Roman lieutenant of Britain from 78 to 85. As well as being very brave and a good general, he was a kind and a far-seeing man. He was anxious to civilize the Celts, and to make Britain a province of the Roman empire. Unlike Ostorius and Seutonius, he did not wish to kill its inhabitants; but he was determined to master them, and also to do all he could to bring them into the ways of the Romans.

Agricola, 78 to 85.

Fortunately for posterity Agricola's son-in-law was the famous Roman historian Tacitus. They were fond

[1] The Annals of Tacitus, book xiv. chap. 37.

and proud of each other; and Tacitus wrote an account
of the doings of Agricola in Britain and elsewhere.
From this account we learn that in his days the
inhabitants of Britain were of three kinds: the Caledonians in Scotland, with red hair and large limbs, British
of German descent: the Silures, with dark complexion Races.
and curly hair, probably a colony from Spain: the rest
of the people Tacitus thought were of the same race
as the Gauls, as they had the same religion, the same
language, and the same character of boldness to stir
up danger and want of determination to face it when
present.[1] He states that some of the tribes fought on
foot and others in chariots; and that, instead of being
under the rule of kings as formerly, they were split
up into parties among their chiefs, who would not join
together against the common enemy. The climate was
pleasant and the soil fertile.

It was in the summer of 78 that Agricola landed in
Britain. At that time the Roman soldiers, thinking
there would be no more expeditions that year, were
anticipating a winter of enjoyment and ease; while
the natives were making preparations to take advantage of their inactivity, and of the inclemency and
darkness of the season. Not long before his arrival, The
the Ordovices, who inhabited North Wales, had sur- Ordovices,
prised a troop of cavalry which was stationed upon 78.
the border of their territories, and had put almost
every man of it to the sword. Agricola determined
to commence active operations against the foe without
undue delay. Notwithstanding the fact that the winter
season was fast approaching, and that the soldiers were
scattered throughout the Roman portion of the country,

[1] The Life of Agricola, by Tacitus, chap. 12.

the General assembled together certain veterans[1] from the legions and a small body of auxiliaries; and, placing himself at their head, he boldly advanced into the territories of the victorious Celts. The latter declined to meet the Romans in the plain; thereupon Agricola divided his forces into two bodies. He led the advanced party in person, in order to excite the confidence and to arouse the enthusiasm of his followers. The engagement that ensued was a most sanguinary one, as the Ordovices, scorning to yield, were almost extirpated by the well-armed and well-disciplined invaders. Agricola was resolved to follow up this success by an invasion of Anglesey. Its people expected to see the Romans cross the Menai Strait by means of a fleet; they were therefore astonished and affrighted when they saw the auxiliaries plunge into the sea[2] upon horseback, and manage their horses and arms whilst swimming across the channel. The islanders at once sued for peace, and surrendered their land to Agricola.

Submission of Anglesey, 78.

In order to remove the causes of war, Agricola now began to remove abuses which existed in his own household and throughout the Roman provinces of Britain. Neither slaves nor freedmen were allowed to transact public business. He promoted the best men, and would not suffer himself to be influenced by private favour or the recommendation of his captains. He insisted upon knowing everything that went on,

The removal of abuses.

---

[1] These were a distinct body of soldiers termed Vexilla, who served under a flag of their own (Vexillum). They were free from the military oath and regular service, but they were called upon to assist the regular army in case of need. Their customary duty was to guard the frontiers, or to occupy forts in recently conquered districts.

[2] The Life of Agricola, by Tacitus, chap. 18; they were probably Batavians; Tacitus mentions them in his History, book iv., chap. 12.

but some things he allowed to pass by unnoticed. He was able to pardon small faults, and to be severe with those who committed grave ones; yet he would not always punish, as repentance satisfied him. With true greatness of mind he tried to excite the emulation of all, and to raise their characters and dispositions, by rewarding the good and the just, rather than by punishing offenders.

Before the time of Agricola the taxes in Britain were collected by a Procurator, who ground down the tribes, and compelled them to pay private exactions as well as public taxes. The people were obliged to buy their own corn out of their own granaries from the Romans, and afterwards to sell it to their conquerors at a fixed price; and they were also obliged to carry corn and to drive cattle to distant places, instead of to the nearest quarters of the Romans. Agricola did away with these cruel and vexatious iniquities.

He encouraged learning, and was much pleased *Encouragement of the Celts.* with the natural genius of the Celts. Before his arrival the Celts did not wear much clothing, nor did they cultivate much land. They hunted and fished, and enjoyed themselves greatly. They loved their native tongue and their own mode of living in huts; but, believing in the justice and humanity of Agricola, they did what he desired them to do. Some of them forgot their own habits, and tried to dress, to speak, and to live like the Romans. They were encouraged to build temples, baths, and houses; and after awhile, from a desire to be polite, they learnt the vices[1] of their conquerors, and soon became unfit for warfare, and were obliged to depend upon the Romans for protection

[1] The Life of Agricola, by Tacitus, chap. 21.

Ireland.

Agricola built a chain of forts[1] between the Firths of Forth and Clyde, and a dyke from the river Tyne to the Solway Firth. He thought to conquer Ireland, which he viewed from the coasts of Galloway: and, as Cæsar was helped by the customary traitor, so a petty Irish king fled to Agricola to urge him to invade his native land.

Agricola kept the Irish prince in his company for some time under the plea of friendship; but he only wished to make use of him, should he invade his country. He was of the opinion that one legion of soldiers and a few auxiliaries would be sufficient to conquer and to hold Ireland; and he was the more inclined to invade it, as its annexation to the Roman Empire would overawe the Britons, as they would then be surrounded by the arms of the Romans, and liberty would be banished from their sight.[2]

The Caledonians.

Agricola's attention was drawn from Ireland by the Caledonians, whom he attacked by land and sea. He had a most difficult task to perform, as the Caledonians were a brave and determined people. They were alarmed at the sight of the Roman vessels, lest, being vanquished upon land, their escape by sea would be cut off. They did not, however, give way to despair. In the year 83, Agricola advanced beyond the Firth of Forth. The Caledonians did not wait to be attacked, but, advancing against the outposts[3] of the Romans, they endeavoured to capture them. Their boldness intimidated some of the invaders, who, upon the pretext of prudence, desired to retreat to the south of the

---

[1] The Life of Agricola, by Tacitus, chap. 23.   [2] Ibid, chap. 24.

[3] These were situated in the vicinity of the Firth of Tay. The Life of Agricola, by Tacitus, chap. 22.

Firth of Forth, lest they should be overwhelmed by the foe. Their fears did not affect the Roman general, who arranged his forces into three divisions, so as not to be surrounded, as he had heard that the enemy were about to attack him in several bodies. The Caledonians became acquainted with Agricola's arrangements. They changed their plans at once, and uniting their forces, they swept down in the dead of night upon the ninth legion, which was the weakest Roman division. For a time success attended this bold and well concentrated attack. The Romans were asleep when the Caledonians, having slaughtered their sentinels and burst through their intrenchments, appeared within their camp. But the unequal combat was not of long duration. Agricola was informed by his scouts of the onslaught of the enemy: he gave orders for the swiftest of his horse and foot to attack them in the rear. This was done. At the break of day the whole Roman army raised a shout, and their standards glittered in the rays of the rising sun. The Caledonians now found themselves between two forces, and, despairing of success, betook themselves to the shelter of the woods and marshes.[1] This engagement inspirited the Romans and the Caledonians; the former were wishful to penetrate into the heart[2] of Caledonia without delay, while the latter, attributing their defeat to chance and the generalship of Agricola, began to arm their youth, to send their wives and children to places of security, and to confirm a general confederacy of their several clans by solemn assemblies and sacrifices.[2] During the summer of 84, Agricola, having sent forward his fleet to ravage

Note attack upon the Roman Camp, 83.

[1] The Life of Agricola, by Tacitus, chap. 26.   [2] Chap. 27.

Agricola's
advance
against
the foe, 84. the sea-shore, advanced against the foe. In his ranks were the bravest of the Celts, who had been trained with the Roman legions, and whose fidelity had been well tried. At the foot of the Grampians they beheld the combined forces of the Caledonians. There were to be seen, under the leadership of the eloquent and heroic Galgacus, an army of 30,000 men, consisting of the tender youth and the hale and vigorous man.

The
Speech of
Galgacus. Galgacus harangued[1] his forces in forcible and telling terms, assuring them that their united efforts on that day would secure " the beginning of liberty throughout Britain." Speaking of the Romans, he remarked —"These plunderers of the world, when the lands have yielded all things to their ravages, even rifle the ocean. They are stimulated by avarice, if their enemies are rich; by ambition, if they are poor. Neither the east nor west has satisfied them : they alone, of all people, behold riches and poverty with equal greed. To ravage, to slaughter, to usurp under false titles, they call empire; and where they make a desert, they call it peace. Nature has ordained that our children and relatives should be the dearest of all things to us. These are torn away by levies to serve in foreign lands. Our wives and sisters, if they should escape the violation of hostile force, are polluted under the names of friendship and hospitality. Our lands and possessions are consumed in tributes; our grain in contributions. Even our bodies are worn out amidst stripes and insults, whilst clearing woods and draining marshes. The wretches born to slavery are bought

---

[1] How Tacitus became acquainted with Galgacus's speech is a mystery, unless it was translated to him by a renegade Caledonian : chaps. 30, 31, 32.

once, and afterwards fed by their masters; Britain every day buys and every day feeds her own servitude." He then alluded to the success of Boadicea, and observed—" Shall not we, untouched, unconquered, and fighting, not for the acquisition but the retention of liberty, show at the very first onset what men Caledonia has reserved for her defence." In conclusion, he referred to the fact that the Roman army was made up of various nations, such as the Britons, Gauls, and Germans, who would desert them, and said —"Here is a leader, here an army; there tributes, mines, and the series of punishments meted out to slaves. This field must determine whether we must eternally endure such things, or instantly revenge them. Forward, then, to battle!, and think of your ancestors and your successors."[1] This address was received with joy by his listeners, who welcomed it with songs, yells, and shouts.

Agricola also addressed his men. He then formed them in battle array: 8,000 auxiliaries on foot occupied the van, with 3,000 horsemen spread out on either side of them: behind these were the three legions, who occupied the space in front of their intrenchments. The Caledonians had been arranged for show and intimidation: their first line stood upon the plain, and the other lines rose one above another along the whole extent of a steep mountain ridge: their chariots and horsemen occupied the space in front of the infantry. Agricola was afraid that the foe would attack him in front and on either side—he therefore extended his

The Battle of the Grampians, 84.

---

[1] This speech is recorded as an interesting evidence of British eloquence, and also as descriptive of the ways of the Roman conquerors, and the fate of their captives.

The Battle of the Grampians, 84. ranks. He dismissed his horse and took his stand on foot[1] before the colours. At first the fight was carried on from a distance: the natives steadily and cleverly avoided or struck down the darts and arrows of the Romans, while they showered upon them a torrent of their own. To bring matters to a climax Agricola ordered the Batavian and other auxiliaries to close upon the Caledonians. They did so, and, by means of their short swords and their shields they were able to overcome their opponents, who were unable to contend against them with any degree of success, as their long swords, which were not sharp pointed, were almost useless at close quarters, while their short targets did not afford the same protection as the bossed shields of the Romans; consequently, the auxiliaries were able to burst through the first line of the Britons, who retreated from the plain to their companions upon the hill side, and were followed by their victors. While the infantry were thus engaged, the cavalry of the Romans were attacked by the British chariots: the former fled precipitately, and were pursued by the charioteers, who suddenly found themselves in the midst of the Roman auxiliaries who were not engaged in the pursuit of the Caledonians. At first their appearance caused some consternation amongst their opponents. The extended ranks of the Romans were now ordered to close: when this order was obeyed the British charioteers were unable to wheel about and career; moreover, as they were inconvenienced by the unevenness of the ground, they were easily overcome in the throng, and chariots without drivers and riderless

---

[1] His example was followed by Harold at Senlac, and by Warwick at Towton and Barnet.

horses rushed through the lines. But the battle was The Battle of the Grampians, 84. not over. The Caledonians, who had up to now remained spectators of the fight, descended from the hill with the intention of attacking the Romans in their rear. Against these fresh forces Agricola despatched four squadrons of horse. The latter were successful; after they had driven back the foe, they were ordered to fall upon their rear. They did so. Then ensued consternation and flight on the part of the Caledonians. Some of the fugitives rallied; but, wherever they did so, Agricola was present with infantry and cavalry to surround and penetrate their forces. The victory was complete. Some of the Caledonians in despair set fire to their dwellings, while others put their wives and children to death. Desolation and conflagration distinguished the day after the battle. Hostages were delivered to Agricola, who slowly retired with both cavalry and infantry; whilst his navy, starting from the Firth of Forth, sailed round the northern part of Great Britain, and ultimately came to anchor in the harbour from which it had set out; and thus discovered Britain to be an island.

Agricola not only conquered but Romanized the greater part of Britain, and left it in peace and safety to his successor.[1]

After the time of Agricola the Romans repaired or

[1] Agricola was infamously treated by Domitian, who was jealous of his military renown. On his return from Britain, he was received by him at night, and in silence, and then suffered to mingle midst the throng of slaves who surrounded the tyrant. Agricola died at the age of 54, and Domitian is suspected of having poisoned him. In his last chapters upon the life of his father-in-law, Tacitus has written some of the most pathetic and eloquent passages recorded in ancient or modern chronicles; and with him we fully believe that, whatever we have loved in Agricola, whatever we have admired, remains and will continue to remain in the minds of men, through the pages of history, to an eternity of years.

re-built his northern fortifications and dyke, in order to keep off the Picts, the descendants of the Caledonians, and the Scots of Ireland, who now occupied Scotland.

400. And about the year 400 the Romans appointed an officer, who was called "Count of the Saxon Shore," to look after the east coast, so as to stop the people who were called Saxons, and from whom the people of England are descended, landing in the country.

Departure of the Romans, 418. After a time the Romans were obliged to return to their own country, to defend its capital, and the Celts were forced to fight their own battles, 418. They were very sorry to see the Romans going away. And as they could not fight without help against their foes, they asked the Saxons, Jutes, and Angles to help them.

Hengist and Horsa, 449. They came, led by Hengist and Horsa, 449. After a time they turned against the Celts, whom they called Welsh, and took a large part of the country from them. The Welsh held a small part of Scotland; Wales; and that part of England now called Cumberland, Westmoreland, Lancashire, Devon, and Cornwall; and parts of the bordering counties. The rest of the country the Saxons divided amongst themselves into eight parts :— Kent, Mercia, Sussex, Wessex, Essex, East Anglia, Deria, Bernicia. Wessex was on the south; East Anglia on the east; Deria and Bernicia in the north-east; Mercia, was in the middle of the country, and along the side of Wales. The fighting men of the Welsh and many of the Welsh families left those parts of their country that the Saxons had conquered, and went to live with their fellow-countrymen who were in the unconquered parts. But a great many of them gave in to the Saxons, and lived among them. Some of these Welsh people became the servants of the Saxons. Others

BRITAIN

ABOUT THE YEAR 350 A.D.

English Miles

Roman Territories ... Purple-Green
Scots .... Green
Picts .... Light Red

PICTS

CALEDONIA
(Celtic origin)

Tools of the
Caupania 84 A.D.

Firth or Tay

Agricola's Forts 80 A.D.

Firth or Forth

VALENTIA

Wall of Hadrian

S U T L O N S

Moorfoot

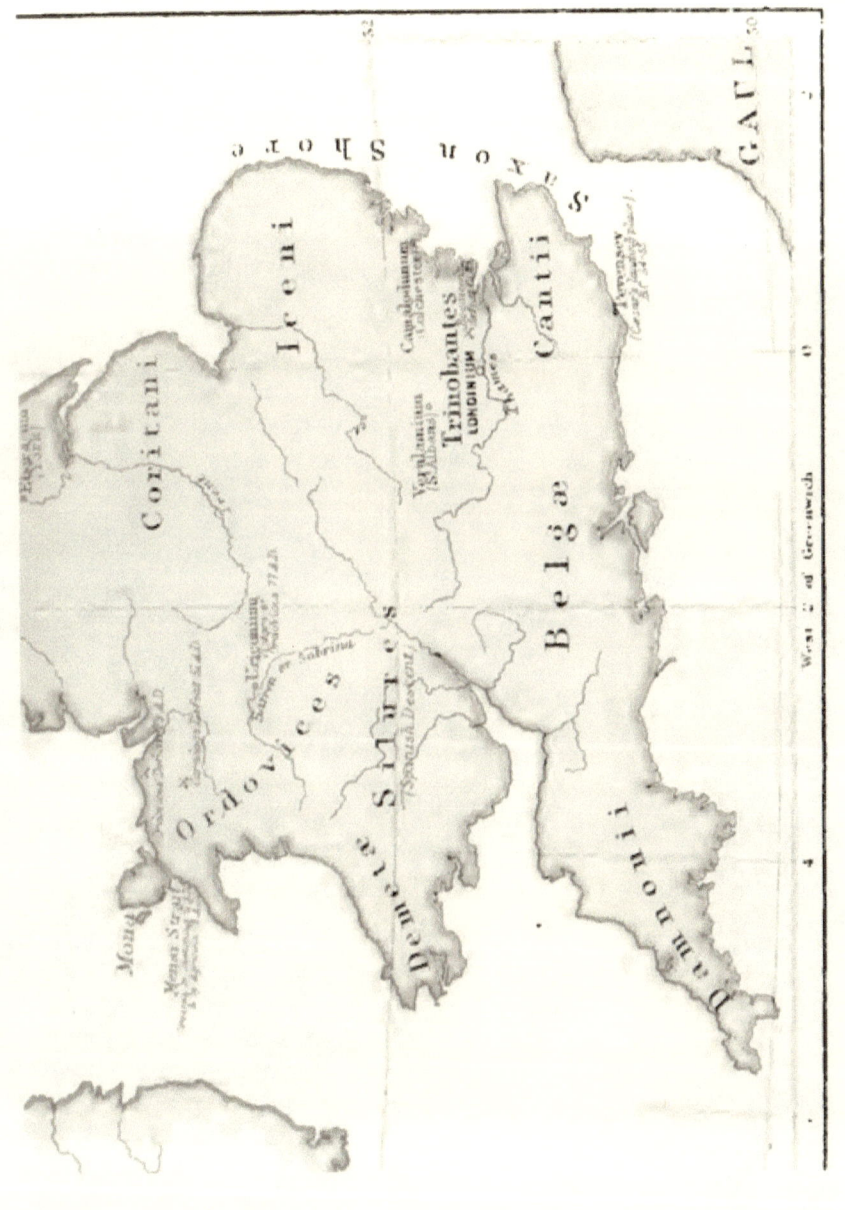

GAUL

Saxon Shore

Iceni

Coritani

Cantii

Belgæ

Trinobantes

Ordovices

Demetæ Silures

Damnonii

Mona

West 3 of Greenwich

became their wives or husbands. Of the eight divisions of the country under the Saxons, for a very long time the largest and most important was Mercia.

LEADING EVENTS.

THE HOUSE OF OFFA.

Pybba : 10th in descent from Woden.

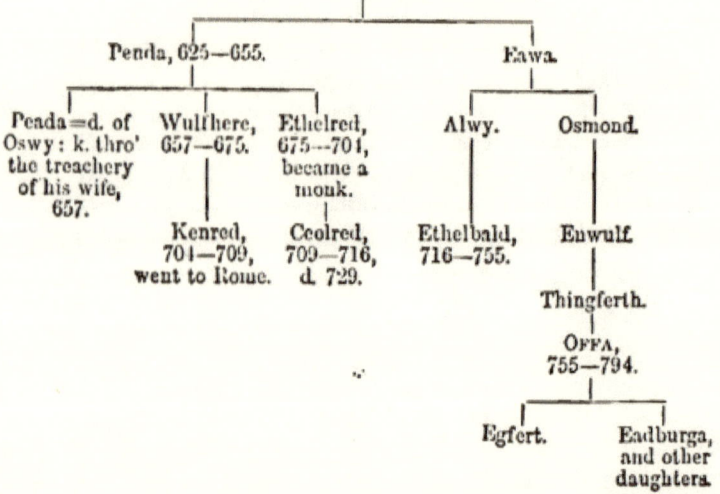

Penda, 625—655.   Eawa.

Penda=d. of   Wulfhere,   Ethelred,   Alwy.   Osmond.
Oswy : k. thro' 657—675.   675—701,
the treachery   became a
of his wife,   monk.
657.
                Kenred,   Ceolred,   Ethelbald,   Enwulf.
                704—709,   709—716,   716—755.
             went to Rome.   d. 729.   Thingferth.

                                                            OFFA,
                                                          755—794.

                                            Egfert.   Eadburga,
                                                          and other
                                                          daughters.

CHAPTER II.

FROM THE MASSACRE AT BANGOR TO THE OVERTHROW OF THE KINGDOM OF MERCIA.

FIERCE, frequent, and bloody were the contests that Wales and Mercia. took place between the Celt and the Saxon, ere the latter had driven the warriors of the former beyond the banks of the Severn, into the narrow vales and among the lofty mountains of Cambria; and as equally fierce, frequent, and bloody were the contests that afterwards took place between the contending powers; and yet, strange as it may seem, the kings of Wales and the kings of Mercia were often stedfast allies and firm friends. Oft did they unite their forces against the foreign foe or the encroaching neighbour. The Welsh remembered that the Mercians had again and again waged war against those who had lifted up the armed hand against the unarmed and defenceless; that Ethelfrid, the pagan king of Northumbria, had at one The Massacre of Welsh Students, 603. fell and foul stroke put an end to the seminary of learning, industry, and piety, with its ancient records, which existed at Bangor Is Coed, and had unjustifiably massacred 1,200 men,[1] whose chief fault was intense love of country, and a still more intense love for the faith and religious customs of their race.

Ethelfrid is described[2] as a most worthy king, and

---

[1] Bede, *Eccl. Hist.*, book ii, c. 2, 603; *Saxon Chronicle*, 607, says 200.
[2] Bede.

The
Massacre
of Welsh
Students,
603.

ambitious of glory. It is stated that he ravaged the Welsh more than all the great men of the English. He is also compared to Saul, king of Israel. This king met the Welsh in battle array at Chester. To the sympathetic and humane no sight could have been more affecting than that which met the eye of the Northumbrian monarch before he gave the word to attack the foe, for he was opposed by a twofold army. The one part was composed of men of war, the other of men of prayer. No incidents in British history is more thrilling than that in connection with the battle which took place in the vicinity of the City of Legions in the year 603. We are informed that the monastery of Bangor, the home of these men of prayer, was divided into seven parts, with a ruler over each, and that some of these parts contained no less than three hundred men who lived by the labours of their hands. They knew that the Northumbrians were approaching, and for three days they fasted, and on the fourth day they went forth and took their stand by their brothers, the soldiers of Wales. On their knees they prayed for their country and their religion. Whilst thus employed, Ethelfrid issued the order to fall upon them. The order was obeyed, and twelve hundred monks gave evidence of their patriotism and their faith with their blood. Bangor was soon deserted. Henceforth the small island of Bardsey, off the Carnarvonshire coast, gave shelter to the religious men of Wales; whilst the ruins of Bangor testified to succeeding ages[1] its once almost incredible prosperity.

Cadwall-
awn.

Vengeance swift and terrible overtook the sacrilegious host of Northumbria. Cadwallawn, the last Celt save

_____
[1] William of Malmesbury.

one who bore the title of King of Britain,[1] formed an
alliance with the redoubtable Penda of Mercia. They   Penda.
united their forces and advanced into Northumbria.
It is stated that, following the terrible example of
Ethelfrid, they harassed the country with fire and
sword, and spared neither age or sex. They killed the
Bretwalda Edwin, and his sons Osfrid and Eanfrid.   Edwin.
Osric, Edwin's nephew, besieged Cadwallawn in a   Osfrid. Eanfrid.
strong town. The Welsh monarch sallied out, and,   Osric.
taking Osric by surprise, destroyed him and his army.
Eanfrid, son of Ethelfrid, met with the same fate,   Eanfrid.
"through the rightful vengeance of Heaven."[2] And
the Welsh King reigned over the North of England
for the space of one year, "like a rapacious and bloody
tyrant."[3] Cadwallawn fell by the hand of the Bret-

---

[1] Powel's Historie of Cambria, 688.

From Matthew of Westminster we learn that Edwin defeated Cadwallawn. The latter fled to Ireland, but was unable to return, because an
astrologer made known all his plans to Edwin. Then the Welsh King
went to Brittany. From Brittany he sent his nephew Brian to York, to
kill the astrologer. Brian met his sister at York. She pointed out the
revealer of Cadwallawn's plans. Her brother succeeded in his design,
and then fled to Exeter, where his fellow-countrymen received him. He
was here besieged by Penda, who was defeated and captured by Cadwallawn. As the price of his liberty Penda swore fealty to the Welsh King.

At this time the Welsh held part of Yorkshire and the whole of England
west of a line drawn from Exeter to Winchester, thence to the Pennine
Chain, and into part of the south-west of Scotland.

Later on, this part of the country was known as:—
 (1) West Wales—Cornwall, Devon, and the Borders of the latter.
 (2) Wales—its present limits, together with Monmouth and Hereford,
     and parts of Gloucester, Worcester, Salop, and Cheshire: its
     capital was Shrewsbury.
 (3) Cumbria—Lancashire, Westmoreland, Cumberland, and part of
     Yorkshire: its capital was Carlisle.
 (4) The country between the Firth of Clyde and the Solway Firth,
     and which was known as Reged and Strathclyde.

[2] Bede. This writer states that Cadwallawn determined to cut off all
the race of the English within the borders of Britain. Religious zeal must
have warped Bede's judgment, for it was not likely that Penda, a Saxon,
would ally himself with a Welshman to kill all the Saxons, himself included!

[3] Bede.

Oswald. walda Oswald, Ethelfrid's second son. Penda killed Oswald in the vicinity of the town now called Oswestry,

Oswy. and was himself overcome and slain by Oswy, the brother of Oswald, and seventh Bretwalda, who reigned in his stead for three years. The chronicler[1] considers the date of the death of the hoary ruler of Mercia as an epoch in the history of his people, for he remarks that from the beginning of the world to this time 5,850 years were gone.

Peada.
Wulfhere.
Ethelred.
Ethelbald. Peada, Wulfhere, and Ethelred succeeded their father upon the throne of Mercia, and, like him, lived at peace with their Celtic neighbours. But Ethelbald, their nephew, coveting the rich and fertile land that lay between the Severn and Wye, began to extend his dominions towards the west. He was stoutly opposed by the ancient possessors of the soil. Ethelbald fell

Offa,
755. by the hand of an assassin,[2] and was succeeded by Offa the Terrible, who completed the task which had been begun by his grandfather's cousin. The chroniclers unite in praising Offa. His descent was traced to Adam and Eve.[3] He was a most gallant youth,[3] the terror and dread of all the kings of England,[3] most warlike and very religious,[4] a man of great mind,[5] and unanimously chosen king by the clergy and people.[3] He extended the commercial relations with the continent by means of embassies, letters, and the influence of Alcuin.[5] Under him Mercia became the most powerful of the Saxon kingdoms. London was its capital.[6] Coventry, Chester, and Bath were the favourite seats of its rulers, and Derby had the charge of their dead.

---

[1] *Saxon Chronicler*, 655.

[2] Bede, *Eccl. Hist.*, 755.   [3] Matthew of Westminster.
[4] Henry of Huntingdon.   [5] William of Malmesbury, book ii., c. 4.

BRITAIN

ABOUT THE YEAR 750 A.D.

English Miles

0   50   100

These Invasions are by no means permanent ones,
their limits were constantly changing in accordance
with the will & power of their respective rulers

Scots   Green
Picts   Light Red
Welsh   Bright Red
Saxons   White
Jutes   Yellow
Angles   Blue

P i c t s

Tay

Firth of Forth

Forth

Edinsburgh

Tweed

BERNICIA

Clyde

STRATHCLYDE

Picts Wall

Reged

Firth of Clyde

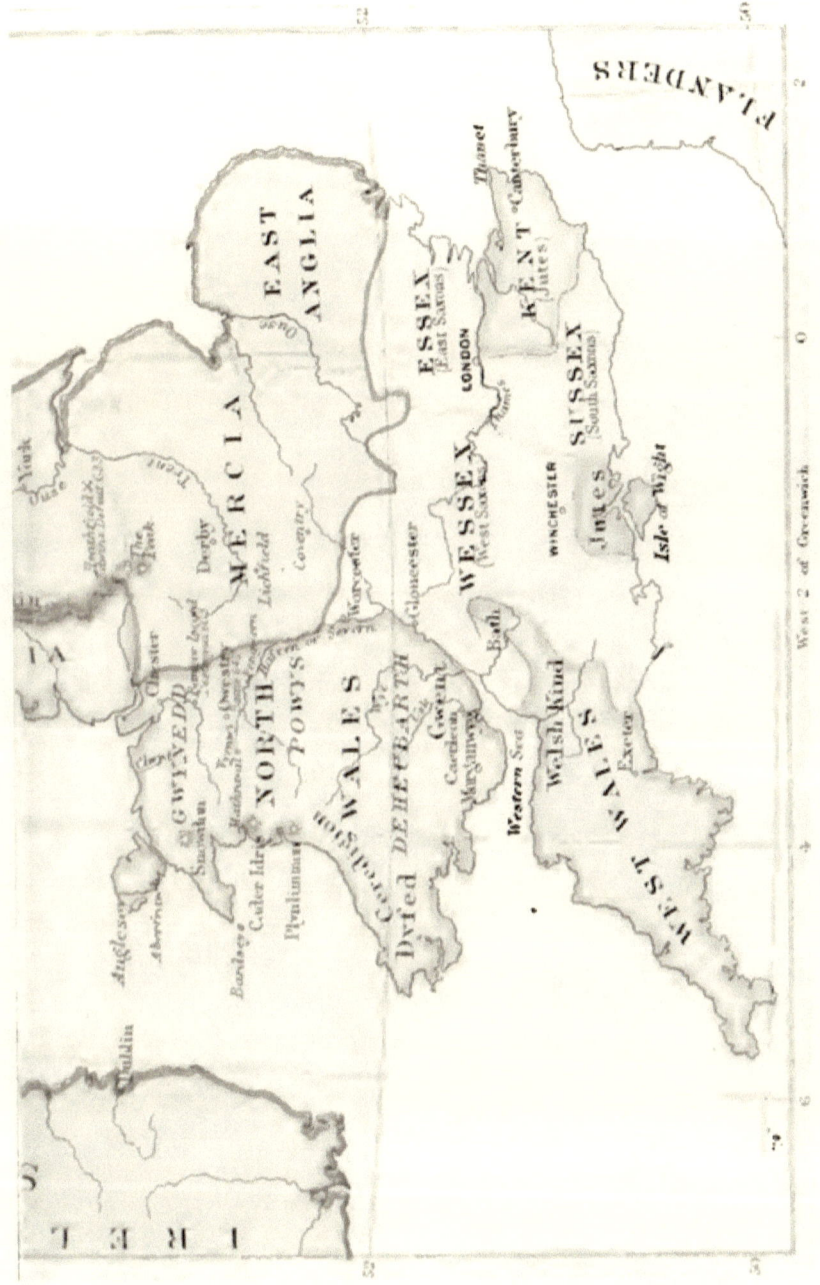

It stretched from the banks of the Severn to the meres **Offa.**
and marshes that bounded East Anglia on the west,
and from the Peak to the waters of the Thames.   Thus
on all sides it was hemmed in by rival kingdoms,
all of which succumbed to the superior skill and ambitious activity of the Mercian monarch.   His subjects
were warlike and renowned for handling the spear and
hurling the sharp dart.[1]   Ere long these weapons were
to be opposed to the terrible bows of the men of
Gwent,[2] and the formidable and death dealing long
lances of the men of Powys.[3]

Offa was the friend of Charlemagne[4] and the benefac-   **Charle-**
tor of the Pope.   He endeavoured to remove the archi-   **magne.**
episcopal see from Canterbury to Lichfield, and succeeded in persuading Adrian to confer the title of Archbishop of the Mercians upon the bishop of that town.
Eight bishops became subject to the see of Lichfield.
By this move Offa obtained a two-fold spiritual aid,
that of the chief of Christendom at Rome, and that of
his representatives in Mercia: so that in a temporal
and spiritual sense Kent had succumbed to the far-
seeing monarch of Mercia.

---

[1] Henry of Huntingdon.

[2] Giraldus Cambrensis, *Itin.*, per Wal., book ii., c. 4.

[3] Ibid., *Des. Camb.*, book i., c. 6.

[4] *Matthew of Westminster* states that Offa and Charlemagne were enemies
at first.   But the wily Mercian soothed the latter by presents and a letter.
In answer to this letter Charlemagne wrote—"Charles, by the grace of
God, King of the French, Lombards, and patrician of the Romans, to
the venerable man and dearest brother Offa, King of Mercia, greeting."
This letter permitted pilgrims to go to Rome, and allowed traders to do
business within his domains.   Among other presents the emperor sent Offa
a belt, a Hungarian sword, and two robes of silk.

From *William of Malmesbury* we gather that the learned Alcuin also
wrote to Offa stating that he was ready to bring the emperor's presents
to him, and thus return to his native land ; but, for the peace of his nation,
he declined to do so.   In another letter he mentions Charlemagne's affections and friendship for Offa.

Offa,
787.

Bertric of Wessex and Ethelred of Northumbria married his daughters. And Ethelbert of East Anglia, whilst seeking the hand of a third, was secretly despatched: his kingdom was added to that of Mercia. Thus with the alliance of the kings of Wessex and Northumbria, with the usurpation of East Anglia, and the conquest of the kings of Kent and of the South Saxons, with the friendship of Charlemagne and the spiritual sympathy of the Pope, Offa had ascended a pinnacle of greatness that no other Bretwalda aspired[1] to.

After a time he turned his attention towards Cambria, as the Celts had frequently crossed the Severn, driving the Saxons before them. Many a time had Offa to

Expedi-
tions
against
the
Welsh.

lead his combined forces against the daring mountaineers, who were so bold and ferocious that even when unarmed they did not fear to encounter an armed force, being ready to shed their blood in defence of their country, and to sacrifice their lives for renown.[2] Cambria presented an undaunted front, and had she been true to herself and not eaten up by internal divisions and perpetual strife, she might have been more than a match for the king who beheaded his allies and forced their subjects to fight his wars.

---

[1] *Matthew of Westminster* states that Offa's wife tried to persuade him to kill Ethelbert, but he warmly rejected her treacherous suggestions. That day the two kings sat down to table, and after the feast they enjoyed themselves with dancing and harp playing. Meanwhile the wicked queen was preparing a hole beneath the chair upon which the royal guest was to sit before going to bed. After the day's pleasure Ethelbert retired to his bedchamber; but he had no sooner seated himself in this chair than he was hurled, chair and all, into the deep hole which had been dug by the queen's orders. Before he could recover himself, pillows, garments, and curtains, were thrown upon him to stifle his cries; he was then quietly strangled The *Saxon Chronicle* states that Offa ordered his head to be cut off, 792.

[2] Giraldus Cambrensis, *Descriptio Cambriæ*, book i, c. 8.

But, even when divided, Offa had to lead army after
army ere he succeeded in defeating the brave de-
fenders of their hearths and burial grounds.   At last
fortune smiled upon him ; the Celts were driven to the
mountains ; the paradise of the Cymry[1] broken into
and acquired ; the King of Powys was forced to retire
from the head of the grove of alders,[2] the fenced
eminence,[3] to the Vale of Meifod,—from the banks of **Offa's dyke.**
the broad and sweeping Hafren, the queen of rivers, to
those of the confined but pure Vyrnwy.   Clawdd Offa[4]
was erected, slight tokens of which still remain as
lasting and tantalising evidences of Offa's might and
Cambria's weakness.   And Caradog of Gwynedd was
routed and slain in the fair Vale of Clwyd.

But, though vanquished, the Celts could not be sub- **Welsh patriot-**
jugated : for ages they continued to contend against **ism.**
the single and combined attacks of Saxons, Danes,
Norsemen, and Normans, and when apparently utterly
crushed, they astonished their foes by their sudden
and vigorous reappearance, when, as if forgetful of
previous disaster, they pushed boldly forward into the
territories of the enemy.   All tribute was sternly and
emphatically refused.   The conviction[5] of a mysterious
eternity reserved for their name and their language,
comforted them when overcome, and cheered them in

---

[1] Powys ; so called by Llywarch Hen.

[2] Pengwern of the Welsh ; Scrobbes-byrig of the Saxons ; Shrewsbury of
to-day.

[3] Thierry's *Conquest of England*, vol. i., book 1.

[4] In the vicinity of Welshpool remnants of this dyke are not to be seen.
It is probable that Offa deemed the Severn a sufficient barrier between
Gwalia and the Marshland.   This work must have taken a long time to
complete.   No doubt those employed upon it had, like the Jews upon the
walls of Jerusalem, to work with arms by their side.   It is a striking
monument of Offa's undaunted determination.   Every Welshman found in
arms upon the English side of this dyke had his right hand cut off.

captivity.   The prediction of the bard Taliesin caused the prisoner to view his bonds with indifference, while he boldly and defiantly informed his victor that he could neither destroy the Welsh name nor language, but that both would endure to the end of time.[1]

Cambria's bitterest curse clung to its conqueror and his race, for with Offa[2] fell the greatness of Mercia. Its star bowed down before the once subject but now triumphant Dragon of Wessex.   Eadburga, Offa's daughter, the last of his blood, begged her bread, and died an abandoned outcast in the streets of Pavia.

[1] It is worthy of interest to note that Taliesin lived about the year 540, so that his grandfather might have witnessed the departure of the Romans from our shores, and the arrival of the Jutes and Angles to aid the British King Vortigern against the Picts and Scots.   Both Taliesin and his father must have had an intimate acquaintance with the successes of the Saxon invaders during the first hundred years after their arrival in Britain, and this acquaintance, no doubt, caused him to give utterance to his famous prophecy concerning the Welsh, whose fulfilment we have to acknowledge in the present day: it ran thus :—

> En Nêr a folant ;
> En Hiaith a gadwant ;
> En Tir a gollant,
> Ond gwyllt Walia.

These lines are expressed in English as follows :—

> Their Lord they shall praise ;
> Their Language they shall keep ;
> Their Land they shall lose,
> Except wild Wales.

His predictions acted as a charm upon those Welsh men and women who believed in them.

[2] *Matthew of Westminster* states that Offa proceeded to Rome two years before his death to record the canonization of the Celtic martyr Alban, and the foundation of a monastery in his name.   In return for this concession and the remission of his sins, he gave to every one of his subjects whose estates did not exceed the value of 30 pieces of silver, if they attended the School of the English at Rome, a piece of silver every day.   To pay this money his kingdom, except the land attached to St. Alban's monastery, was taxed ; and this tax was called Romescot.   In aftertime it was known as Peter's Pence.

Eadburga was a very bad woman. She was surpas-
singly handsome, and had great influence over her
husband. When people offended her she accused them
falsely to him, so as to deprive them of life or of
power. As a rule, her husband did as she wished.
But, unluckily for him, he refused to believe her accusation against a young man whom he loved. His wife
determined to poison her husband's favourite. Not
knowing what was in the wine cup presented to the
object of his wife's hatred, Bertric partook of it and
died. Thus Eadburga by her wickedness lost her husband, her throne, and the society of her friends, for the
people of Wessex rose against her and sent her out of
their country. They also passed a law that henceforth
no king should reign over them who allowed his wife
to sit beside him on the throne. King Ethelwulf broke
this law.

Eadburga crossed over to France with great riches
to the court of Charlemagne. The emperor wished to
marry her, and asked[1] her which she would prefer, himself or his son; she answered—"If I am to have my
choice, I prefer your son, because he is younger than
you." He replied, "If you had chosen me, you should
have had my son, but as you have chosen him, you shall
have neither of us." Thereupon he caused her to become an abbess. For an unchaste act she was expelled
from France. Thence, deserted by all save one faithful
servant, she made her way to Pavia.

It was not unusual in the days of the Saxons for the
King's eldest son to be chosen King during the lifetime
of his father. Doubtless this was done in order to make
sure his accession to the throne. Thus, Egfert, Offa's

[1] Florence of Westminster, under the year 855.

Egfert,
794.

son, was not merely the heir to the throne of Mercia, but he was actually elected and consecrated King nine years before his father's death. And yet the year 794 witnessed the death of father and son. The death of the latter intensifies the forlorn and destitute condition of his sister, the representative of a dozen monarchs, and the last of the race of Offa, in a foreign land.

LEADING EVENTS.

CHAPTER III.

FROM THE DEATH OF OFFA TO THE CONVERSION OF GUTHRUM.

THE Saxons looked upon their kings as generals and administrators. It was necessary for them to be able to lead their subjects to battle, and also to manage the internal affairs of their kingdoms. The Saxons did not acknowledge the hereditary rights of their kings. A son succeeded a father, not because he was his father's son, but because he was elected by the Witan to sit upon the throne. They selected the best man they could find. Thus it was that Egbert, son of Elmund,[1] King of Kent, was elected by the Witan, composed of the ealdormen, thanes, clergy and people of Wessex, to rule over that state. And these facts explain why Alfred and Edred became kings instead of their nephews.

Egbert, 800.

Egbert had been the rival of Bertric, but Offa took the part of his son-in-law, and caused Egbert to leave the land. He went to the court of Charlemagne, where he learnt many useful things. No doubt Offa's influence with the emperor prevented Egbert's return to England during his lifetime. Egbert was looked up to because he was the last descendant of the house of Cerdic. He changed the name of the country from Britain to England, either on account of its shape, which resembles that of a triangle, or because it was inhabited chiefly by the descendants of the Angles.

[1] *Sax. Chron.*, 784.

Egbert,
823.

In 823 Egbert defeated the Mercians; and his son Ethelwulf annexed to his father's territories those of the men of Kent, of the men of Surrey, and of the South and East Saxons: in the same year the East Anglians sought Egbert's alliance, and also his pro-

827.

tection against Mercia. In 827 Egbert conquered Mercia, and the whole of the country south of the Humber; he also led an army against the Northumbrians, and forced them to swear allegiance and obedience to him. He was the eighth and the last Bretwalda. In the same year he was crowned at Winchester as first king of the Saxons. And in a

828.

charter of 828 he is styled King of England.

His reign was distinguished by many battles, for as Offa, to establish his kingdom, "shed a deluge of blood;" so Egbert won and rescued the kingdom of Wessex by the shedding of much blood. Egbert was succeeded

Ethelwulf,
836 to 858.

by his son Ethelwulf, who also fought many battles. One of these battles was against the Welsh of Wales, as Burhred, King of Mercia, who afterwards married his daughter, besought Ethelwulf to help him against his aggressive neighbours, who stoutly[1] opposed the forces of the Mercians. The Welsh were unable to withstand the combined forces of the Kings of Mercia and Wessex—they were defeated, and forced to submit[2] to their Saxon neighbours.

Ethelwulf went to Rome, and on his way back he married Judith, a girl of twelve years of age, daughter of Charles the Bald of France. During his absence in Italy and France, his eldest son Ethelwald, with the

---

[1] Flor. of Worcester.

[2] *Saxon Chronicle.* The writer of this chronicle, under the year 855, had evidently a high opinion of Ethelwulf, as he traces his descent to Adam

help of the bishop of Sherborne and the Ealdorman of Civil Dis-
sension,
855.
Somerset, schemed[1] to prevent his father re-assuming
the government of his kingdom. Ethelwald was not
altogether successful in his ambitious projects, as the
nobles did not wish to see the land rent asunder by
civil strife; they therefore would not help him in his
designs to prevent, by force of arms, the return of his
father to England. Ethelwulf, religiously inclined, and
solaced by the presence of his girl wife, was induced
to divide the kingdom between himself and his son.
Ethelwulf took the eastern part of the kingdom, and
Ethelwald[2] the western. The former seemed to have
consoled himself at his curtailed rule by making Judith,
contrary to the custom of the West Saxon Kings from
the days of Offa's daughter, to sit beside him on the
royal throne—and this was done without arousing the
hostilities of his nobles by word or deed.[1]

Ethelwulf was a pious man: he left land[3] for the
glory of God and the salvation of his soul; and he
commanded his heirs to look after the poor.

In addition to Ethelwald, he was the father of
Ethelbald, Ethelbert, Ethelred, and Alfred, all of whom
reigned as kings. The first died before his father.
The second son married his father's girl-widow. But
the people cried shame upon him, and she was sent
to her home, 859. There she ran away with Baldwin,
the great forester of France. He became Earl of
Flanders. From Baldwin and Judith descended Ma-

---

[1] Flor. of Worcester.

[2] The *Saxon Chronicle* terms him Athelstan, and states that his father
gave him in 836 the kingdoms of the Kentish men, of the East Saxons, of
the men of Surrey, and of the South Saxons; it further states that in 858
Ethelbert ruled over these districts, and that his brother Ethelbald ruled
Wessex.

[3] *Sax. Chronicle.*

tilda, who married William of Normandy, and Judith, who first married Tosti, son of Earl Godwin, and afterwards Guelph IV. of Brunswick, the direct ancestor of Her Imperial Majesty Queen Victoria.

The third and fourth sons of Ethelwulf were but ordinary men. Like their predecessors they had to struggle against the Danes. Ethelbald died in 860, and Ethelbert in 866. Upon the death of Ethelred, his sons were put aside, and his brother Alfred was elected king by the will of his father, by the election of the Witan, and with the consent of Ethelred: this took place in the year 871.

Moreover, he was specially set apart for the throne; for when he was barely four years old his father sent him to Rome with great pomp and many followers, and, at his request, Pope Leo[1] consecrated and anointed the baby-boy King; he also received him as his son by adoption, and confirmed him. Thus, like David of old, he became the Lord's anointed: and it would appear that his father foresaw, with the eye of faith, the great things he was destined to do for his country. No other King of England ascended the throne fortified with so many rites, or with brighter hopes and expectations, than did Alfred in the year of grace 871. It is needless to state that he was his father's favourite.[2] In the year 855 he visited Rome for the second time. On this occasion he was protected by his father. They remained in Rome a whole year. When young the people did not like him. It might have been that the great favour shown him by his father and the Pope caused him to be proud and overbearing. No doubt

[1] Florence of Worcester.

[2] Florence of Worcester states that Ethelwulf loved Alfred more than his other sons; this chronicler traces Alfred's descent to Adam.

he was too busy with his books and devotions to take an active part in sports;[1] while his infirmity obliged him to seek repose; and so those who were better sportsmen, and more stalwart and hardy than Alfred, might have treated him with contempt. And, on the other hand, their ignorance of what he had learnt might have caused him to treat them with coolness. But after a time this feeling changed for one of mutual respect and affection, and, throughout the greater part of his chequered and eventful existence, his people remained faithful to him in the hour of trial and adversity, and suffered themselves to be guided by him when he sought to improve their condition. This change of feeling took place after Alfred's defeat at Chippingham, on the Chistmas Eve of 878. Before that disaster befel him he was inclined to act arbitrarily and cruelly towards his subjects; and he was also guilty of lustful and immoral conduct. During his sojourn upon the Isle of Athelney he visited St. Neot, who advised him to give up his former course of life. The King determined to follow the good man's advice; and we are informed[2] that after that visit his followers flocked to him, and that success attended his every effort.

Alfred's flight, 878.

---

[1] Florence of Worcester states that he had no rival in the huntsman's craft. The same writer states that he was *twelve years of age when his mother excited his love for learning by showing him and his brothers a book of Saxon poetry, and saying to them* "I will give this book to whichever of you first learns to read it." This story is incredible for the following reasons: (*a*) When Alfred was twelve years old, 861, his mother, Osburh, was dead; (*b*) his step-mother, Judith, had been driven in disgrace from the land; (*c*) all his brothers, except Ethelred, were also dead. Most probably he was encouraged by Judith in his desire for learning, and that she, a mere girl in years, would feel as much interest as the boy Alfred in "a beautifully-illuminated and initial-lettered volume." William of Malmesbury also states that Alfred was twelve years of age when he began to study; this chronicler makes the extraordinary statement that his mother was with him in the Isle of Athelney, 878!   [2] Matthew of Westminster.

C

Alfred fortified[1] this isle. From thence he went forth against the Danes, and had frequent encounters with them. He determined to spy out their camp; and in order to do so he disguised[2] himself as an harpist. With one faithful follower by his side, he boldly approached their resting place. They were admitted into the tent, and also into the banqueting room of Guthrum, the leader of the Danes. They remained in the Danish camp several days, and whilst there, the Saxon king, as his fingers played with the strings of his harp, tried with ears and eyes,[2] to make himself acquainted with the secrets of his listeners. When he had obtained as much information as he desired to know, he returned to his anxious friends at Athelney. He assembled his companions, and assured them that the enemy was indolent, and could be easily defeated. All were eager for the enterprise. At Egbert's stone,[3] in the eastern part of the forest of Selwood, he was met by the men of Somerset and of Wilts, and a portion of the men of Hants, who received him with joy.[4] The king, having ascertained from his scouts the exact position of the Danes, attacked them suddenly, and

The overthrow and conversion of Guthrum, 878. defeated them with great slaughter.[3] After this victory Alfred besieged the Danes in their fortified position for fourteen days,[4] when Guthrum surrendered, and delivered hostages to him. He was afterwards christened, Alfred being his godfather, under the name of Athelstan, and received East Anglia for himself and such of his followers as became christians. A portion of the Danes would not be baptised: they left England under the

---

[1] Henry of Huntingdon.   [2] William of Malmesbury.

[3] Florence of Worcester.

[4] *Saxon Chronicle.*

leadership of Hastings, of whom we shall read in the next chapter.

Matthew of Westminster gives a most interesting account of King Alfred's life upon the Isle of Athelney. This isle was situated at the junction of the rivers Tone and Parret, and was surrounded by marshes; no one could arrive at it except by boat. It consisted of a wood and a level space of less than two acres, and was inhabited by a poor man and his wife, and by some stags, goats, and pigs. The poor man took pity upon Alfred when he told him that he was a servant of the king, and that he was pursued by the enemy. Alfred lived with these people several days, and did what they told him to do. One day the wife was so busy that she forgot to attend to some loaves that were baking in the ashes of her fire, and, when she saw that they were scorched, she put the fault upon the king, saying:—

> " You see the cakes burn,
> But never give them a turn ;
> Though you won't be so slow
> To eat them, I know."

Her husband is supposed to have become a bishop. This supposition is founded upon a statement made by Florence of Worcester, who writes that one Danewulf was, during the early part of his life, not only ignorant, but a swineherd. King Alfred, overcome by the onslaughts of his enemies, had taken refuge in a forest, where by chance he met him as he was feeding his swine. The king was struck with his intelligence, caused him to be educated, and afterwards made him bishop of Winchester, a See once held by his father, Ethelwulf.[1] As Alfred took refuge but once, and that

---

[1] Henry of Huntingdon.

Alfred at
Athelney,
878. once upon the Isle of Athelney, and as his entertainer thereon was a swineherd, it is not unreasonable to conclude that the swineherd of Athelney and the swineherd of the forest were one and the same person. It is also not unreasonable to entertain the pleasing fancy that the Queen and the swineherd's wife became bosom friends, and that whilst living together at Winchester, the former often entertained the latter in the king's palace, and now and again visited her in the palace of her husband the bishop: if so, they were privileged to listen to the voice of King Alfred, who, so the chronicler[1] informs us, was in the habit of relating to his companions, in a lively and agreeable manner, his perils upon the Isle of Athelney.

LEADING EVENTS.

[1] William of Malmesbury, book ii., chap.

CHAPTER IV.

FROM THE FIRST LANDING OF THE DANES IN ENGLAND TO THEIR ARRIVAL UNDER HASTINGS.

THE same year, 787, in which the marriage of Bertric, King of Wessex, with Offa's daughter was celebrated, the Danes first landed in England,[1] and began that system of slaughter and plunder which ended with the foundation of the dynasty of Sweyn, and which was revived after the wanton and horrible mangling[2] of the body of the last Saxon king, the heroic Harold, around the hoar apple tree at Senlac.[3] The Danes began by killing one man, but before their swords were finally sheathed thousands had fallen before them.[4]

The Danes, 787.

The northern rovers were perfectly at home upon the billows, and when in the trough of the sea they would sing aloud, "The force of the storm is a help to the arms of our rowers; the hurricane is in our service, and carries us the way we would go." The Danes looked upon the Saxons as renegades from the faith of their forefathers. When the Saxon priests and their followers were pierced through by the spear, cloven with the sword, or crushed with the battle-axe, the

Their habits

---

[1] Her nom Beorhtric cyning Offan dohtor Eadburgae to wive. And on his dogum cuomon aerest 3 scipu Northmanna of Haeretha lande.—*Saxon Chronicle.*

The reeve wished to take the crew from these strange ships to the king's town, as he did not know who they were; they killed him.

[2] Guy of Amiens; William of Poitiers.

[3] *Saxon Chronicle*, 1066.   [4] Henry of Huntingdon, 787

Danes shouted forth, "We have sung the mass of spears, it began at the rising of the sun."[1]

Regner Lodbrog. One of the earliest and most renowned of the sea-kings was Regner Lodbrog. After ravaging the shores of the Baltic, the North and Irish Seas, and the coasts of France, and sacking Paris, he landed in England, **Ella.** and was captured by Ella of Northumbria, who hurled him into a pit which swarmed with adders and snakes. While their venom filled his veins, and their fangs gnawed his vitals, he composed that song,[2] which ought to live for ever in the memory of his countrymen, and excite the horror and sympathy of the humane.

The news of Lodbrog's death roused up the ardent spirits of the Norsemen. They rushed to join the standard of his sons, Halfden, Ingwar, and Ubba, who threw themselves upon the shores of England with such relentless fury, that she writhed more and endured greater agony than did the mighty rover and poet, Regner Lodbrog. Northumbria, East Anglia, and Mercia were overrun by them. They captured Ella, their father's murderer; and the "cubs of the boar" avenged his death, for they cut Ella's ribs from his spine, drew his lungs through the opening, and then **Helpless state of England.** threw salt into the wounds.[3] There was no power[4] in England to oppose the progress of these desperate men. Wessex was in a state of thraldom to the priests; its martial spirit had fled, and its throne had become a

---

[1] Thierry, vol. i., book 11.

[2] Sharon Turner's *History of the Anglo-Saxons*, vol. i., book 4, chap. 3.

[3] They also captured Edmund, King of East Anglia, and having used his body as a target for their arrows, they cut off his head.—Matthew of Westminster, 870.

[4] Alfred had fought nine battles against the invaders in 871, at Reading, Ashdown, Basing, and elsewhere, so that his forces were unable to contend successfully against the almost incessant attacks of the Danes.

mere stage, across which a phantom line of kings flitted, they disappeared so rapidly one after another. The whole country was sunk in the slough of despair, and utterly exhausted. Alfred had indeed appeared, shedding around him the same short-lived and dazzling brilliancy that a meteor does as it flashes across the sky, dark with a blackness the more awful in contrast to the unexpected streak of fire. As the sky after such an appearance relapses into a darkness that might be felt, so did England, after the fatal and disastrous rout of Alfred and his few forces by Guthrum, on the unpropitious Christmas Eve of 878, present the unusual phenomenon of a land without a king or government, the former being a fugitive, and the latter but a memory of the past. But though the king was a fugitive and contemned by his own subjects,[1] the Danish rule was not to be as yet; that catastrophe was postponed for almost another half century. It was necessary to contend with Alfred even after he was overcome, after he was prostrate; insomuch that when he might be supposed altogether vanquished, he would escape like a slippery serpent from the hand that held him, glide from his lurking place, and, with undiminished courage, spring on his insulting foes. After flight he became more circumspect from the recollections of defeat, more bold from the thirst of vengeance.[2] The refuge at the swamp[3] amidst the waters of the Tone and Parret; the revilings of the swineherd's wife;[4] the overthrow of Ubba, the last surviving son of

Alfred's flight, 878.

Ubba.

---

[1] Asser. [2] Will. of Malm., book 2, chap. 4.

According to William of Malmesbury, Alfred's mother (who had been dead many years) was with him in the isle of Athelney!

[4] Matthew of Westminster, 878.

Lodbrog, a man of terrible obstinacy and unheard of
valour ; with the slaughter of twelve hundred of his
followers,[1] and the capture of the mysterious banner
called the Raven, which was woven in one noontide by
the daughters of the mighty Jarl ;[2] the king's secret visit
to the foemen's camp ; the discomfiture and blockade

The Danes of the Danish host; and the peace with Guthrum,—were
followed by several years of comparative rest, during
which time Alfred struggled to repair the great ills
that had afflicted the country. He erected camps and
forts. He built ships, and gathered around him such
a force as would for the future defy the combined
attacks of his foes. Well was it for England that she
had for her ruler such a vigilant and prudent monarch.

The years employed in internal reform were succeeded
by a complete inundation of the land by the countless
hordes from the North, under the guidance of the re-

Hastings. doubtable and far-famed Hastings, the son of a labourer
at Troyes,[3] the pupil of Lodbrog, the tutor of his son
Biorn, the vanquisher of Count Robert the Strong,[4] the
scourge of France, and the terror of Italy. Satiated
with the spoils obtained from the imbecile French and
Italians, and disappointed of the French crown and the
imperial diadem, Hastings thought to hurl from the
throne of England its king, seize the kingdom for himself, and found a dynasty. This was a mighty project.
It was undertaken with all his might. But he was
more mightily opposed by the far-seeing and ever alert
Alfred, with the aid of the Royal Ethelred, and the
princes and warriors of Wales and of the Welsh borders.

---

[1] Flor. Wig., 878 ; Henry of Huntingdon and the *Saxon Chronicle* say 850.

[2] Asser.   [3] Thierry, vol. i., book 2.

[4] Sharon Turner, vol. i., book 4. chap. 11.

It must be allowed that Hastings had a fair chance of success, when we recollect that his followers did not consist of the factious or lukewarm, but of the choice spirits of the North, of veterans who had fought, bled, and triumphed with Regner Lodbrog, of men who venerated their leader as a descendant of Wodin,[1] and who scorned to abide at home. In his ranks, too, were youths flushed with the first bloom of liberty, and burning to gain the approbation of their chief, outdo their comrades, and emulate the heroes whose exploits had been the theme for praise in their northern homes, while the snow covered the land and the storm howled around their rude abodes, and lashed into fury the elements, which they were taught to regard as the servants of their will and their guides to immortal renown.

Exploits of Hastings.

Before the birth of Alfred, Hastings had won for himself a name which, when mentioned, struck terror into the hearts of his enemies, but filled his admirers and followers with the fiercest enthusiasm. He had routed the forces of the Frankish King, accepted his gold and pillaged his subjects. Failing to stir up Guthrum to revolt,[2] and not contented with harassing the shores of Britain and of France, Hastings destroyed the inhabitants of Paris and other cities. He afterwards shaped his course into the Mediterranean, for the express purpose of feasting his men amidst the palaces of Papal Rome. The worshipper of Wodin was desirous of looking into the face of the Pope, and of obliging him to confer upon himself the imperial title; or, in default of compliance with his wish, he determined to witness the dying agonies of the Chief

[1] Matt. of Westm. 887.   [2] Will. of Malmesbury, book 2, c. 4.

of Christendom. Happily for Rome, Hastings' geographical knowledge was not equal to his ambition, for the town of Luna[1] was mistaken for the city of the Tiber. Upon his return to France he defeated the progenitor of the Capetian dynasty. But having been repulsed by the Bretons,[2] and afterwards by the Emperor, he gathered around him a mighty host for the conquest of England, and set sail from Boulogne. The

Hastings invades England. whole force consisted of three hundred and thirty vessels, which were filled with men and horses; for not only were the Danes intrepid sailors, but also, when occasion required, they were the most daring and dashing of cavalry. This fact will account for the celerity of their movements, and the consternation that their vicinity inspired. Some time after their arrival they were joined by the Danish settlers of Northumbria and East Anglia, who ravaged the southern shores and besieged Exeter. Alfred, at the head of his cavalry, set off to relieve the capital of the west, and Hastings hastened to succour his own followers, and build a strong fortress at Shoebury, in Essex. Here he was joined by Sigefert, grandson of Lodbrog, at the head of a great force,[3] and then, setting himself at the head of his vast army, he proceeded through Mercia to the borders of Wales. No doubt they were accompanied by their three usual attendants, fire, slaughter, and pillage,[4] for bloodshed and murder afforded them the same delight as the continued feast.

At length they came in sight of that river—the Hafren of the Celts, the Sabrina of the Romans, and

---

[1] Sharon Turner, vol. i., p. 499. [3] Flor. of Wig., 891.
[2] *Saxon Chronicle*, 894: Sharon Turner. [4] Henry of Huntingdon, 1003.

the Severn of the Saxons[1]—which the Welsh then
looked upon with almost the same love and reverence
as did the Hindoo the Ganges, or the Gael the Forth;
and with the same ambitious, regretful, and revengeful
longing as did the Teuton the Rhine. Onward it
flowed, with a mighty and majestic sweep, from the
fenny marsh at the base of Plynlimon, afterwards the
dangerous stronghold of Owain Glyndwr[2]—over rocks
and huge boulders, amidst flowers, fern, and furze
beautified with perpetual bloom—through narrow glens,
hemmed in by gloomy and lofty mountains, along
whose slopes the wild goat frolicked in undisturbed
security; widespreading vales, where the native kine,
black with brown faces, wantoned in freedom and
plenty; and forests crowded with trees of a variety of
growth and beauty of leaf, from the feathery foliage
of the pine, the dark shades of the yew, to the bright
green of the oak and poplar, and the silvery white and
rich blood-red of the beech—past Llanymynech rocks,
with their dread associations;[3] Oswestry, with its
recollections of a past greatness, and the fond credulity
of a monarch's[4] sanctity and miraculous worth—
strengthened by the water of the Vyrnwy, which had
rushed by Mathraval, the last abode of the Princes of
Powys, and the tombs of that race—past Shrewsbury
once Pengwern, and the capital of Powys—past grim
and solitary Wrekin, the last[5] brave stand of a desper-

Description of course of the Severn.

---

[1] Camden's *Britannia*, "Montgomeryshire."   [2] Pennant's *Tours in Wales*.
[3] It is supposed to have been a stronghold of the Druids.   [4] King Oswald.
[5] Hartshorne's *Salopia Antiqua*. It is the opinion of a credulous few
that Caradog made his stand against the Roman legions upon the Wrekin
But all who are acquainted with this hill will conclude that the credulity
of these people far surpasses their judgment. About seven places have the
credit of being the scene of Caradog's last battle; most probably this battle
took place in the heart of North Wales.

The
Severn.

ate man at the head of a desperate band, looking like
a deserted giant, or like one who had lost his way, or
had been overtaken with perpetual sleep when about to
join his brethren of Wales—past Bridgnorth, with its
Danish fort, doomed to be demolished and re-erected
by the Lady of the Mercians—through the forest of
Morfe, where the stag browsed, the wild boar whetted
his tusks, and the swineherd whiled away his days—
past Worcester, fated to experience the brutal ferocity
of the last Danish king and the gentle charity of the
wife of Ealdorman Leofric, the Lady Godiva of Coventry notoriety—by the hut of the churl, the rude
dwelling of the ceorl, the fort of the Thane, the castle
of the ealdorman, and the burgh of the free—until it
mingled its sweet water with those of the Western Sea,
which now and again rushed up its channel with the
overwhelming roar and force of an avalanche, and the
velocity of a troop of wild horses, as though they
longed to embrace its pure depths or do battle with
its descending tide for the favour of the God of the
Sea.

Hastings'
advance
into Wales

The news concerning the approach of the spoilers of
Saxondom towards Shrewsbury was, no doubt, received
by those in power along the borders of Wales with
very different feelings, many of whom bore a rancorous
hatred against the Mercians on account of past and
recent[1] depredations. These men, as a matter of course,
would far sooner unite with Hastings for the purpose
of sweeping the Saxons from the land, than aid the
latter in this their hour of dire necessity. Others
might have remembered that the Black Pagans[2] had

[1] *Annales Cambriæ.*
[2] The name given to the Danes, because of their terrible cruelty.

strangled Cyngen,[1] ravaged Mona,[2] slain Cynan, and harassed the Borders up to the town of Montgomery.[3]

But when the Danes advanced towards and even endeavoured to pass the sacred boundary of the Severn, then we may feel assured that even those Welshmen who had counselled co-operation or neutrality, were eager to oppose to the death their further progress. They might have been willing to join the Dane against the Saxon in England, but they would not join with the invader of England upon the soil of Wales, lest, after the overthrow of the Saxons, the Danes might turn upon themselves. They had heard, too, that their race in Brittany had checked[4] the before unchecked career of the successful Sea-king, and a glow of pride flushed their cheeks at the news; while they mentally resolved that, as the Bretons had saved the throne of France, so would they help to rescue the Saxon crown from the baffled Dane. At the sight of the burning country that marked the approach of Hastings and his followers, the mother clasped her babe to her bosom; she shuddered at the thought that her little one might be tossed from spear point to spear point;[5] and the father, after looking upon both with feelings of the acutest agony, rushed forth to oppose with his comrades the approaching army, rather than wait to witness the probable destruction of the one and the worse than destruction of the other.

Upon the arrival of the Norsemen at Buttington, we are informed by Matthew of Westminster[6] that they were received with great respect by their fellow-

Hastings at But-tington, 894.

---

[1] *Annales Cambriæ.*   [2] *Sharon Turner*, vol. i., p. 411.
[3] *Brut y Tywysogion.*   [4] *Flor. of Wig.*, 894 ; Henry of Hunt., 890.
[5] *Henry* of Hunt.; Math. of West.   [6] *Flowers of History*, vol. i., 895.

countrymen, who had built a town there. Probably they were the remnants of "the black Normans"[1] who had visited Tre Valdwin[2] in 890. Other authorities assert that they either entered a fortress,[3] or fastness,[4] or threw up for themselves a fortification.[5]

The further or western banks of the Severn were guarded by the forces of Powys under their Prince Mervyn. His brothers, Anarawd of Gwynedd and Cadell of Deheubarth, afforded no help to their suzerain. They were too busily engaged in hastening the downfall of their country by attacking each other.[6]

Hastings besieged at Buttington, 894.

Thus in front of the Danes were posted the Celts. And the smouldering embers of ruined villages, hamlets, and huts had scarcely been quenched, and the last breath had hardly left the desperately wounded, ere Ethered of Mercia, the earldormen Athelm and Athelnoth, Alfred's minister Ordhelm, and a great many king's thanes, hurried up at the head of a huge army gathered from every town and fortified place in Wessex and its dependencies.[7] They were soon followed by the king himself with such vessels from the royal navy as were used in the ascent of rivers. Very likely at that time the Severn was deeper and broader than it is at present.[8] Alfred surrounded the Danes with his fleet and also with his army.

---

[1] *Brut y Tywysogion.*   [2] The town of Montgomery.   [3] Flor. of Wig.
[4] *Saxon Chronicle.*   [5] Henry of Hunt.   [6] Powel, 893.
[7] Flor. of Wig.; *Saxon Chronicle.*   [8] Matthew of Westminster.

In the time of Bede the island of Thanet was divided from the rest of Kent by a channel almost a mile in width: now a mere brook separates this island from the mainland. Perhaps somewhat similar influences have been at work since the days of Alfred to reduce the width and depth of the Severn. In his time, according to *Matthew of Westminster*, Buttington was washed on all sides by the waves of the Severn. A few years ago a large heap of human remains were found there.

Hence at Buttington, in the year 894, were assembled some of the mightiest and most renowned chiefs, and the bravest warriors that England has ever seen. With-in the vale floated for weeks the rival banners of Celt, Dane, and Saxon,—the Red Dragon of Cambria showed the position of those who stood to guard their crops, their goods, and the honour and lives of those who were dear to them; the mystic Raven of the Norsemen swung ominously in the breeze, with drooping[1] wings and dejected appearance ; and the White Dragon showed that the "almost invincible army" of the Saxons still lay along the eastern banks of the fastness, and that their vessels were still washed by the waves of the Severn.[2]

The struggle that ensued was to decide the supremacy of Alfred or of Hastings. From this remote vale the fiat was to go forth which would call upon the inhabi-tants of Britain—Saxon, Celt, Norse, Pict, Scot, and Dane—to acknowledge the control of the Saxon mon-arch or the Danish sea-king. No wonder, therefore, that both parties waited so patiently, and prepared themselves so well for the death grapple. Alfred now experienced the full benefit of having left unmolested the ancient possessors of the soil of Wales.

The bards of Cambria no doubt seized upon so favourable an opportunity for the exercise of their charms. And who knows but that the kingly harper of the camp of Guthrum solaced his followers as they lingered before the fastness of Buttington with the same music that had beguiled his first great antagonist

---

[1] The Raven of the Danes is said to betoken victory by outstretching its wings ; but when defeat awaited their arms its appearance was woeful and despondent.—Asser.

[2] Matthew of Westminster.

Hastings
besieged
at But-
tington,
894.
and his forces, while the Celts stood enraptured around,
and the gentle summer breeze carried the soft notes to
the ears of the beleaguered Norsemen ?

But what must have been the thoughts that occupied
the hearts of the fiercely brave men cooped up within
the barriers they had erected in self-defence ?   Many
a one, as he lounged about, or sharpened his weapons,
or kept watch, must have thought of the dear ones at
home, of the aged parents, or of the wife and children,
of the lover, of the companions of their boyhood, and
the associates of their adventures by land and sea—
many, too, must have longed with a desperate longing
for the ocean open and free, for the stirring breeze, the
lazy calm, but, above all, for the intense excitement of
a hand-to-hand encounter, as their small and lightly-
built crafts were linked together in the embrace of
death,[1] as if the very planks, cordage, and sails partook
of the fierce enthusiasm that animated the beings that
guided them.   Not a few were roused from the pur-
poseless life of inactivity by the remembrance of terrible
encounters, of victories barely won by sheer brute force,
or by single examples of wanton daring, of the burning
of houses, the sacking of towns, the division of the
spoil, the endless carousal and the listless apathy that
necessarily followed.   Some must have shuddered as
they hastily brought to mind the brave men who had
fallen since they had left the far north, from which
they had launched forth as light-hearted as a lark, for
would they not return enriched[2] with the riches of the
effeminate, degenerate, and factious Saxon ?   But they
were not to return.   The riches they had gained were
the waters of the fathomless ocean, which would be

[1] Turner, vol. i., p. 387.   [2] Ingulfus.

theirs to all time, or the earth with which they com-
mingled.

It was with a start that they returned to the stern
realities of their own position. And as they watched
the camp fires of the opposing armies, or listened to the
howl of the prowling wolf, the screech of the owl, the
cry of the wild cat, the sighing of the wind, and the
rushing ripple of the Severn, a creeping terror, such as
lays hold upon those who are in the shadow of death,
must have prostrated their bold hearts. Others looked
upon their position with utter indifference. Come
attack or listless endurance, life or death, why should
they embitter the present by the sad recollections of
the irrevocable past, or by the gloomy forebodings of
the inscrutable future? Their murmurings were loud
and oft-repeated at the prolonged confinement, and
Hastings and Sigeferth were often blamed for not
leading forth the host and risking the hazard of an encounter. Could they not rush forth, and, having overcome their present foes, spoil once more the French,
beard the Spaniards, sweep the Mediterranean, scatter
the Saracens, overawe the Italians, and menace the
Greeks? Why die like sheep in ranges, or rot like
carrion? Such questions as these, no doubt, were often
asked by the indignant and starving host. Their supplies were at length exhausted : some died of hunger,[1]
and the rest were obliged to kill their horses for the
sake of their flesh.[2] The wolf lingered around in anticipation of the coming struggle, while the vulture, the
kite, and hawk, hovered overhead and eyed the thousands beneath them with many an impatient scream at
the delayed slaughter.

[1] Flor. of Wig.   [2] *Saxon Chronicle;* Matthew of Westminster.

Hastings
besieged
at But-
tington,
894.

And yet Alfred, Mervyn, and Ethered dared not attack the famished Norsemen. They might as well
enter unarmed a jungle infested by hungry tigers and
expect to overcome them; as well try to scale the dizzy
height and rob the eagle's eyry in her very presence;
as well spring from the vessel's side into the midst of
a shoal of sharks and hope to return unhurt, as expect
to kill or subdue a band of men inflamed with the
pride of an almost unbroken series of victories, brave
to desperation, and looking upon life simply as a pawn
which, when lost in the throng of battle, was succeeded
by the full and unchecked enjoyment of the passions
in the halls of Walhalla, the palace of the dead. The
king and his helpers bore in mind that the Danes were
becoming mad from hunger, unwonted restraint, baffled
hopes, and disappointed succour. They did well, therefore, to try to subdue the foe by starvation. No doubt
they were in full expectation that ere long their dearest
hopes would be realised in the unconditional surrender
of the enemy. Delusive expectation! Vain hope! Instead of receiving the white flag and the peaceable
envoy, the blockading forces on the eastern banks of
the Severn were suddenly struggling with the strongest
and boldest of the Danes. Sigeferth may have cheered
the Northumbrians and East Anglians by the sight of
that spear with which his grandsire had been wont to
announce the distant enterprise,[1] while Hastings blew
his ivory horn, whose harsh and terror-inspiring notes,
termed "the thunder" by the affrighted Gaulish
serfs,[2] echoed again and again by the wooded slopes of
the Rhallt,[3] and, mellowed by the waters of the Severn,

---

[1] Lodbrog's *Quida*, Turner, vol. i., p. 409.
[2] Thierry, vol. i., p. 120.   [3] A hill near Welshpool.

announced to the astounded Saxons and Celts that the
Norsemen were upon them. We may feel assured that
the fight was both fierce and bloody. The woods and
hills resounded with the clashing of arms, the dashing of
shields, the flight of arrows, the whirl of the sweeping
battle-axe, and the loud thud as it smashed through
armour and laid low its wearer, the shouts of the combatants, the yells and groans of the dying, and the rush
of the Danes as they pushed onwards steadily and ir-
resistibly.

The slaughter was great on both sides. Ordhelm fell
at the first onset.[1] Many king's thanes followed him.[1]
Of the Danes thousands[2] were slain in that terrible retreat. The waters of the Severn[1] and the soft mud
and tall rushes of the swamp became the shroud of
hundreds; and as the summit of Voel y Golva,[3] rising
abruptly from the vale, became gradually dim to their
sinking sight, the minds of many must have fled back
through years of hardship, careless want, rude plenty,
and wanton deeds of horrible cruelty, to pine-clad hills
or the snow-enveloped heights of the rugged north,
the home of their race.

The hoary Hastings and a great part of his army
escaped. He rallied his forces in Essex, swept across
the country, by day and by night, at one stretch[4] to
Chester, back to Essex and again to Quatford, retired
to France, where he acquired the peaceable possession
of the town of Chartres in the following manner.
Hastings laid siege to Poitiers. He failed to storm it.
Shortly afterwards he sent a messenger to the bishop
and count of the town, to tell them that he was upon

The
Defeat
and
Flight of
Hastings,
894.

---

[1] Matt. of West. [2] Flor. of Wig.; *Saxon Chronicle.*
[3] A beautiful hill near the town of Welshpool. [4] *Saxon Chronicle.*

Hastings in France. the point of death, and that he was very wishful to become a Christian. The bishop and the count were very glad to learn of the repentance of so terrible a man.

They believed his statement, and his men were allowed to enter the city. After a time he was carried into the church and was bathed in the sacred font, and the bishop and the count raised him out of the water. His servants carried him back to his ship. Some time afterwards he pretended to be dead. And on a dark night at midnight he was placed on a bier, but he was fully armed with sword and breastplate. His men began to lament aloud. They, too, were armed. And in this manner they carried Hastings upon the bier from his ship into the church. The bishop thought he was really dead, and hastened to perform the rites of his church over him. But the awful man suddenly jumped down from the bier and killed both bishop and count with his sword. Of course, as the people of the town never suspected such wicked treachery, they were completely at the mercy of the Danes, who fell upon them like a pack of wolves. No one was spared. Old and young men were killed by them. They made the city a waste, and even threw down its walls to their very foundations. After this Hastings went to Charles, king of France, and made peace with him. He then received the city of Chartres as a present from the king.

Hastings lived to greet the arrival of the successful freebooter Rollo,[1] the founder of the duchy of Normandy, whose descendant, the Conqueror of England, was no doubt inspired by Hastings' lofty deeds and mighty projects. Between the days of Hastings and

---

[1] Thierry, vol. i. p. 154.

those of William of Normandy, both England and France were subjected to foreign invasions and serious civil strife, all of which tended to the overthrow of Saxon, and to the establishment of Norman rule in England.

LEADING EVENTS.

CHAPTER V.

FROM THE OVERTHROW OF HASTINGS TO THE DAYS OF THE "LADY OF THE MERCIANS."

King
Alfred.
THE last chapter entered somewhat fully into the habits, thoughts, and aspirations of Hastings and his host. After their defeat at Buttington the land had comparative rest for many years. But the good and brave King Alfred was never idle. After he had overthrown the foreign foe, he tried to overcome the ignorance of his people, and also to make them better than they were. He stimulated them with rewards and punishments,[1] and no ignorant person could hold any position of dignity at his court. He made into one book the different laws and judgments of other Saxon kings. He was a student: he was fond of reading Saxon books, and particularly fond[2] of committing to memory Saxon poems. He translated the history of Bede, part of the Psalms, and other works into Anglo-Saxon.

King Alfred divided the country into hundreds[1] and tythings, and he made the people of each division responsible for the good behaviour of their fellows; and this obligation was so eminently successful, that gold bracelets, hung up in the public way where roads crossed each other, were not stolen. He built a monastery at Winchester[1] and at Athelney,[2] and a nunnery at Shaftesbury,[2] and sent presents by the Bishop of Sherborne to Rome, and even to India;

---

[1] William of Malmesbury.   [2] Florence of Worcester.

he was regular, both night and day, in his devotions. The twenty-four hours Alfred divided into three parts—eight for writing, reading and prayer; eight for refreshment of body; eight for the despatch of public business.[1] He had a knowledge of naval and structural architecture: by means of the former he caused ships to be made which were twice[2] as long, and more swift and higher than those of the Danes, and thus he laid the foundation of the British navy; by means of the latter he erected buildings[2] more stately and costly than those erected by his predecessors. His fleet defeated that of the Danes, and captured twenty of their ships in 897.

His court[2] was the home and school of the sons of his nobles. He formed schools for the instruction of his people. He asked clever men, amongst others the Welshman Asser, who wrote an account of his life and deeds, to live with him, and to help him to govern and improve his subjects. Alfred looked upon the Bible as the best law book. He was fond of sports. He measured time by burning candles.[1] He was kind to the good, but stern with the wicked. He freely gave away both money and goods to the clergy, and to other people as well.[2] His subjects showed their love for him and their confidence in his bravery and skill by taking his part as one man when the terrible Hastings visited England in 894. For twenty-five years he was, Asser tells us,[2] subject to great pain, which came on now and again. When we bear this fact in mind, and that he was only fifty-two years old when he died, we do not feel surprised that posterity venerate his name, and that to him alone of all the kings and

King Alfred.

---

[1] William of Malmesbury.   [2] Florence of Worcester.

queens of this kingdom the title of "Great" has been heartily and unanimously ascribed.

He was born in 849, began to reign 871, and died 901. He had a son who was called Edward the Elder, and a daughter, Ethelfleda, who married Ethered, who ruled Mercia in King Alfred's name, and so he was called a sub-king. Ethelfleda bore the title of "Lady of the Mercians." Another daughter, Ethelswitha, married Baldwin[1] of Flanders, the son of Alfred's step-mother, Judith.

[1] William of Malmesbury.

LEADING EVENTS.

Victory of the Saxon Fleet .... 897 A.D.
The Death of King Alfred 901

CHAPTER VI.

ETHELFLEDA, "THE LADY OF THE MERCIANS."

THERE are many quiet country places in England and Ethelfleda. Wales which a traveller might unconcernedly pass by, although, as Cicero happily and eloquently observed,[1] a history was beneath his feet. If by accident, or out of mere curiosity, he observed any peculiarities in the natural or artificial features in the vicinity of these places, no doubt his observations would not arouse any recollections of the past, or excite his imagination to conjure up and clothe again the crowd of beings who once took a prominent part in the affairs of the country. In such a case the mind of the observer would be deprived of food for reflection, if not for guidance and instruction.

Not a few of these places are connected in some way or other with Ethelfleda. It must be borne in mind that in her time only a small part of the country was cultivated. A great part of it was forest, jungle, or bog. A forest extended, with occasional open spaces, from the borders of Wales to the North Sea. In these open spaces forts were erected. And around these forts clustered a certain number of huts. A ditch with a palisaded mud wall protected fort and huts, which collectively were called a Burgh or Bury by the Anglo-Saxons.

In the time of the Romans these forests and desolate places afforded refuge to the Britons. Within their

---

[1] Quacunque enim ingredimur in aliqua historia vestigia ponimus.

Ethelfleda. gloomy depths they were at liberty to enjoy their civil and religious rights. Under the shadow of the oak were enacted the mysterious solemnities of Druidism, whilst the surrounding trees echoed the shrieks of the victims of this gory superstition, or the neighbouring stream wafted along its waters their dying sobs. In after time these forests were the abode of the Saxon wolf-head,[1] and the ever restless Celt—men who rivalled the wolf in ferocity and unbending hostility.

Several Burghs were built in various parts of the country by the Lady of the Mercians. It will be recollected that upon the death of Bertric of Wessex, the Witan decreed that for the future the wives of their Kings were not to be called queens, nor were they to share their thrones. This fact may explain the term "Lady" as applied to the wife of Ethered, Sub-king of Mercia. In many respects she was a really wonderful person. She was the delight of her brother's subjects, and the dread of his enemies.[2] And we are further informed that she was a woman of a comprehensive spirit,[2] of wonderful prudence, and eminent for her just and virtuous life, and also for her firm and equitable government of Mercia.

Unlike the daughter of Offa, she carefully nurtured the youths brought up at her husband's court. Like the empress-countess,[4] she drained to the very dregs the evils connected with a divided rule, and the horrors of a civil war. Unlike the "She-wolf of France,"[5] she both honoured and loved her husband. Like the pos-

---

[1] This term was applied to those who had been outlawed on account of some grievous crime.

   [2] Will. of Malmesbury.   [3] Florence of Worcester.

  [4] Matilda, wife of the Emperor Henry V., and of Count Geoffrey of Anjou.

      [5] Isabella, wife of Edward II.

sessor of the "tiger's heart wrapt in a woman's hide,"[1] **Ethelfleda.**
she levied armies, led men, won battles, but never
experienced a repulse. Unlike the youthful Jane,[2] she
did not fall a victim to the ambition of a renegade
father-in-law. Unlike the mate[3] of the grim-visaged
and grim-souled foreigner, she did not experience the
agonies inflicted by a morbid, jealous, thwarted, disappointed heart. Unlike the foundress[4] of our navy
and colonies, she despised the fawning and sickening
flattery of a court. Like the present "Lady" of
England, she wept over the untimely death of her
husband, and her presence was ever welcomed by all
who met her.

Ethelfleda was a great help to her brother Edward,
who became King upon the death of his father in 901.
His right to the throne was disputed by his cousin Ethelwald, who was helped by the Danes and the people of
East Anglia and Northumbria. After fighting for some
years, Ethelwald was killed in battle by his cousin.

In the year 913 Ethelfleda built a fortress at Bridg- **913.**
north, and three years later,—ere Germany had hailed
its first king in the person of Henry the Fowler;[5]
while Rollo, the Conqueror's ancestor, was laying the
foundation of a permanent hold upon the soil of north-
west France;[6] and while Berenger, the grandson of
Charlemagne, was contending in the north of Italy
with the numerous descendants[7] of the Sorcerer of the

---

[1] Margaret, wife of Henry VI.
[2] The Lady Jane Grey, daughter-in-law of Dudley, Duke of Northum-
berland. [3] Queen Mary. [4] Queen Elizabeth.
[5] Carlyle's *Frederic II.* [6] Matt. of West.
[7] The Hungarians: they came from Scythia; their object was devasta-
tion itself; by some they were looked upon as the Gog and Magog of
Scripture; and to others their approach betokened the end of time.—
Gibbon's *Decline and Fall.*

Ethelfleda. North and his wolfish dame, barbarians of barbarians, who had vanquished both Greeks and Teutons, and in the south of Italy with the blood-stained and impetuous followers and propagators of the Crescent,—her forces advanced still further west, and penetrating the great forest, they marched through its marshy thickets as far as the place now known as Chirbury, in Shropshire, and there a Burgh was erected. And the hollow thud of the axe as it fell upon the trees, and the loud talk of the workman, succeeded the ringing of battle-axes and the shouts or groans of the combatants as they struggled on or fell in the combat. The Mercians must have worked armed, or with their weapons close at hand, and companions on the watch, for they knew full well the perils of their position, as it was upon the very threshold of Wales. It must have been with an anxious and careful gaze that the sentinels scanned the surrounding country at the close and breaking of each day. Ethelfleda no doubt visited the armed host which her husband commanded before the fortress of Buttington in 894, and the royal navy which, under the charge of her father, had sailed up the Severn, and assisted in cutting off all succour from Hastings. While there she might have accompanied some of the various foraging parties which were sent forth to procure the necessary provisions during the lengthened blockade. And it is highly probable she visited Chirbury on one of these expeditions. If so, the eye, which afterwards looked upon so many battle-fields and fortified positions, must have perceived the importance of its situation in a military point of view ; and the mind which afterwards planned so many successful arrangements, no doubt even then formed

designs which after years were to see realised. Chir- Ethelfleda.
bury was excellently situated to keep the Welsh in
check.

In the year 916, shortly after Christmas,[1] when its 916.
vicinity was subject to down-pouring showers, or when
it was closely gripped by the unrelenting king frost,
trees were felled, trenches dug, mounds thrown up, and
a fortress, burgh or bury, with its rugged but strong
wooden walls, was raised, and stood alone amidst the
sylvan desert, with its stout occupants who were
appointed to guard this perilous quarter, and to drive
back the Celtic bands that endeavoured to make their
way either to the site of their former capital[2] or to the
city of Hereford. It also barred the way if the Northern rovers should attempt to repeat their visit of 890
to the town of Montgomery, or to rebuild the fort[3]
which had given shelter to the most famous of their
Sea-kings. Ethelfleda's object in raising fortresses
along the whole course of her dominions, from the
banks of the Severn to those of the Welland,[4] and
from Runcorn in the north to Canterbury in the south,
was to overawe the neighbouring districts, and to check
the almost incessant depredations of the Danes. With
places of defence to shelter and protect them, the
Saxons took heart, and were able to hold their own
against the wild cavalry raids of the North-men.

Ethelfleda continued to build towns, found monasteries, restore cities, and erect forts. To a certain
degree she became to Athelstan what Judith had been
to Alfred. The influence these ladies had over their
pupils was not long lived, but it was productive of many

[1] Henry of Huntington: *Saxon Chronicle.*
[2] Shrewsbury.   [3] Buttington.   [4] Matthew of Westminster.

Ethelfleda, lasting benefits to themselves and their country. The one taught her pupil the art of warfare, and set him an example of patient endurance, stubborn determination, great policy, unshaken fidelity, and a perfect scorn of the pleasures of the flesh; after the birth of her first and only child, Elfwina, she deserted her husband's bed; from that time they appeared more as companions in arms than as husband and wife.[1] The other taught her pupil the delights of learning, and guided his boyish ambition towards objects which were ultimately destined to raise the social and moral standard of his subjects; though she also set him an example of girlish attachment, and easy observance of the codes of Christianity, a delight in the pleasures of a court procured at any sacrifice, and a fondness for the concerns of wifehood, however infamously attained.

Her death, 919. Henry of Huntingdon becomes enthusiastic while describing the reign of Ethelfleda, and finally bursts forth into verse :—

> " Ethelfleda, terror of mankind !
> Nature, for ever uncoufin'd,
> Stampt thee in woman's tender frame,
> Tho' worthy of a hero's name.
> Thee, thee alone, the muse shall sing,
> Dread Empress and victorious King !
> E'en Cæsar's conquests were outdone
> By thee, illustrious Amazon !" [2]

At this time Hywel Dda (Howell the Good), grandson of Rhodri Mawr (Roderick the Great), was King of South Wales and of Powys, and his cousin, Idwal Voel, reigned over North Wales.[3]

[1] Ingulphus gives the following explanation of this extraordinary conduct : " Pariendo, suam sobolem primam difficultatem perpessa, tanta indignatione carnalem concubitum abhorruit, ut nunquam deinceps ad viri sui thorum rediens, se caelebitu castissimo contineret."

[2] Pennant's *Tour in Wales*, p. 121.

[3] Warrington's *History of Wales*, book iv., pp. 158, 159.

Edward honoured his sister's memory by depriving her daughter, Elfwina, of all authority, and by conduct- Elfwina. ing her into Wessex,[1] under the pretence that she was about to wed[2] a Danish prince, to whose brother his own daughter was afterwards given in marriage by his son Athelstan. History is silent concerning the fate of this ill-used maiden. She may have lived in solitary confinement to extreme old age, or she may have fallen a victim to the vindictive jealousy of her uncle the king.

Upon the death of Ethelfleda, Mercia became a fief The Ealdor- of the kingdom of Wessex, and its caldormen, though men of they sometimes took a prominent part in the affairs of Mercia. the country, could no longer wield full authority like Penda the Cruel, Ethelbald the Arrogant, Offa the Terrible, and Ethered the vice-King, within the dominions entrusted to their charge. The Mercian caldormen were Elfere the Regicide, Elfric the Treacherous, Edric the Arch-traitor, Leofric the Pious, Algar the Fiery, and Edwin the Dilatory. Elfere stabbed Edward the Martyr, helped Elfrida, wife of Edgar and mother of Ethelred the Unready, to overcome Dunstan and the Monastics, and was eaten of vermin.[3] Elfric repeatedly betrayed the Unready King. Edric did the same, and waded through pools of noble blood,[4] until he rivalled Canute himself in power: his victims were Gunhilda, sister of Sweyn, her son, and her husband Palling; the caldorman Elfhelm, father of Canute's first wife; Sigeferth and Morcar of the Five[4] Burghs;

---

[1] Flor. of Worcester, 920.
[2] Professor Barlow's Lectures; University of Dublin.
[3] Will. of Malmesbury.
[4] Lincoln, Nottingham, Derby, Leicester, Stamford. —*Florence of Worcester.*

King Edmund the Ironside, and his brother the Atheling Edwy.

The chief events in connexion with the lives of
the Ealdormen of Mercia will be given in succeeding
chapters.

LEADING EVENTS.

CHAPTER VII.

FROM THE DEATH OF ETHELFLEDA TO THE TIME OF DUNSTAN.

EDWARD the Elder, Alfred's son, was the first king to take the title of "King of England." While the Atheling he married a peasant girl. This marriage was a grave scandal, and shook the credulity of those who looked upon the royal race as descended from Woden. In the year 894 a son was born of this marriage. He was called Athelstan. Athelstan was the solace of his grandfather's declining years.[1] When seven years old Alfred conferred the honour of knighthood upon his grandson, and gave him at the same time a scarlet cloak, a belt, and a Saxon sword studded with diamonds. At the request of his grandfather he became the pupil of the Vice-king and the Lady of the Mercians, under whose charge he was instructed in those military exercises which afterwards enabled him to overthrow the united forces of Gael, Scot, Celt, Norse, and Dane,[2] at Brunanburgh, and to consolidate the various sections of the Saxon Community, 937.

Edward the Elder, 901 to 924.

The Battle of Brunanburgh, 937.

The *Saxon Chronicle* celebrated in verse Athelstan's great victory, and stated that :—

> The field deluged
> with warrior's blood,
> since the Sun,
> up at morning-tide,
> glided o'er lands,
> God's candle bright,
> sank to her settle.

---

[1] Will. of Malmesbury. [2] *Saxon Chronicle.*

E

Five lay
on the battle field
youthful kings,
by swords in slumber laid;
so seven also
of Anlaf's (Olave's) jarls;
of the army countless
shipmen and Scots.

Constantine,
hoary warrior,
had no cause to boast
in the communion of swords;
and his son he left
in the slaughter-place
mangled with wounds,
young in the fight.

King[1] and Atheling[2]
their country sought
in the war rejoicing.
They left behind them
the corse to devour,
the yellow kite
and the black raven;
the corse to enjoy,
the greedy war-hawk
and the grey beast
wolf of the wood.
Carnage greater has not been
in this island,
of people slain
by edges of swords,
since from the East hither
Angles and Saxons
came to land.[3]

---

[1] Athelstan.   [2] His brother Edmund.

[3] The above lines are taken from the first piece of poetry that appears in the *Saxon Chronicles*. The writer describes the events of the battle-field and the results of the contest with patriotic enthusiasm. Henry of Huntingdon translated this poetry into prose. His account of the Battle of Brunanburgh is unrivalled for majesty of language and brilliancy of description. Mentally, the reader beholds the various scenes of that bloody fight —as the spears transfixed the Danes through their shields; as the West Saxons hewed with their swords the flying foe; as the Mercians engaged the

It will thus be seen that the Battle of Brunanburgh was a terrible one. There were four distinguished leaders engaged in it—Athelstan and his brother Edmund at the head of the Saxons, the Norwegian Anlaf, and Constantine, King of the Scots. No quarter was given. The ferocious and unchristian character of the combatants is strikingly evidenced by their treatment of the dying and the dead, as both were left upon the battle-field to become the food of birds of prey and wild beasts. According to William of Malmesbury, Anlaf, following the example of King Alfred, visited the camp of the Saxons in the disguise of an harpist, and played in the presence of Athelstan. He was recognized by one of his former followers, who advised the King to remove his tent: Athelstan did so, and the following night Anlaf burst into the Saxon camp and killed a bishop, whose tent occupied the space upon which that of Athelstan had stood. A miraculous sword alone saved the King and his host. The battle continued to rage until the next night: Constantine,[1] twelve jarls, and almost the whole of the attacking force were killed. Anlaf sailed for Dublin, and Constantine fled to Scotland after their defeat. After Athelstan's victory the land had comparative rest for upwards of fifty years, when it was visited by Sweyn and Olave.

Athelstan favoured commerce and encouraged private enterprize by admitting merchants who had made three

---

heroes of Anlaf's forces; as the dead and dying strewed the ground; as Constantine and Anlaf sought safety in flight; as mothers wailed for their dear ones; as bird, toad, dog, and wolf gorged upon the flesh of the slain. He termed Anlaf King of Ireland.

[1] The chronicler confounds Constantine with his son: the story of the miraculous sword is a pious fiction.

successful voyages on their own account to the rank of thane; they were the first of our merchant princes. He **Athel-stan's sisters.** was a great match-maker. He had eight sisters. One married Charles the Simple of France. One became a nun. Athelstan arranged the marriages of the others with (1) Sihtric[1] of Northumbria; (2) Hugh the Great, founder, by his second wife, of the Capetian dynasty; (3) Otho, Emperor of Germany; (4) a German duke; (5) an earl of Poitiers; (6) Louis the Blind of Aquitaine. These Saxon ladies were the pioneers of Saxon trade and influence on the Continent.

As the Court of Ethelfleda gave shelter and in- **Athel-stan's Court.** struction to Athelstan and others, so that of Athelstan became the home and school of his nephew Louis of France; of Haco, son of Harold of Norway, who is known in history as King "Haco the Good;" and of Alan, grandson of Alan of Brittany. Athelstan helped these princes to ascend the thrones of their ancestors. He died in the year 940, at the early age of forty-six.

LEADING EVENTS.

The Birth of Athelstan .... 894 A.D.
The Death of Edward the Elder.................................. 924
The Battle of Brunanburgh 937
The Death of Athelstan 940

[1] Will of Malmesbury states that Athelstan gave her in marriage to Sihtric.

CHAPTER VIII.

DUNSTAN.

THE Monkish chroniclers, cut off as they were from public intercourse, could not have been eye-witnesses of the events they described. They wrote of what was described to them by others. Under these circumstances it is surprising that they wrote so well. Fervid feelings, highly wrought imaginations, and grateful hearts, with a ready credulity and faith in those they trusted, took the place of direct information concerning the persons they praised or blamed, and the events chronicled in their pages.

Upon the subject of Dunstan they are particularly feeling and eloquent. And it must be readily allowed that the career of this really wonderful man afforded them every material for meditation and stirring recital. Born in the year when Athelstan began to reign, 925, he was the guiding principle during the reigns of his successors, Edmund the Atheling, Edred, Edwy, Edgar, and Edward the Martyr. His ready tongue, daring energy, and wily conspiracies, were more than a match for the fighting, hunting, drinking, and lewd kings and nobles of his days.

Dunstan first came into notice in the eighteenth year of his age, when King Edmund gave Glastonbury[1] into his charge, 943. From this time up to the reign of Ethelred the Unready, he ruled both Church and State.

Edmund the Atheling succeeded his brother as king

Dunstan, 925 to 988.

943.

---

[1] *Saxon Chronicle.*

in 940. In 946 he was killed in a drunken brawl by Leofa, a wolf-head. Dunstan declared that a dancing devil[1] forewarned him of the King's death. He afterwards secured his Satanic Majesty by the nose, because he had appeared before him in the form of a beautiful woman, and had, thus disguised, tempted him to do evil.[2] These intercourses with the unseen greatly added to Dunstan's reputation and power. Thus it came to pass that Edred, who succeeded his brother Edmund, devoted his life to God and Dunstan.[1] He was a sickly man, and passed his life in repeating long prayers, and receiving stripes at the advice of Dunstan.[1] The latter was told of Edred's death by a voice from heaven.[1]

At this time the Abbot of Glastonbury was very busy with political affairs. And when Edwy became King in 955, he wished him to be, as the other kings had been, a mere puppet in his hands. Edwy, who was a beautiful youth, offended Dunstan in two things —he married Elfgiva, a near relative, and preferred on the evening of his marriage the society of his wife to that of the Abbot and the drunken nobles. Dunstan treated him as a boy, and forced him back to the banquet. The King resented this conduct. In his quarrel with Dunstan he was helped by the secular priests, while the regular priests took the part of Dunstan. The seculars lived among the people, and were allowed to marry. The regulars, however, lived together in large buildings, and did not marry.

The King was wishful to bring Dunstan to judgment,[3] but he refused to appear, and fled to Flanders.[4]

Edmund the Atheling, 940 to 946.

Edred, 946 to 955.

Edwy, 955 to 958.

---

[1] William of Malmesbury. [2] Matt. of Westminster.
[3] Florence of Worcester.
[4] According to the *Saxon Chronicle*, Dunstan was driven away over the sea by Edwy, 957.

Perhaps he was unable to give an account of the public Dunstan's Intrigues. treasures entrusted to him by Edred. From Flanders, by means of Archbishop Odo, the monks of Mercia, and the traders between the two districts, he incited the Mercians to rebel against Edwy, and to fix upon Edgar as their ruler. Thus the union of England by Egbert and others was undone through the powers of the regulars, headed by Dunstan. And this was not enough; Elfgiva was seized, branded on the face, and sent to Ireland. Returning, she was again seized and tortured to death. Edwy, who had been excommunicated, soon followed his beloved wife to the grave, 958. Edwy's death, 958. Certain writers,[1] upon the authority of some obscure and unreliable MSS., use words of a terrible nature against Edwy and his wife. On the other hand, we are assured that his reign was a happy and prosperous one.[2]

Edgar now became sole King of England; and Edgar, 958 to 975. Dunstan once more ruled the land. The seculars were treated with the greatest severity. Edgar built forty[3] new monasteries. Dunstan was made Bishop of Worcester and London, and afterwards Archbishop of Canterbury. A large fleet was built, which sailed along the coast, to protect the country. The Archbishop was very energetic on behalf of the King, and we read in certain books that all was peace and happiness throughout the land whilst Edgar reigned, and that even Welsh wolves and princes were subdued by him.

But the Saxon Chronicle,[4] while mentioning Edgar's peaceful reign, his love for God's law, his erection of religious houses, and the honour in which he was held

---

[1] Will. of Malmesbury; Matt. of Westminster; Lingard, the historian, &c.
[2] Henry of Huntingdon.   [3] Matt. of Westminster.
[4] Under the year 959.

by other nations, mourns over his foreign vices, and his introduction of heathen customs, outlandish men and harmful people into England.

LEADING EVENTS.

CHAPTER IX.

AN EXAMINATION CONCERNING THE TRIBUTE OF WOLVES' HEADS, AND EDGAR'S TRIUMPH AT CHESTER.

WE shall now leave Dunstan for awhile. History books **Edgar and the wolves** inform us that the Welsh princes were so completely subdued by Edgar, and that the Saxon king had such regard for the Welsh people, that he obliged their princes to hunt down the wolves in their domains, and present the heads of three hundred of them every year to him : thereby acknowledging him as their lord, and, at the same time, freeing their own people from these fierce animals.

This story envelopes Edgar with a twofold mantle, that of the autocratic king, and that of the humane man. If it were a true story, one's imagination could easily picture the great hunting parties throughout Wales, and the anxiety of its princes, lest they could not make up the stipulated number of Heads. But it must be put aside as one of the interesting legends concocted by Edgar's monkish admirers. It might be true that foreigners came to witness[1] his glory and to hear the words of wisdom that fell from his lips, but neither his glory nor his wisdom could have much influence over Welsh wolves. In fact, this story rests upon the authority of one chronicler. The same writer[2] states that Athelstan drove Idwal Voel from his kingdom, and afterwards restored him to it, with the words—

---

[1] Flor. of Worcester, 959. [2] Will. of Malmesbury.

Edgar upon the Dee.

"It was more glorious to make than to be a king!" No allusion is made to this tribute by any Welsh or Saxon writer. Even upon the showing of the Norman monk, this story cannot be true, for he states that Edgar commanded Judwall to pay him yearly a tribute of 300 wolves. Judwall, no doubt, stands for Idwal Voel. And the Welsh chroniclers assert that Idwal was killed in battle by the Saxons in 943, whereas Edgar began to reign in 959.

Dr. Lingard, and very many other historians, aver that once upon a time a most interesting spectacle was witnessed on the Dee at Chester—the appearance of no less than nine kings in one boat. The steersman was Edgar of England, and the eight oarsmen were the monarchs who held sway over almost the whole of the Celtic inhabitants of the British Isles. What a day that must have been at Chester when this most interesting and significant event took place! The River's mouth must have been thronged with vessels. There must have lain at anchor the ships of the Saxon monarch who had navigated the whole of the seas encompassing Great Britain. There, too, must have been anchored the vessels that brought to Chester the kings of Cumbria and of Scotland, "that prince of pirates, Maccus" (what fierce looking and broad-chested fellows they must have been! but what must he have been himself?), not to mention the small craft of the sight-seers. It certainly was in the opinion of the inhabitants and of the lookers-on a day of days—a day from which to chronicle all subsequent events as long as their lives lasted. But what must have been the happy and proud thoughts that tenanted the breasts of the Saxon king and the Saxon premier, Dunstan of

Canterbury (if he were present), as the one steered Edgar upon the Dee. "to the admiration of many," and the other officiated in the monastery of John the Baptist? To the one it was a regal, to the other an ecclesiastical triumph.

Such a train of thoughts as the above would probably enter the mind of the readers of Dr. Lingard's account of this, to him and to many others, historical fact.

It is almost a pity to try to dispel the mists that surround this interesting legend—for legend it must be pronounced to be—and so disbelieve the magnificent effects of Edgar's declaration to his nobles in the words "that now at last all his successors might boast that they were kings of England, since he had enjoyed a procession of such honour and triumph in the obedience of so many kings."[1]

Had this procession actually taken place, the chroniclers would, doubtless, have agreed upon the date of its occurrence, the number of tributary kings, the town near which, and the river upon which, it took place. They would, moreover, have coincided as to the names of the performers. But there is no unanimity amongst them in these particulars. There are also other facts and points which tend to throw doubt upon the story of King Edgar and his contemporary princes at Chester.

Florence of Worcester[2] says that the reputed occurrence took place in 973; Matthew of Westminster says in 974; William of Malmesbury[3] does not give the date; the *Saxon Chronicle*[4] says Edgar was at

---

[1] Matthew of Westminster; he wrote his chronicle in the 13th and 14th centuries.   [2] He wrote in the 11th and 12th centuries.

[3] His chronicle was written in the 12th century.

[4] We have evidence to conclude that facts were recorded in its pages contemporaneous with their occurrence; hence the great reliance placed upon its statements.

Chester in 972; Henry of Huntingdon[1] says he was there in 970.

Florence of Worcester, Matthew of Westminster, and William of Malmesbury, say there were eight tributary kings at Chester; but the *Saxon Chronicle* and Henry of Huntingdon give six as the number.

In the *Brut y Tywysogion* (Chronicle of the Princes) we read that in the year 971 "Edgar, King of the Saxons, collected a very great fleet at Caerleon upon Usk." It gives no information about his visit to Chester, and the procession upon the waters of the Dee; it simply states that Edgar collected a very great fleet, and that that fleet lay at anchor before Caerleon, a town in Monmouthshire, situated on the river Usk.

All that the earliest authorities state is that Edgar held a Court at Chester, and that he there received the homage of the kings. Henry of Huntingdon says that six subordinate kings pledged him their fealty there: but he does not give their names, nor does he say a word about the triumphant procession by water. The *Saxon Chronicle* is equally silent on these two vital points. Nor does Humphrey Lloyd, in his *Historie of Cambria*, or any other Welsh historian, allude to this matter.

The names given by the monkish chroniclers do not correspond with the names of the Welsh kings who were contemporary with Edgar up to the year 974, except that of Howell, given by Matthew of Westminster; and it will be borne in mind that 974 is the year given by this chronicler as the one in which Edgar's triumph took place at Chester. This is a curious coincidence.

[1] Written in the first part of 12th century.

The Welsh princes contemporary with Edgar were
Meyric, Ieuaf, Iago, Idwal, Rhodri, Ionaval, Hywel,
Cadwallawn, Cystenyn, Seisyllt, Llewelyn, Cynan,
Owain, Einion, Meredith, Edwyn.

Edgar upon the Dee.

William of Malmesbury names the so-called tributary
kings as follows:—"Kinad, King of the Scots;
Malcolm, of the Cumbrians; that prince of pirates,
Maccus; all the Welsh kings, whose names were Dufnal,
Giferth Huval (perhaps Hywel, i.e., Howell, is here
meant), Jacob (Iago?), Judethil."

Matthew of Westminster says they were—"Kined,
King of the Scots; Malcolm, King of Cumberland;
Maco, King of Man, and many other islands; Dufnal,
King of Demetia; Siferth and Howel, Kings of Wales;
James, (Jacob or Iago?), King of Galwallia; and Jukil,
King of Westmaria."

Florence of Worcester says they were—"Kenneth,
King of the Scots; Malcolm, King of the Cumbrians;
Maccus, King of several Isles; and five others, named
Dufnal, Siferth, Huwal, (Howel?), Jacob, and Juchil."

From the Iolo MSS. we gather that Edgar did
attempt to persuade at least one Welsh Chieftain to
help to row him on the Dee. This potentate was
Gwaethvoed, Lord of Cibyr and Ceredigion. In reply
to Edgar's summons he said "he could not row a barge;
and if he could, that he would not do so, except to
save a person's life, whether king or vassal." When
a second message begged for some sort of a reply to
return to the king, "Say to him," said Gwaethvoed—

"Ofner na ofno angau."
(Fear him who fears not death.)

It is not to be supposed that the kings of the three
chief divisions of Wales would have been outdone by

one of their subordinates in declining such an igno-
minious position as oarsmen to King Edgar.

There is another strong reason why even the statement of the monkish chroniclers concerning Edgar
must be refused as independent testimony. He was
completely in their hands; and so it will be found that
his reign, as described by them, is scarcely anything
more than a record of the doings of the monks; that
an abbey was founded here, that such an abbot, bishop,
or archbishop began to rule—

> New temples crowned the hills at his command,
> Heaped with rich gifts the sacred altars stand,
> And hoary minsters owned his lib'ral hand. [1]

Like Henry VIII., he permitted nothing to stand
between him and his lust. Neither husband, nor vows
of sanctity, nor the rights of hospitality, were any protection to those whom he fancied. And yet, notwithstanding his licentiousness, his cruelty, and the atrocity
of his criminal laws, one[1] monkish chronicler states
that he was beloved both of God and man, and that he
invited his people to the practice of virtue by word and
deed; another[2] termed him the flower and glory of a
race of kings; another[3] affirmed that his sanctity broke
the neck of an abbot and cured a blind lunatic; and
another[4] declared that he exchanged his earthly kingdom for an eternal one. He was also likened unto
Solomon, Romulus, Cyrus, Alexander, and Charlemagne!
Wherefore? Because he was the ready tool of the
king-maker of his age, the Wolsey of his time—
Dunstan.

[1] Henry of Huntington.   [3] Flor. of Worcester.
[2] Will. of Malmesbury.   [4] Matt. of Westminster.

The last argument against the supposition that Welsh and other kings rowed Edgar upon the Dee is of a conjectural character. What would their subjects think of such an ignoble exhibition? While the kings were at Chester, what became of their subjects at home? Who protected them? Had Dunstan inaugurated a year of jubilee, and guaranteed peace and security to the dominions and subjects of the eight kings? Indeed, such a fair opportunity of advancing their own interests would not have been neglected by their rivals. And in those days scarcely a Welsh prince sat securely upon his throne. Treachery and murder, and not goodwill and harmony, distinguished those days. The Welsh would not have obeyed a prince who had submitted to the imperious mandate of the Saxon Cæsar with the same tameness that a naked captive followed the chariot of the Roman Cæsar. Why, the very spirit of Caradog would have burst its bonds at such a debasing sight, and confronted such craven-hearted creatures as the Welsh princes are represented to be! But they were no cravens, but bold and brave men. Gwaethvoed's reply may aptly be put into the mouths of each one of them. Perhaps Hywel Ddrwg (Howell the Bad) was there from interested motives. A man who could imprison his father, blind one uncle, drive another into exile, and murder a cousin, would not hesitate to handle an oar to tickle the fancy of the vanity-struck monarch. Perhaps, too, other princes, out of curiosity, or from some other motive, visited at Chester the king who never led an army, or won a battle, and whose days were passed in lewdness and penance. Such being the case, it was no difficult matter for certain of the chroniclers, out of gratitude for the benefits he conferred

Edgar upon the Dee.

Edgar upon the Dee. upon their order, to assert that " he (Edgar) exhibited them (eight princes) on the River Dee in triumphant ceremony."

LEADING EVENTS.

CHAPTER X.

INTESTINE STRIFE IN WALES.

WE return once more to the affairs of Wales. We have **The Welsh** read that Cadwallawn was the last Welsh Prince who was called King of Britain ; that Offa obliged the princes of Powys to remove their seat of government from Shrewsbury to Mathraval in the Vale of Meifod, and that he tried to cut them off from England by means of a large mound made of earth, timber, and stones, and which extended from the top to the bottom of the district now known as Wales, where it borders upon England.

We should imagine that the erection of this bulwark would soon lead to the conquest of Wales. But it had the contrary effect, as it led to a Welsh nationality amongst the ancestors of the people who now live in Wales. But this nationality was not of a comprehensive kind, as the people were never thoroughly united : they never joined together *as a people* to fight against the common foe. As it was in the days of Agricola, so it continued until they were altogether overcome. A combination of two or three princes to repel the common danger was rare ;[1] thus while they fought the foe singly they were all subdued. With such characteristics it was surprising that they were ruled by their own princes up to the time of Edward I.

Various reasons may be assigned for the final overthrow of the Welsh, and the loss of their independence

---

[1] The Life of Agricola, by Tacitus, chap. 12.

F

The Welsh as a nation. Foremost among these was the system of
gavelkind. By this system princedoms and estates
were parcelled out amongst the various members of
each family. This led to disputes, to deeds of cruelty
and treachery. Brother rose up against brother. The
ties of kith and kin were snapped asunder. Those
bonds of sympathy that usually draw together the
various members of one family into an impenetrable
phalanx were succeeded by feelings of revenge. Patriotism, that ethereal flame that tenants the hearts of the
noble-free, and supports them under every difficulty,
gave way to the spirit of self-aggrandisement. While
the Saxon or Norman were upon the Borders, busily
engaged in harrying the same; while Norse, Erse, or
Gael were attacking the lands along the sea-shore—
Celt was engaged in mortal strife with Celt.

Many of these contests took place in the district now
constituting Montgomeryshire. This county may aptly
be termed the battlefield of Wales.[1] Many Welsh mountains and streams are consecrated by the memory of
historic deeds, but none more so than those of Montgomeryshire. Plynlimon ranks among the former.
This mountain was the debateable land between North
and South Wales, in consequence of its being a natural
bulwark separating these divisions. Oft its carn-
crowned summits are enveloped in mist, as though
it mourned over the slaughter of the well-beloved,
whose blood had tinged its coarse grass, and inter-
mingled with the dark-brown moisture of its peat beds.

---

[1] Among the battles that have taken place within its borders may be
mentioned those of (1) Carno; (2) Buttington; (3) Rhyd y groes; (4)
Cyveiliog, 844, Mervyn Vrych fell in this battle—he was succeeded by
Rhodri Mawr; (5) Mechain: in this battle Idwal ap Griffith ap Llewelyn
and Rhiwallawn ap Cynvyn were slain, 1067.

It was on one of its offshoots that overlooks the Vale The Battle of Carno, 949. of Carno and Tref Eglwys, and at a spot equally distant between the former village and that of Dylife, that a desperate battle was fought in 949. It was waged between the North and South Walians. The former were led by Ieuaf and Iago, Owain ap Hywel Dda, and other princes, commanded the South Walians.

Unfortunately, the historian has but scanty accounts of the events that took place in Wales and along its borders prior to and even after the year 949. In those days everybody's motto was strictly and literally—*Facta, non verba.* The deeds were often startling and momentous; but the words with which they were, not described, but simply recorded, were the quintessence of brevity. The Saxon and the Welsh chroniclers alike were but a step removed from the Peruvians: these primitive people recorded events by simply knotting a piece of cord; thus, twenty knots upon a piece of cord in the possession of a Peruvian would readily recall to his mind as many events of his life. One Welsh chronicler[1] hands down to posterity an account of the feats performed at the first battle of Carno in the words, "Gwaith Carno,"—exploit or work at Carno.

In order to understand the causes that led to this battle it will be necessary to state that, during the early part of the reign of Alfred the Great, the whole of Wales was under the rule of one prince, who was termed the Pendragon. This term was somewhat similar to that of Bretwalda. The Pendragon and the Bretwalda was the chief ruler of a number of rulers. In certain cases they settled disputes. They were the rulers over certain districts which were altogether un-

[1] Brut., O.C.

The Welsh der their control, and they also exercised a certain amount of authority and jurisdiction over other districts which were under the immediate control of other princes. These titles were not hereditary ones, for the Saxon Bretwalda was sometimes the King of Wessex, Mercia, or Northumbria: in like manner the Welsh Pendragon was Prince of North or South Wales.

Rhodri Mawr.

Anarawd.

Cadell.

Mervyn.

The Pendragon of Wales in the time of Alfred was Rhodri Mawr. He was killed in battle by the Mercians, 877. Upon his death Wales was divided among his three sons. The eldest, Anarawd, became King of Gwynedd, which comprised the counties of Anglesey, Carnarvon, Merioneth, and parts of Denbigh and Flint. The Kings of Gwynedd before the days of Rhodri Mawr lived under Snowdon, but Rhodri removed the royal residence to Aberfraw in Anglesey. Cadell, the second son, obtained Deheubarth, which extended over the counties of Pembroke, Cardigan, Carmarthen, and parts of Brecon and Glamorgan. The youngest son, Mervyn, became King of Powys. Powys was the smallest of the three divisions. Because of its bordering on Mercia, it was the most exposed to attacks by land; whereas Gwynedd and Deheubarth were exposed to the attacks of the Scotch, Irish, and Danes by sea, and also to the attacks of the Saxons by land. Powys consisted of the counties of Montgomery and Radnor, and parts of the counties of Salop, Denbigh, and Flint. After the days of Caradog, in the time of Offa, Mathraval, in the Vale of Meifod, was the residence and the burial place of the princes of Powys.

In addition to these princedoms there were lordships in certain parts of Wales, as for instance that of Gwent, which consisted of parts of the present counties of Gla-

morgan and Monmouth; and that of Brecon. Under The Welsh
these lords were local chieftains. With so many sub-
divisions of so small a country as that of Wales, and
with natures so excitable and irascible as those of the
Welsh, it is not surprising that intestine strife was so
frequent in Wales. The various chieftains rallied around
their lords, and the latter supported the cause of the
prince of their choice.

Anarawd revenged the death of his father in 880.
He was helped by refugees from Westmoreland and
Cumberland, which formed in those days a Welsh district called Strath-Clyde. These Welshmen from the
North settled down in that part of North Wales that
lies between the mouths of the rivers Conway and Dee,
and they called their new home Y Ystrad Clwyd.

Anarawd and Mervyn acknowledged Alfred as their
superior lord. The former visited the Saxon monarch
and received gifts from him.[1] We have read that the
Welsh helped Alfred to defeat the Danish leader
Hastings. Nine years afterwards, doubtless in revenge
for the help given by Mervyn to Alfred at the siege
and battle of Buttington, he was killed by the Danes.

Upon the death of Mervyn his brother Cadell seized Death of Mervyn, 903.
upon Powys. Thus in 903 Wales was under the rule
of two chief princes. Upon the death of Cadell,
909, his son Hywel Dda became king of Powys Hywel Dda 909.
and Deheubarth. And in 915 Idwal Voel[2] succeeded Idwal Voel 915.
his father as king of Gwynedd. Both Hywel and
Idwal acknowledged the supremacy of Edward the
Elder.[2] But they joined their forces with those of the
Scots, Irish, and Danes against Athelstan, and were
routed with them at the terrible battle of Brunanburgh.

---

[1] Asser.   [2] Flor. of Worcester.

Idwal Voel   William of Malmesbury asserts that Athelstan had
obliged Idwal to meet him at Hereford in the year
926, and to give him annually, in token of vassalage,
Defeat of   gold, silver, dogs, and hawks.   And Florence of Wor-
Hywel,   cester states that the Saxon king defeated Hywel in
926.   the year 926.

Idwal Voel   Idwal of Gwynedd was killed by the Saxons in 940.
killed,   Upon his death Hywel Dda became the Pendragon of
940.   Wales, and well did he deserve the title.   With the
help of the bishops and wise men of his land he drew
up a number of laws for the guidance of his palace,
and for the country at large.   Several of these laws
were in existence before the days of Hywel.   He
altered some of them : others he did not change : and
new ones took the place of those old laws he abolished.
It is supposed that the Pope approved of Hywel's
legislature.   He was one of the few Welsh princes who
died a natural death.   Hywel was, in a certain sense,
amongst Welsh what Alfred was amongst Saxon rulers :
both were the chief and glory of their respective
nations.

Death of
Hywel Dda   Upon the death of Hywel in 948, Iago and Ieuaf, the
948.   sons of Idwal Voel, laid claims to the sovereignty of
Iago and
Ieuaf, sons   the whole of Wales.   They made this claim as the
of Idwal   representatives of the eldest branch of the family of
Voel.   Rhodri Mawr : and also because they were the heirs to
two out of the three princedoms of Wales, as their
father's father was Anarawd, and their mother's father
Mervyn of Powys.   Upon the whole their claim has
been denounced on the ground that Rhodri had himself
made a three-fold division of the land.   But it is highly
probable that Iago and his brother simply wished
to assert and secure the supremacy of the crown of

Gwynedd over that of Deheubarth, and to remind the
king of that district, and the other Welsh princes, that
the head of the House of Idwal was the Pendragon.

The sons of Hywel naturally resented such a claim.
Had not their father's authority extended over Deheubarth and Powys, and even into Gwynedd? In a word,
had not Hywel Dda been Pendragon since the death of
Idwal Voel? Had he not also framed a code of laws
which were acknowledged throughout Cambria? Had
he not visited Rome and done other things that had
caused his name to become a byeword for good in the
mouths of its utterers? And were they to submit
tamely to the dictates of the Princes of Gwynedd?
Certainly not. Idwal might have fallen gloriously
while battling against the common foe. Hywel, their
father, might have admired such conduct. But with
them national rights were forgotten, and personal pique
and vanity were intensified to such a degree that
nothing but an intestine war could assuage their
wounded pride and importance.

Iago and Ieuaf assembled their forces, and marched
through Montgomeryshire. But their further progress
was checked by the appearance of Owain, Rhodri, and
other sons of Hywel, with their warriors. Then ensued
"Gwaith Carno." The men of Gwynedd obtained the
victory. After their exploits at this battle Iago and
Ieuaf appear to have pursued the discomfited South
Walians, and to have invaded South Wales on two
occasions. But the latter were by no means crushed,
for they afterwards ravaged North Wales as far as
Conway. We are not informed whether they sailed
to this place, or whether they arrived there by land.
They were attacked and again overcome, and driven

The Welsh southwards by the successful northmen, who once more visited South Wales in an hostile manner.

After ten years' warfare, Owain ap Hywel, and other princes, acknowledged Ieuaf and Iago as paramount sovereigns of Wales. Ieuaf and Iago could not agree, **Death of** and at length Iago got rid of his brother, either by **Ieuaf, 964.** blinding, hanging, or imprisoning him. This happened in 964. Iago did not enjoy his undivided sway more **Expulsion of Iago, 974.** than ten years, for in 974 he was driven forth by his nephew, Hywel Ddrwg, son of Ieuaf.[1]

LEADING EVENTS.

---

[1] This Hywel was one of the Welsh princes who are reported to have rowed the puny-bodied, lustful-minded, Dunstan-guided Edgar at Chester.

CHAPTER XI.

FROM THE FALL OF DUNSTAN TO THE RISE OF EDRIC OF MERCIA.

WE have read that Dunstan was the chief man in the **Dunstan.** kingdom. He continued to hold this position up to the accession of Ethelred, the second son of King Edgar. During all these years he appears to be the only man of great ability in the country. We do not read of a single layman of mark, except the king, in those days. Hence Dunstan must have the credit of keeping the land in quietness.

A great fleet was built, consisting of 3,600 stout ships according to one authority,[1] and of 4,800 according to another authority.[2] Following the example of Agricola, the King caused his fleet to sail round the island : this was done during the summer months. Its appearance had the desired effect of showing all who saw it the power of the Saxon king. Dunstan had friendly intercourse with the Pope and foreign potentates. He showed his influence in the Church by the promotion of his friends and partisans to important bishoprics. He was the means of raising Oswald, nephew of Archbishop Odo, to the see of Worcester, and Ethelwold to that of Winchester. It is worthy of note that members

---

[1] Flor. of Worcester. Dr. Lingard, forgetting that these ships were small ones, observes: "The number appears to me enormous, I have therefore retrenched a cipher." This retrenchment was most unjustifiable.

[2] Matt. of Westminster.

Dunstan. of the same family held the most important sees: thus, Dunstan was the successor of an uncle as Archbishop of Canterbury; and Oswald became Archbishop of York. Both Oswald and Ethelwold worked with a will to expel the secular clergy from their abodes, and to place regulars in the large monasteries.

The Coronation of Edgar, 973 Unlike that of other kings, the coronation of Edgar did not immediately follow his election. He was a boy of sixteen[1] when he ascended the throne: this fact contradicts the statement that his coronation was delayed to the thirteenth[1] or fourteenth[2] year of his reign, through the influence of Dunstan and the power of the Pope,[2] *in consequence of his misdeeds.* We see the master mind of Dunstan in this: an uncrowned and unanointed king would have less authority than one fully armed by the pomp and ceremony of coronation and sanctification; the former would be in a state of pupilage to the Church; the latter would be free and independent, for he was king by the blessing of the Church as well as by the election of the Witan and the voice of the people.

If Edgar was careless as to his own acts, he was kind to the middle and poor classes, and encouraged temperance.[2] In his manner he was cautious, mild, humble, liberal, and merciful;[3] and so brave that, though he was both short and thin, he challenged the King of Scotland to meet him in single combat, because he had called him "a sorry little fellow."[2] In summer he joined his fleets. In winter he travelled throughout the land, in order to see that the laws were observed, and justice administered:[2] and in his days there was no private thief or highway robber[2].

[1] *Saxon Chronicle.*   [2] Will. of Malmesbury.   [3] Flor. of Worcester.

Upon the death of Edgar the *Saxon Chronicle* Death of
pathetically observed :— Edgar, 975

> " God grant him
> that his good deeds
> be more availing
> than his misdeeds
> for his soul's safety
> on the longsome journey."

The month of July, in the year of grace 975, was a grievous month to Dunstan, for Edgar died in that month and that year. With the death of his pupil and obedient king fell the power of the great churchman. Dunstan has been called the Becket and the Wolsey of his days. But neither Becket nor Wolsey established fleets and courts of law, and administered justice through the medium of their respective kings. And both Becket and Wolsey fell the victims of their Sovereign's ingratitude and hate. Whereas Dunstan ruled the land, and at the same time established the ascendency of his order, while professing to honour and obey four puppet kings.

Upon the death of Edgar, his son Edward became king, through the influence of Dunstan.[1] His step- Edward, the mother Elfrida and some of the nobility opposed his Martyr. election.[1] Edward was Dunstan's nominee. But 975 to 978. Elfrida was determined to remove the former, and to compass the overthrow of the latter. Woman's wit was more than a match for the Archbishop's power. Elfrida had sacrificed her first husband in order to wed Edgar. And she now determined to rule once more as queen through her son, a boy of seven years of age. She was helped by Elfere, ealdorman of Mercia.

Elfere took the part of the secular priests, and drove

---

[1] Will. of Malmesbury.

The Secu-lars and Regulars. the regulars out of the monasteries of Mercia.[1] The religious question, concerning the Seculars and Regulars, appears to have agitated the whole nation. Three[2] synods were convened for the purpose of asserting the supremacy of one of these Orders, or of arriving at some arrangement which would put an end to their unseemly and unchristian strife. The first was held at Winchester: there the crucifix spoke[1] in favour of the Regulars.

Synod at Calne, 978. The second synod was held at Calne, and was attended by all the members of the chief[3] Witan; the king was absent on account of his youth.[4] The subject in dispute was debated with great zeal and diversity of opinion.[4] It appears that several of those present took advantage of the opportunity to show their distrust of Dunstan, for "like arrows"[4] their reproaches were directed against him. He was opposed by the whole Witan.[4] Its members were, doubtless, indignant at their exclusion from the management of state affairs. They must have borne in mind that their country was garrisoned with monks, and that the erection of monasteries had emptied the king's exchequer. By taking the part of the Seculars they aimed a blow against the personal rule of the Archbishop.

Undaunted, Dunstan withstood their reproaches. Suddenly the floor upon which they stood, boards and rafters, gave way, and all, save Dunstan, who stood upon a single rafter, were hurled to the ground: some were killed,[5] and others crippled for life. Some people

---

[1] Will. of Malmesbury.   [2] Flor. of Worcester.
[3] *Saxon Chronicle.*   [4] Matt. of Westminster.
[5] *Saxon Chronicle.* During the reign of Frederick Barbarossa a similar catastrophe took place in Germany, when several of the nobility were killed.

believe the boards and rafters of the council room gave Synod at Calne, 978. way through a miracle.[1] Others are of the opinion that Dunstan's mechanical skill had something to do with it, and that before the council had met he had caused the supports of the room, except the beam upon which he stood, to be loosened, and that he had control over the machinery that temporarily supported its floor.

If the Synod at Calne had been convened for the purpose of refuting the arguments of the Regulars or of the Seculars, surely Dunstan would have been supported by his sturdy colleagues, Ethelwold,[1] Bishop of Winchester, and Oswald,[2] Archbishop of York, and by the other heads of the Regulars: but they were all absent.

If the Witan had been summoned to take into consideration a question of national importance, the King would have presided: but he was absent.[3] The fact that this gathering was of national importance, and that it met for the express purpose of settling the disputes between the Seculars and Regulars; and the fact that the king and the supporters of Dunstan were not present at it, and that Dunstan was the only one who escaped unhurt, might lead us to the conclusion that the catastrophe at Calne was the contrivance of one who allowed religious zeal and partisan feelings to override his humanity and warp his judgment, and that Dunstan's victory was the result of a desperate effort to retain his own power and that of his order over the

---

[1] Matt. of Westminster.

[2] Ethelwold died 984, and Oswald in 992: *Saxon Chronicle.*

[3] Matthew of Westminster. Dr. Lingard says he was present: this writer states that the floor of the council room at Calne gave way, as the weight upon it was too great: if so, it is strange that only one man escaped.

ecclesiastical and civil affairs of the realm. The assembly at Calne, 978, is an epoch in the history of the Saxon people. With it the supremacy of the Church ceases for more than half a century.

Whilst Dunstan ruled the land, civil strife and foreign invasion were almost unknown to it. And the best testimony in his favour was the confusion and the terrible sufferings that followed his days.

Murder of Edward, 978. In the year 978 King Edward was brutally and treacherously murdered. He had been hunting. Upon his return he visited his step-mother. She received him with a kiss,[1] and gave him to drink out of a cup; whilst drinking he was stabbed by the ealdorman Elfere,[2] or by one of the household[1] of Elfrida. The king set spurs to his horse, but, falling to the ground, one foot got entangled, and he was dragged to death by his frightened steed. The *Saxon Chronicle* simply states that he was martyred, and makes no mention of the hunt, or of his visit to his step-mother. Henry of Huntingdon is also silent concerning the hunt, and he merely remarks that he was killed by *his own family* at Corfe-gate, at eventide. As Ethelred was a mere lad, he could not have been guilty of the death of his half-brother, consequently the guilt of this terrible crime must be laid at the door of his wickedly ambitious mother. According to William of Malmesbury, Elfrida plotted against the life of Edward, and that her cruel design was successful after the following manner:—the king was returning home tired with the chase, and gasping with thirst, while his companions were following the dogs in different directions, when he was told that his relatives lived in a neighbouring

---

[1] Matt. of Westminster.   [2] Will. of Malmesbury.

house; he proceeded towards it at full speed, unattended Murder of Edward, 978. and without suspicion, as he judged others by his own feelings. On his arrival Elfrida, enticing him with female blandishments, caused him to lean forward to receive her kiss; afterwards, whilst he was eagerly drinking from the cup which had been handed to him, he was pierced through the body by the dagger of an attendant.[1] Edward, dreadfully wounded, with all his remaining strength clapped spurs to his horse in order to join his companions, when one of his feet slipped, and he was dragged by the other foot through the trackless paths and recesses of the wood, while his streaming blood made known his death to his followers. Edward is known in history as "Edward the Martyr" —no doubt the Regulars bestowed that appellation upon him, because he was their choice, and also because he fell through the machinations of Elfrida, the leader of the Seculars.

Ethelred, son of Edgar and Elfrida, succeeded his half-brother. His life is said to have been cruel in the beginning, because of the death of his brother; wretched in the middle, by reason of his flight and weak conduct; and miserable in the end,[2] in consequence of the circumstances that attended his death.

At the coronation of Ethelred, Dunstan foretold[2] with Dunstan's Prophecy. a loud voice the evils that were about to fall upon the land, saying to the youthful monarch:—"Since you have aspired to the kingdom by the death of your brother, hear the word of God. Thus saith the Lord, the sin of your wretched mother, and that of the

---

[1] William of Malmesbury, in book 2, chap. 9, does not give the name of Elfrida's attendant; but in chap. 10, under the year 1012, he describes Elfere as—"Elfere, who had murdered the late king."

[2] William of Malmesbury.

accomplices of her wicked plot, shall not be blotted out except by much blood of the wretched people; and such evils shall come upon the English nation as they have not experienced since they came to England until now." This prophecy was fulfilled to the very letter.

Ethelred, 978 to 1016 From the accession of Ethelred in 978 to the accession of Canute, in 1016, the affairs of our country seem to have revolved around the person of Edric, ealdorman of Mercia.

LEADING EVENTS.

[1] Florence of Worcester.

THE HOUSE OF GODWIN,

Showing its connection with Eldric of Mercia.

ETHELRIC.[1]

| Brihtric.[1] | Ethelmere.[1] | Elfric.[1] | Three other sons.[1] |

Ednic,[1] ealdorman of Mercia, = Elgitha, d. of Ethelred the Unready.

Wulfnoth, "Child of the South Saxons,"[2]

Elfric the Forester,[1] or the Wild.[3]

GODWIN,[4] earl of Wessex,=Gytha, sister of Ulf, Canute's brother-in-law.

| HAROLD, king of England, k. at Hastings. | Sweyn, k. by Saracens. | Tosti, k. at Stamford Bridge | Gurth, k. at Hastings. | Leofwine, k. at Hastings. | Wulfnoth, a hostage. |

Elgitha=Edward the Confessor.

Haco.

Harold, and other sons exiles.

[1] Florence of Worcester.
[2] Saxon Chronicle. Dr. Lingard states "The descent of Harold can be traced no further back than his grandfather Wulfnoth."
[3] Ingulfus.
[4] William of Malmesbury states that Godwin's first wife was Canute's sister, and that their son was drowned in the Thames.

CHAPTER XII.

EDRIC OF MERCIA, OR THE STRUGGLE BETWEEN SAXON AND DANE FOR SUPREMACY.

Edric of Mercia.

EDRIC was the master spirit of his time. In days of cruelty and treachery, he was the most cruel and treacherous of his contemporaries. By means of subtle genius, persuasive eloquence, matchless perfidy, and relentless cruelty, he ruled the land. Two kings[1] he betrayed time after time: one[2] king he killed: two[3] kings he placed upon the throne. Had Edric not lived, there would have been no Danish Conquest of England: ancient writers look upon him as the cause of the subjugation of their country.[4]

In very truth Edric was the fit successor of Penda, of Offa, of the regicide Elfere, and of Elfric. It seemed as if the very soil of Mercia bred traitors and rebels. In after time Algar of Mercia allied himself with Griffith of Wales, and fought against his own countrymen: his sons, Edwin and Morcar, were passive traitors to Edward the Confessor, active ones to Harold, son of Godwin, and compulsory ones to William of Normandy. We must, however, recollect that treachery appeared to be studied in those days as a fine art. The catastrophe at Calne was the result of treachery. The king's mother had been won by treachery and murder; his half-brother had been sent to an early grave by guile and the dagger. Moreover, the king himself endea-

---

[1] Ethelred the Unready, and Edmund the Ironside.   [2] Edmund.
[3] Sweyn and Canute.   [4] Lingard, vol. i., p. 157.

voured, by one foul and sweeping act of cruel treachery, Edric of
to destroy his enemies in one day.[1] It will thus be Mercia.
seen that treachery was practised in church and state,
in the camp and at the court. Edric, however, determined to out-Herod them all. He soon became known
as " a new traitor, but one of the highest order."[2]

We have no information concerning Edric's forefathers: neither their names nor their positions in
life are mentioned by the chroniclers, except that we
are informed that he was of low origin,[3] and further
that he was the lowest of the people.[4] One writer[3]
gives the names of his brothers and that of his father.
One of his nephews, Wulfnoth, became the ealdorman
of Sussex, in which position he was succeeded by his His rela-
son Godwin, and by his grandson Gurth. Henry of tionship
Huntingdon and the *Saxon Chronicle* style Wulfnoth to Godwin
" Child of the South-Saxons," a term equivalent in
some respects to that of Atheling: Matthew of Westminster styles him " the king's servant." It is stated[5]
that Wulfnoth was a herdsman in early life, and that
Godwin[6] helped him. Another nephew, Edric the Forester,[3] was as successful against the Normans amidst
the woods and hills along the Welsh borders as Here-
ward was amongst the Fens. From these particulars
we gather that Edric belonged to an historic family,
many of whose members were perfectly free from guile
and cruelty, and who willingly sacrificed their lives for
their country.

Ethelred began to reign when ten years old. His

---

[1] St. Brice's Day, 1002.   [4] Matt. of Westminster.

[2] Henry of Huntingdon.   [5] The MS. Chronicle of Radulphus Niger.

[3] Florence of Worcester.   [6] Lappenberg: Sharon Turner.

youth was the chief cause of the disasters that happened to the Saxons during his reign. He had no general to lead his soldiers to war: he had no one to give him sound advice in the council chamber. When he heard of the death of his half-brother Edward he wept aloud: his tears so irritated his mother, that, not having a whip at hand, she beat him with candles in so savage a manner that he dreaded candles to the end of his life, and could not suffer the light of them to be brought into his presence.[1] This incident shows that in his youth he could not go to his mother for comfort and advice.

Olave and Sweyn, 994.

The unprotected state of England soon became known to the Danes and Norwegians, who invaded its shores under Olave of Norway and Sweyn of Denmark in 994. They were bought off, and some of them were allowed to winter in the land. In the year 1002 two events took place in England: each event led to a change of dynasty. The first was Ethelred's marriage with Emma, "the Pearl of Normandy," daughter of Richard I., Duke of Normandy, called by the Saxons Elfgiva ("the gift of the fairies"). This marriage was an act of policy[2] in order to secure the aid of the Normans against the Danes. It paved the way for the Norman Conquest. One chronicler[3] observed that this marriage, in conjunction with the attacks of the Danes, was a double chastisement and a snare, and that if the Saxons escaped the open attacks of the Danes, they would not have the firmness to break the meshes in which the subtlety of the Normans would entangle them unawares. The

---

[1] Will. of Malmesbury.

[2] Ethelred married Emma for the same purpose that Vortigern married Rowena.   [3] Henry of Huntingdon.

second event was the massacre on St. Brice's Day: this
led to the Danish Conquest.

Edward the Elder began the perilous custom of em-
ploying Norwegian and Danish auxiliary forces; they
were called huscarls.   Under Ethelred several of these
northern soldiers held posts of trust in the army and
the navy.   Palling, a Dane, whose wife was Gunhilda,
Sweyn's sister, was an admiral of the king's fleet.
Naturally the huscarls had a kindly feeling towards
their own countrymen.   The king's marriage was
hateful to them, for they feared that the son of this
union might become king of England and Normandy,
and so, sufficiently powerful to drive them out of the
country.   Thereupon they determined to take the
king's life[1] by treachery, to kill every member of
the Witan, and afterwards to seize the kingdom "without any gainsaying."[1]   This is one reason why Ethelred
ordered the Danes throughout the land to be killed.
From another source[2] we learn that this massacre was
brought about through the insolence of the Danes,
who, after peace had been declared, insulted and violated
the wives and daughters of the nobles.   One chronicler[3]
stated that Ethelred ordered the massacre of the Danes,
because he was "elated with pride" after his marriage
with Emma; and another[4] asserted that he did so "from
light suspicion."   According to Florence of Worcester,
it was plot against plot, and a simple question as to
which party should strike the first blow, for he
distinctly states that Ethelred gave orders for the

Massacre
on St.
Brice's
Day, 1002

---

[1] *Saxon Chronicle.*   [2] Matt. of Westminster.   [3] Henry of Huntingdon.

[4] Will. of Malmesbury: he does not mention what the king suspected;
no doubt his suspicion had reference to some Danish plot against his life or
authority.

Massacre
on St.
Brice's
Day. 1002. massacre of all the Danes of every age and of both
sexes, because the Danes had formed a conspiracy to
kill him and his nobles, and to reduce the whole of
England under their rule. We must not, therefore,
forget the circumstances that surrounded the king when
he issued his fiat against the Danes. In fact, this
massacre, unlike the dynastic one in Italy[1] and the
religious one in France,[2] was a political or race
massacre: it was brought about from fear of loss of
life and of supremacy, rather than through a spirit of
wild revenge or of wanton cruelty.

The slaughter of the Danes was not so great as is
commonly believed, as the king's order could not have
been executed in Northumbria, East Anglia, or the
seven Burghs,[3] as the Danes formed the bulk of the
population in those parts. And it is not unlikely that
those Danes who had accompanied Olave and Sweyn,
and who had been allowed to settle in England, alone
were killed.[4] Amongst the slain were Palling, Gunhilda,
and their son. They had been put under the protection
of Edric.[5] With a refined cruelty, he caused both
husband and child to be killed in Gunhilda's very
presence,[5] and then ordered[6] her head to be cut off,
though he stated that her death would bring great evil
upon the whole kingdom.

The massacre of the Danes upon St. Brice's Day
may be looked upon as the first move in the game of
slaughter instigated by Edric, and as the first thread of
that web in which he hoped to mesh those who stood
between him and supreme power, for he was the ruling

---

[1] The Sicilian Vespers, 1272.   [2] St. Bartholomew's, 1572.
[3] The towns of Leicester, Stamford, Derby, Nottingham, Lincoln, York,
and Chester.   [4] Lappenberg.   [5] Matt. of Westminster.
[6] Will. of Malmesbury.

THE DESCENDANTS OF ETHELRED THE UNREADY.

Ethelred=(1) Elfleda, a Saxon lady: (2) Emma of Normandy.

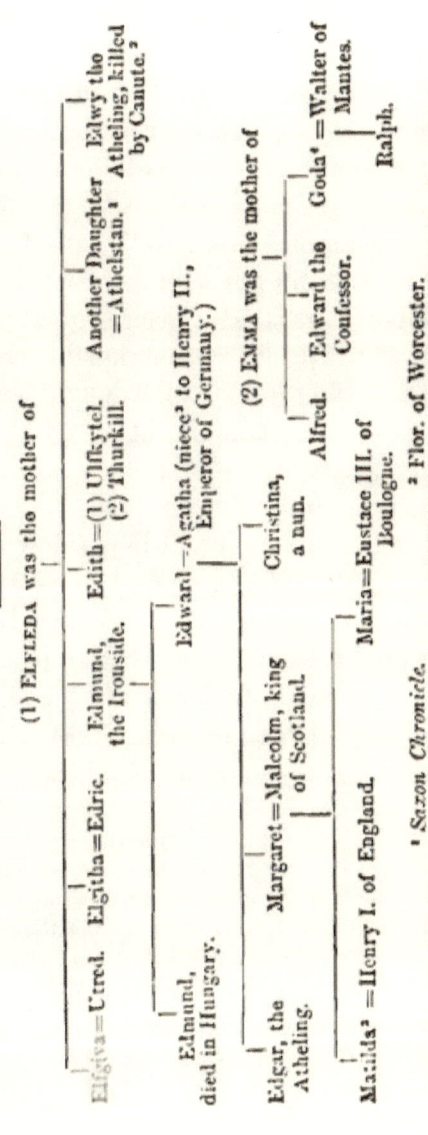

(1) ELFLEDA was the mother of

Elfgiva=Utred. Elgitha=Edric. Edmund, the Ironside. Edith=(1) Ulfkytel. (2) Thurkill. Another Daughter =Athelstan.[1] Edwy the Atheling, killed by Canute.[2]

Edmund, died in Hungary.

Edward=Agatha (niece[2] to Henry II., Emperor of Germany.)

Margaret=Malcolm, king of Scotland. Christina, a nun.

Edgar, the Atheling.

Matilda[3]=Henry I. of England.

(2) EMMA was the mother of

Alfred. Edward the Confessor. Goda[4]=Walter of Mantes.

Maria=Eustace III. of Boulogne. Ralph.

[1] Saxon Chronicle. [2] Flor. of Worcester.

[3] William of Malmesbury states that Henry married Matilda "in our time," thus showing that he was their contemporary.

[4] She also married Eustace II. of Boulogne, of Dover notoriety: by his second wife, Ida, Eustace became the father of Eustace III., and of Godfrey and Baldwin, successively kings of Jerusalem.

spirit upon that barbarous day. His next victim was

Elfhelm, caldorman of Mercia. Edric invited him to a great feast at Shrewsbury. During the hunt which followed, a ruffian, known as "the town's hound,"[1] suddenly sprang upon Elfhelm[2] and killed him. The assassin had been bribed by Edric.

Edric had gained the king's favour by his riches,[3] by his smooth tongue,[4] and persuasive language.[5] He was made caldorman of Mercia 1007; and he also obtained

the hand of the king's daughter, Elgitha. Ethelred appears to have been as great a match-maker as Athelstan. The latter married his sisters to ruling princes: the former married his daughters to the leading men in the land, whom he attached to his cause by these marriages.[6]

In the year 1004 Sweyn paid his second visit to England, and plundered and burnt down Norwich and other places. In 1006 he again landed upon our shores, and England is said to have trembled before him like the rustling of a bed of reeds shaken by the west wind.[5] King Ethelred, naturally indolent,[3] was sick with sorrow and perplexity at his manor in Shropshire.[7] His army was a mere rabble, ignorant of military discipline, and

---

[1] Flor. of Worcester.

[2] Canute married his daughter Elfgiva. She was the mother of Harold Harefoot, King of England, and of Sweyn, King of Norway.

Florence of Worcester states that Sweyn was the son of a priest, and Harold the son of a cobbler; and that they were adopted by Elfgiva, who assured the king that she was their mother,—hence Mary of Modena was not the first suspected of having deceived a royal husband.

No doubt Elfgiva informed Canute of her father's assassination through Edric's instrumentality; but she did not live to see her husband revenge the death of his father-in-law.

[3] Matt. of Westminster.   [5] Will. of Malmesbury.
[4] Flor. of Worcester.   [6] See previous page.
                    [7] Henry of Huntingdon.

without a leader.[1]   The days of peace under Edgar had made the Saxons unfit for war : and his fleets had been allowed to decay.   In his desperation the king had been advised to buy off the invaders.   He had already on three different occasions paid them 10,000, 16,000, and 24,000 pounds of silver; and in the year 1007 Sweyn consented to a peace upon the receipt of 36,000 pounds of silver.   These ruinous sums of money bought off the invader only for a short time.   In 1008 the Witan, at which the King presided, determined to build a large fleet for the defence of the country, and to get armour for the sailors.   It was decreed that the whole of England should contribute in the proportion of one ship for three hundred and ten hides of land, and a breast-plate and helmet for nine hides.   A hide was as much land as one plough could till in a year.   This was the first direct tax levied in England : it was a thoroughly voluntary one.   With the money thus raised one thousand vessels were built.   After their construction they were brought together at Sandwich, with supplies of provisions and chosen troops[2] on board, and there they laid at anchor.   Such a naval force had never been seen in England before.   But the money and the labour of the nation were brought to nought through the conduct of Brihtric, who falsely accused his nephew Wulfnoth to the King.   Wulfnoth fled with twenty vessels, and was pursued by his uncle with eighty, who vowed he would bring him back "dead or alive."[3]   A storm arose and shattered the fleet under Brihtric.   The wrecks were set on fire by Wulfnoth.   The evil tidings soon reached the rest of the fleet, which returned to London.

The Danes bought off

The Saxon fleet, 1008.

Wulfnoth.

[1] Matt. of Westminster.

[2] Florence of Worcester.   [3] Henry of Huntingdon.

The army was also broken up. Henceforth Ethelred took no active part in the defence of his kingdom.

Destruction of Canterbury, 1011.

We now pass on to the year 1011, when Canterbury was betrayed to the Danes, who put some of the men to the sword, others perished in the flames that enveloped the town, several were thrown headlong from the walls, women were dragged by their hair through the streets and then burnt to death: infants, torn from their mother's breasts, were caught on the point of spears, or crushed beneath the wheels of waggons.[1] The venerable Archbishop Elphege was loaded with fetters and tortured. For seven months[1] he was kept in prison, as the Danes expected he would pay the sum of three thousand pounds of silver for his release. He

Archbishop Elphege's martyrdom, 1012.

refused to pay it. Thereupon they dragged him before their popular assembly, and pelted him with stones, bones, and ox skulls, and finally, one of them, who had been confirmed by the archbishop the day before his martyrdom, put an end to his sufferings, out of pity, by splitting his head with an axe.[1] Thus fell this noble man, whose courage and consistency excites the admiration of mankind.

Sweyn: his successes and death, 1014.

In 1012 Edric[1] and other members of the Witan prevailed upon the Danes to leave England for 48,000 pounds of silver. The following year Sweyn entered England for the last time. His track was marked by blood, famine, and pestilence. The whole country was at his mercy. Oxford fell before the Danes. Winchester opened its gates to Sweyn. At Bath he was proclaimed king. The Londoners alone stood firm, and resisted his attacks as long as the king remained with them; but when[2] he fled from the city in order to join

---

[1] Florence of Worcester.   [2] William of Malmesbury.

his wife and children in Normandy, they too surrendered
to the Danish conqueror. The queen had left England
two years before her husband, under the protection of
Edric, who attended upon her at her brother's court " in
splendid style."[1] Shortly afterwards Sweyn was killed
whilst assaulting the Burgh[2] that contained the remains
of St. Edmund, by the martyr himself, so the chroniclers
assert.[3] Most probably a patriotic assassin, or a ruffian
in the pay of Edric, taking advantage of the inoffensive
credulity of the people of the locality, despatched the
gigantic[4] and cruel-hearted Sweyn. Upon his death
the Witan with one voice determined to recall Ethelred, **Ethelred's return.**
on condition[3] that he would govern more justly and
more gently than he had done before.[4] The king
promised to be a loving and gentle lord to them, to
consult their wishes, to act according to their advice,
and to forgive and forget the past. These promises
were made by word of mouth and by treaty.[3] Thereupon Ethelred returned to his native land, and was
received with great honour,[3] and joy.[1]

To avoid capture Canute was obliged to leave England **Canute's flight.**
in haste; but, before he did so, he cut off the hands and
ears, and slit the nostrils of the Saxon hostages who
had been entrusted to his father.

After the return of Ethelred, Edric, through unjusti-
fiable desire for their property,[5] caused Morcar and Sige- **Morcar and Sigeforth.**
forth, the rulers of the seven Burghs, who were attend-
ing a conference at Oxford, to be slain at a banquet[1] to

---

[1] Matt. of Westminster.   [3] Bury St. Edmunds of to-day.

[3] Florence of Worcester, &c.   Edmund was the last Saxon king of East
Anglia; he was killed by the sons of Regner Lodbrog in 870. Guthrum
became King of East Anglia in 878.

[4] This is the first symptom of that spirit that eventually secured for us
the privileges embodied in Magna Charta.   [6] Will. of Malmesbury.

which he had invited them. Their followers took refuge in a church, which afforded them no protection, as it was burnt to the ground, and all within its walls perished in the flames. Edric was baulked of the fruits of his stratagem and guilt by the king's son Edmund the Ironside, who married Sigeferth's widow, Elgitha, a lady remarkable for her rank and beauty.[1] Edmund also seized upon the rights and property of the Danish nobles who were slaughtered at Oxford.

Attempt upon the life of Edmund the Ironside.

In revenge, Edric made an attempt upon the life of the Atheling Edmund, but his designs were frustrated And yet, despite his manifold treacheries, he managed to regain the confidence of all. This can only be explained by the fact that, if he did not actually hold the balance of power between the contending parties, he was at least at the head of a considerable party, and had much influence over the crowd that follows fortune's smile.

Shortly after his attempt upon the life of the Atheling, Edric enticed the crews of forty ships of the royal fleet, which were manned by Danes,[2] to follow his fortunes. He then joined Canute. The West Saxons now submitted to the Danes, delivering hostages and supplying them with horses. The Ironside tried to induce the Mercians to attack Edric and Canute, but they refused to do so unless they were joined by the King and the Londoners. Thereupon he disbanded his forces. But in a short time he was at the head of another army, which was joined by the King. The latter soon returned to London, as he had been informed that some of his auxiliaries intended to betray him to the enemy.

---

[1] Will. of Malmesbury.   [2] Flor. of Worcester.

In the year 1016 death seized upon the King. He had been unfortunate from his very birth. The disasters that surrounded him through life were predicted by Dunstan at the font. At Ethelred's coronation Dunstan addressed him as follows:—"Because you have aspired to the kingdom by the death of your brother, whom your mother murdered, the sword shall never depart from your house, but shall rage against you all your life, killing your offspring, until your kingdom is given to another family, whose manners and language the nation you govern do not know."[1] The ghost of the slaughtered Edward seemed to have pursued the fickle king to the day of his death. And the sword never departed from his house. Three[2] of his sons were tortured to death. Two[3] sons and two[4] grandsons suffered the miseries of exile. One[5] alone ascended the throne of his ancestors, but only to become, like his father before him, a tool in the hands of favourites. Both father and son were equally out of place upon the throne, and mocked its dignity. Both were succeeded by brave and energetic monarchs,[6] each of whom died in defence of his country.

Death of Ethelred, 1016.

The fate of Ethelred's family.

And now we come to one of the most memorable years in English History—that of 1016. In many respects it resembles the year 1066. In fact, the similarity between the events connected with the Danish and Norman Conquests is particularly striking. Before the year 1016, five[7] kings had hired Danish troops.

A comparison of the years 1016 and 1066.

---

[1] Matthew of Westminster.
[2] Edmund, the Ironside; Alfred, his first-born by Emma of Normandy; and Edwy, the Atheling. [3] Edward the Confessor, and Alfred.
[4] The Ironside's two sons, Edward and Edmund.
[5] The Confessor. [6] The Ironside; and Harold, son of Godwin.
[7] Edward, Athelstan, Edmund, Edred, Edgar.

One[1] endeavoured to get rid of them all at once. The last Saxon king[2] before the Danish conquest fought many battles, but was slain and succeeded by his conqueror.[3] Five[4] kings favoured Normans. A Norman force was almost extirpated.[5] The last[6] Saxon king before the Norman Conquest vainly endeavoured by a series of battles to prevent his country's overthrow, and he, too, was slain and succeeded by his conqueror.[7]

The year 1016 is also distinguished by the supreme efforts made by Edric to compass the destruction of every member of the stock of Cerdic.

Edmund the Ironside.

The hero of this period was Edmund,

Who Ironside was called
for his valour.[8]

No defeat daunted his brave heart. No treachery quelled his proud spirit. No fatigue wearied his iron frame. Victory or defeat alike found him prepared to renew the contest. Wherever he fought in person, his skill and bravery, unless thwarted by guile, were always crowned with victory. Six[9] pitched battles were fought, Edmund won five, but was defeated in the last. Upon the death of his father Ethelred, the citizens of London and the few nobles that were in the city at the time elected him king. The majority of the nobles and bishops took the part of Canute, and swore fealty to him at Southampton.[10]

The battle of Sherston.

The battle of Sherston lasted two days. On the first day the ealdorman of Mercia joined the Danes at the head of a large force, but as this act had not the desired

---

[1] Ethelred.   [2] The Ironside.   [3] Canute.
[4] Ethelred, Canute, Harold, Hardicanute, and Edward.
[5] The force under Alfred the Atheling.   [6] Harold, son of Godwin.
[7] William of Normandy.   [8] *Saxon Chronicle.*
[9] Pen; Sherston; London; Brentford; in Kent; Assandun.
[10] Matthew of Westminster.

effect of bringing disaster upon the Saxon host, he determined upon a more daring stratagem. The next day the fight was continued, and Edmund surpassed his former feats of valour, for, quitting his usual position by the standard, he rushed impetuously upon the foremost rank of the Danes, and fell upon it like lightning. Wielding a chosen sword, he hewed a passage through the very centre of the foe, and charged right on to Canute's bodyguard. Then Edric frustrated the effect of Edmund's daring conduct, and snatched the victory from his very grasp, for he struck off the head of one Osmer, who bore a striking likeness to the king, and, holding it up, shouted to the Saxons, "Flet Engle, flet Engle, ded is Edmund."[1] On the instant a dart sped like a thunder-bolt from the hand of the Ironside against the cruel traitor, but, unfortunately, he avoided it, and two soldiers were transfixed by the terrible missile. Edmund immediately proceeded to an eminence, and taking off his helmet, an act afterwards imitated by the Norman duke at Senlac, showed his face to his comrades. Confidence was restored, the battle was resumed, and at the fall of night Canute retired.

Treachery of Edric.

One writer[2] asserts that Edmund was assisted by a body of Welshmen at the battle of Sherston, and that he was rescued by them at the time that Edric pretended he had been killed.

The Welsh help Edmund.

After this encounter Edric deserted the Danes and swore fealty to King Edmund. But at the battle of Assandun—the Danish Hastings—he fled at the head of his forces.[3] The slaughter at this battle was very

Battle of Assandun

[1] Flee English, flee English, Edmund is dead.—*Henry of Huntingdon.*

[2] Geoffrey Gaimar.   [3] *Saxon Chronicle.*

great, as no quarter was given: all[1] the Saxon nobles
were destroyed. A small number remained firm upon
the battle-field after the flight of Edric and the retreat
of Edmund, and, glorying in the death of the brave,
were cut off to a man.[2]

Flight of
Edmund.

Edmund fled almost alone[2] to Gloucester, where he
was joined by Saxon and Welsh partisans. Canute
pursued the fugitive. A battle was imminent; Edmund
and his forces were on the Welsh[3] side of the Severn,
Canute and his army were on the opposite banks of the
river; but the people cried aloud[2] for peace. Edric is
reported[4] to have averted a general battle, and to have
brought about a personal encounter between Canute
and Edmund. In an assembly of nobles he spoke

Edric's
speech.

thus[4]—" O, senseless nobles, men mighty in arms, why
do we expose ourselves to death in battle for our kings,
who, notwithstanding our slaughter, neither succeed in
becoming masters of the kingdom, nor put any limits
to their greed. My advice is, that they (Edmund and
Canute) should fight, yes, fight in single combat, since
their object is to reign singly. What is the meaning
of such lust for kingly power? Is England not large
enough for *two* kings, when formerly it was large
enough for *eight?* Therefore, let them singly make
peace, or singly fight for the crown." This masterly
oration pleased everyone.[5] Another writer[2] states that

---

[1] *Saxon Chronicle.*   [2] Will. of Malmesbury.   [3] Flor. of Worcester.
[4] Matt. of Westminster.

[5] *Matthew of Westminster.* This writer gives a full account of the
encounter upon the small island of Olney, between Edmund and Canute, in
the sight of the two armies; and so does Henry of Huntingdon. They
state that their spears were shattered to pieces against their fine armour;
the fight was continued with swords: the people heard the dreadful clang
and saw the flashing of their arms, and they shouted approval and encouragement, or groaned aloud in sympathy with the combats. At length Edmund

Edmund demanded a single combat, in order to put a stop to the shedding of the people's blood, but that Canute refused to meet him as he was so small[1] and Edmund so big, and suggested that England should be divided between them. This suggestion was carried out. The kings met at Olney, an island in the middle[2] of the river Severn, and agreed upon a treaty of peace, love, and brotherhood.[2] Edmund was to hold the crown with Wessex, East Anglia, Essex, and London; the rest of the country was to be held by Canute. The two kings parted. Canute returned to his ships, and Edmund marched to London.

Combat between Canute and Edmund.

Shortly afterwards Edric surpassed all his former cruelties by the assassination of the brave Edmund the Ironside. The unholy deed was done either by Edric's son,[3] or by Edmund's personal attendants,[1] who had been bribed by the arch-traitor. The king was attacked when alone, and entirely defenceless—a dagger or iron hook was thrust into his body.[4]

Assassination of Edmund.

Canute was immediately acknowledged king of all England. He began at once to remove by death or banishment the members of the royal family, and in this undertaking he was eagerly assisted by the Mercian ealdorman. Edwy the Atheling, brother of Edmund, was banished and afterwards murdered.[5] Edward and

Canute the King

The Exile of the family of Ethelred.

redoubled his blows on the head of his enemy like thunder. Canute, beginning to quail, suggested that they should be brothers and govern the kingdom between them, and Denmark also in like manner. The people gave their consent to the suggestion "with tears of joy;" and the kings kissed and became friends.

[1] Will. of Malmesbury.

[2] Flor. of Worcester: the *Saxon Chronicle* states the result "of their coming together" was a confirmation of their friendship by pledge and oath.　　　[3] Matt. of Westminster.

[4] Adam of Bremen states that he was poisoned.　　[5] Flor. of Worcester.

Alfred, sons of Ethelred and Emma, fled into Normandy. Edward and Edmund, the infant sons of the Ironside, contrary to Edric's advice—for he wished them to be despatched at once—were sent to Olave, King of Sweden, who was requested to put them to death: he refused to do so, and sent them to the court of Stephen, King of Hungary. Edwy, King of the Churls, a kind of tribune of the people, the Robin Hood of his day, was also driven into exile, but was afterwards reconciled to the king.

Edric. Edric now aspired to the crown. His object all along had been to crush Edmund by means of Canute, and so weaken Canute that, by stirring up the popular prejudices against the Danes, he might succeed in driving them out of the country. He could the more easily take the lead on account of the slaughter of the nobles at Assandun. He was now the only Saxon that ruled one of the four great divisions of England. Two were ruled by Danes, and the fourth by a Norwegian. And now only one person stood between him and that object, to attain which he had shed rivers of blood, had broken every tie of humanity, had approached, as far as it was possible for man to approach, the utmost bounds of iniquity, and had exhibited those characteristics which are universally acknowledged to be the special attributes of the Prince of Darkness.

Like Count Robert of Artois,[1] Edric, in the pride of his heart, boasted of his services to the king; thereupon the latter determined upon his destruction. We now arrive at the last scene in the eventful life of the

---

[1] Great-grandson of the brother of Saint Louis of France: he was the chief means of raising Philip VI. to the throne of France. He took the part of Edward III.

ealdorman of Mercia. At the Christmas festivities[1] of Edric. 1017 the court was held in London. A numerous and brilliant assembly was gathered together, headed by the "gift of the fairies." This "flower of Normandy,"[2] forgetting the injuries inflicted upon her family and the exile of her two sons, had bestowed her hand upon Canute in the previous month of July.[1] Edric was present at the feast of our Lord's Nativity,[1] which was celebrated at the royal palace. In his company were many noble Saxons. The king evidently dreaded the daring and unscrupulous cunning of the Saxon ealdorman, and was prepared to accomplish his destruction with his own weapons,[3] and we read[1] that he feared he would some day fall a victim to Edric's treachery. Notwithstanding the joyful and solemn occasion, treachery, cruel and unrelenting, was enthroned in the heart of Canute. Whilst the wine-cup went round and laughter and music resounded throughout the banquetting hall, he was meditating over the assassination of his guests. Edric had received a mysterious intimation of his impending fate, for when he presented himself before Canute after the assassination of Edmund, he saluted him thus—"Hail! thou who art the sole King of England;" and when he had explained the meaning of his strange salutation, Canute enigmatically replied—"For this deed I will exalt you, as it merits, *higher than all the nobles of England.*"[4] It is possible that Edric did not

---

[1] Flor. of Worcester.   [2] Henry of Huntingdon so terms Queen Emma.
[3] William of Malmesbury.

[4] Henry of Huntingdon: according to this chronicler Edric was beheaded "*then*," that is, *immediately* after his salutation; this was in 1016. But according to Florence of Worcester, Edric was slain in the king's palace *whilst* Canute was keeping the Feast of our Lord's Nativity, in London, on 25th December, 1017. Matthew of Westminster distinctly states that Edric was strangled *directly after* he had attacked the king for having de-

perceive from the king's reply that he was to be exalted
after the manner of Haman's exaltation; still, it is
quite probable that he fully understood the implied
threat, but that, having implicit confidence in his own
cunning, influence, and power, he attached no importance to the enigma, and, therefore, visited his
sovereign in his palace without fear or suspicion of
foul play. But on the evening of the feast he was told
that he was no longer[1] caldorman of Mercia. Whereupon
he bearded the king to his very face, and tauntingly reminded him that to his services alone he owed his
exaltation to the throne, and that the death[2] of King
Edmund was caused through his fidelity to Canute.
The King became red[1] with rage; and, to prevent a
tumult,[1] for, doubtless, Edric's retainers and partisans
were both in and without the palace, he ordered a Norwegian jarl[3] to fall upon him there and then. The
order was obeyed upon the instant. William of Malmesbury states that Edric was strangled in Canute's
presence, and that his body was thrown out of a win-
dow into the river Thames. Florence of Worcester
writes that his dead body was thrown over the city
walls and left unburied. Henry of Huntingdon states
that his head was placed upon the highest[4] battlement
of the Tower of London. For "battlement" Matthew
of Westminster writes "stake," and remarks that
Edric's head was fixed upon it—as a prey to the birds.

Death of
Edric.

prived him of his earldom; it would therefore appear that this altercation
and assassination took place at the Feast.

[1] Matt. of Westminster.

[2] Matt. of Westminster; Canute left money to be spent in masses for the
repose of Edmund's soul: this is supposed to indicate a guilty conscience.

[3] Eric, who cut off his head.

[4] Thus Edric was exalted "higher than all the nobles of England."

With Edric fell Norman, nephew of Leofric the ealdor- **Edric.**
man; Ethelward, son of Ethelmar the ealdorman; and
Brihtric, son of Elphege, ealdorman of Devon.

Thus perished this mighty plotter. We do not read
that he ever used the sword, except against Osmer; yet
his influence over kings, Witans, and the people was
apparently unbounded. In the art of ascending the
ladder of fortune upon the passions and weaknesses of
his fellows, he has no rival in ancient or modern
history.

LEADING EVENTS.

CHAPTER XIII.

CANUTE, THE KING.

Canute,
1016 to
1035.

WE have read that Canute crushed at one blow the machinations of the powerful and terrible Edric, ealdorman of Mercia; and that, not content with the destruction of the leader, he slew with him his chief supporters. The hopes of the Saxons perished at the banquet of blood with which Canute terminated the feast of our Lord's Nativity in the year 1017, for with Edric, Norman, Ethelward, and Brihtric, fell the only Saxon confederation that Canute dreaded. The long wars between the Danes and the Saxons had cleared the land of the old nobility, so that when Canute became king, the Saxon Witan had not a single independent member. This representative assembly of the Saxon people decreed anything and everything that was likely to conciliate the Danish conqueror. Canute was determined to remove every rival out of his way. And

Removal
of Saxon
royal
family.

everyone[1] who was related to the Saxon royal family he banished. And we have read that he sent the sons of his brave rival Edmund to Norway, but that Olave, king of that country, refused to comply with his request to put them to death. With their removal, and by the death of Edwy the Atheling, and the exile of Alfred and Edward, there was not a single member of the Saxon royal family in the land to conspire against his

[1] Matt. of Westminster.

authority. The king was most anxious[1] to secure the crown of England for his sons by his first wife,[2] Elgiva of Mercia.

Upon the death of Elgiva, Canute married Emma of Normandy. He was wishful that she should become his wife for two[3] reasons: first, to reconcile the Saxons to his rule by the sight of one seated by his side to whom they had been accustomed to pay obedience: secondly, to acquire the favour of her brother, Richard II., Duke of Normandy, and thus check his inclination to take the part of his nephews, Alfred and Edward. William of Malmesbury is in doubt who deserves greater blame—the uncle who neglected the cause of his nephews, or the woman who had consented to marry the man who had injured her first husband and driven her children into exile. {.marginnote Emma.}

Canute's precautions did not rest with slaughter, banishment, and marriage. He determined to send back to Denmark all his ships except forty; and to reduce his Danish army to 3,000 men. One authority[1] states that this was done at the advice of Queen Emma, and that "all the paid troops" were sent back to Denmark. But they did not go back to their native shores empty handed. Some had sold the lands which had been bestowed upon them; and to pay his[1] Danish army the provinces were obliged to contribute 72,000[5] or 73,000,[6] and London 10,500[5] or 11,000[6] pounds of silver. {.marginnote Dismissal of Danish forces.}

The 3,000 troops that remained in England were particularly well disciplined. It would appear that

---

[1] Matt. of Westminster.
[2] Dr. Lingard, and Mr. Green, in direct contradiction to Matt. of Westminster, state she was not his queen.   [3] Will. of Malmesbury.
[4] Flor. of Worcester.   [5] Saxon Chronicle.   [6] Henry of Huntingdon.

the king was anxious to secure their attachment : with this object in view he placed himself under the same rules which they were obliged to observe, for, killing a soldier in a passion, he pretended to place himself at the mercy of his huscarls and to submit to their judgment. As they were silent, he condemned himself to pay 360 talents of gold, nine times the amount of the usual fine, and nine additional talents. Such conduct as this was highly calculated to win not merely the ready obedience, but also the sincere affections of his trusted followers.

The Witan   Canute summoned all the bishops, ealdormen, and chief men to meet him in London.[1] When they met, he asked them whether Edmund intended that his brothers or his sons were to succeed him. At once they replied that Edmund never intended that his brothers should succeed him : and they also stated that it was his wish that Canute should be the guardian and protector of his sons until they were of age.[1] This was done to gain the king's favour : instead of that, some of these false witnesses were put to death by his orders.

After this enquiry he used every effort to win the Saxon nobility to his cause. He was successful : the members of the Witan elected him king, and swore they would obey him ; and, at the same time, they repudiated the claims of Edmund's brothers and sons, and denied their rights to the throne. Canute also made an agreement with all the nobles and people ; and they made, upon oath, a solemn concord between them, and in this way they ended and put into oblivion all their past animosities.[1]

[1] Florence of Worcester.

Canute was successful in a threefold character—as a soldier, a legislator,[1] and a regulator of church affairs.

As a soldier he was eminently successful in securing the confidence of his own troops, and in winning over to his cause the leaders of the armies to which he was opposed. It was his determination that, undaunted by reverses and repeated encounters, ultimately led to his sovereignty over England, Denmark, Norway, and part of Sweden, and to his lordship over Scotland.

Canute as a soldier.

We shall now refer to his warlike expeditions. In 1019[2] he sailed from England with his forty ships, to Denmark, and spent the winter there. In 1024[3] he fought against the Swedes, who were led by Ulf and Eglaf.

One of his companions in this enterprise was Godwin, son of "Child" Wulfnoth. On the first[4] day of battle the Swedes were victorious. Under the year 1025 the *Saxon Chronicle* states that Ulf and Eglaf came against Canute in Denmark, with a land army and a fleet; and that, in the engagement that followed, very many Danes and English were killed, and that the Swedes remained upon the battle-field. No doubt this passage has reference to the first day's fight mentioned by Matthew of Westminster. On the evening of the next day Godwin addressed his fellow-countrymen, and exhorted[5] them not to forget their ancient fame, but to display their courage before their new lord; and he

Godwin's victory over the Swedes, 1025.

---

[1] Matt. of Westminster states that Queen Emma advised Canute to reconcile the English to him by gifts, and by the promise of good and welcome laws.

[2] *Saxon Chronicle;* Matt. of Westminster.

[3] Matt. of Westminster; Henry of Huntingdon gives 1020 as the date of this expedition; Will. of Malmesbury states that it took place the year before the death of Olave of Norway, that is, in 1029.

[4] Matt. of Westminster.   [5] Will. of Malmesbury.

assured them that it was by an accident on the part of
fortune that they had been conquered by Canute, but
if they defeated those who had overcome him, then such
a victory would be ascribed to their courage. That night,
when both camps were sunk in sleep, Godwin made a
night attack[1] upon the Swedes. He took them by
surprise, defeated and killed a great number of them;
Ulf and Eglaf. and obliged Ulf and Eglaf to surrender and come to
terms of peace. When morning broke, Canute dis-
covered that the tents of the Saxons were empty: he
concluded that Godwin and his men, becoming panic-
struck, had betaken themselves to flight, or that they
had gone over to the enemy. But when he arrived
at the camp of the Swedes, he perceived the results
of Godwin's night attack. As a reward for his victory,
Canute made Godwin an earl; and evermore he held
the Saxons in the highest honour.[2]

Olave of Norway. Having overcome the Swedes, and secured Denmark
from further invasions, Canute directed his attention to
Norway. It will be remembered that its king, Olave,
refused to comply with Canute's request to do away
with the Ironside's sons. Perhaps this refusal was
never forgiven by Canute. Be this as it may, he determined upon the conquest of his kingdom; and, in 1028,
he landed in Norway, and having expelled Olave, he
took possession of the whole land.[3] Before he set sail
for Norway, with his usual caution and knowledge of
the treachery that existed amongst most nations, he
sent as bribes[4] large sums of gold and silver to Olave's

---

[1] Matt. of Westminster; Henry of Huntingdon.

[2] Matt. of Westminster; Henry of Huntingdon. Ulf married Canute's
sister; and Godwin married Ulf's sister Gytha.

[3] *Saxon Chronicle.*   [4] Florence of Worcester.

chief men. They accepted the bribes, and sent messengers to Canute stating that they were prepared to
receive him. In 1030, Olave tried to regain his king- Olave of
dom, but his own people rose up against him and killed Norway.
him.

Olave was the Apostle of Norway, for as king,
teacher, and preacher, he tried to spread a knowledge
of the gospel amongst his people. He also made good
laws. His efforts excited the superstitious prejudices[1]
of his subjects. Olave was the companion of Sweyn,
Canute's father, in his first invasion of England, 994.[2]
Upon that occasion he received part of the 16,000
pounds of silver which had been raised by Ethelred to
induce the invaders to leave the country. He was in-
troduced by Elphege,[3] the martyred Archbishop of
Canterbury, to Ethelred, who presented royal gifts to
him. They made a covenant with one another, and
Olave promised never again to visit England in hostile
array. He kept his promise in a righteous manner.
No doubt he became a Christian through the influence
and administration of the good Elphege. The conduct of
Olave is a bright contrast to that of his contemporaries.

Canute's revengeful spirit, greed, and bribes accorded
with the feelings of the Norwegians. Upon the death
of their sainted king, they acknowledged as his successor Canute's eldest son, Sweyn.

Canute brought his conquests to a close by the
defeat of Malcolm of Scotland, and by the acknowledgment of his supremacy over that country. He does
not appear to have made war upon the Welsh, or
to have interfered with the affairs of Wales.

[1] Matt. of Westminster.   [2] Saxon Chronicle.
[3] At that time he was Bishop of Winchester.

Canute as a legislator. As a legislator, Canute showed that he possessed a comprehensive spirit and a humane disposition. The Danes and the Saxons met at Oxford in 1018, and agreed to live under King Edgar's laws,[1] or those of Edward the Elder.[2] Another meeting was held at Winchester: this gathering resulted in the compilation of a code of laws founded upon those of previous sovereigns. They enacted, (i.) that mercy should be shown the poor, and the penitent ill-doer; but that the impenitent criminal, and the rich should be treated with sternness. (ii.) they prohibited the sale of natives upon the continent, lest they should be prevailed upon to forsake their faith : (iii.) witchcraft was forbidden, as well as the worship of natural objects: (iv.) purveyance[3] was abolished: it was enacted that neither widows nor spinsters should be forced to marry against their will. Canute also equalized the rate, and lowered the amount, of money which the representatives of tenants were obliged to pay to their lords upon the death of the former.

Canute as a churchman. As a patron of the Church, Canute was most liberal and also just. He built churches at all places where he had fought battles,[2] and placed ministers in them, who were to perform divine service for the salvation of those who had been killed in their vicinity.

To the monastery of Glastonbury, which contained the body of his heroic antagonist, Edmund the Ironside, he was particularly noble and liberal. It would appear that he paid a pilgrimage to that shrine in the year 1026.[2] He prayed over the tomb of King Edmund for

---

[1] *Saxon Chronicle.*   [2] *Matt. of Westminster.*

[3] Purveyance enabled a king or his representatives to journey through the land at the expense of the subject.

the *salvation of his soul:*[1] and he presented it with a
cloak of various colours. And this he did in order to
remove the supposition that he had consented to the
death[2] of the man with whom he had made a treaty at
the time when they met in single combat. He also
granted the abbots of this monastery the immunities
of their predecessors with the words—" I, Canute, king
of England, by the counsel and decree of Archbishop
Ethelnoth, and of all the priests of God, and by the advice
of our nobility, do, for the love of heaven, and the
pardon of my sins,[1] and the *remission*[1] of the *trans-
gressions*[1] of my brother, King Edmund, grant to the
Church at Glastonbury its rights and customs throughout my kingdom."[3]

He was also, at the entreaty of his wife, very liberal
to the monastery at Winchester: so much so, that
strangers were astonished[2] at the sight of the quantity
of gold and silver with which it was adorned.

In 1031,[4] Canute journeyed from Denmark to Rome
with great pomp.[5] As going to and returning from the
imperial city, he was most kind to the poor; and he
also purchased, at great cost, the abolition[6] of the tolls
which were extorted from pilgrims at different parts of
their journey. No king from the west of Europe had
visited Rome with so magnificent a display[5] as Canute.
His offerings, alms, and banquets were countless.[5]

In a letter in which he describes the results of his
journey to Rome, he styles himself King of all England,
Denmark, Norway, and part of Sweden: and states that

Canute's
letter.

---

[1] Hence it has been inferred that he had arranged with Edric to bring
about Edmund's death.　　[2] Matthew of Westminster.
　　[3] Will. of Malmesbury.　　[4] Saxon Chronicle.
　　[5] Henry of Huntingdon.　　[6] Flor. of Worcester.

his journey was made for the forgiveness of his sins,
and for the welfare of his dominions and subjects ;[1] that
he was received with honour, and presented with gifts
by the Pope John, and the Emperor Conrad; that he
had arranged with the various princes he met there to
obtain for his people, merchants and pilgrims, better
justice and greater security whilst they journeyed to
and from Rome. He also stated in his letter that he
had expressed his high displeasure that the archbishops
in his domains were forced to pay immense sums of
money when they went to the apostolic see to receive
the pallium, and that it was decreed that such extortions should cease.

He remarks :—" Be it known, therefore, to all of you,
that I have humbly vowed to the Almighty God henceforth to amend my life in all respects, and to rule the
kingdoms and the people subject to me with justice and
clemency, giving equitable judgments in all matters.
If, through the intemperance of youth or negligence,
I have hitherto exceeded the bounds of justice in any
of my acts, I intend, by God's aid, to make an entire
change for the better. I, therefore, adjure and command my counsellors, to whom I have entrusted the
affairs of my kingdom, that henceforth they neither
commit themselves, nor suffer to prevail, any sort of
injustice throughout my dominions, either from fear of
me, or from favour to any powerful person. I also
command all sheriffs and magistrates throughout my
whole kingdom, as they tender my regard and their
own safety, that they use no unjust violence to any man,
rich or poor, but that all, high and low, rich and poor,
shall enjoy alike impartial law ; from which they are

[1] Flor. of Worcester.

never to deviate, either on account of royal favour, respect of persons in the great, or for the sake of heaping up money wrongfully."[1]

The letter further remarks:—"May God, of his merciful kindness, uphold my sovereignty and honour, and ever scatter and bring to naught the power of all my enemies."[1]

He then states:—"I have sent this letter before me that my subjects may be gladdened at my success, because, as you know, I have never spared, nor will I spare myself, any exertions for the needful service of my whole people."[1]

Canute endeared himself to the Church, as we have read, by the erection of churches, and the restoration and adornment of monasteries, and also by his munificence whilst on his pilgrimage to Rome. But one of his acts deserves special mention, and that was the part he took in connexion with the removal of the body of St. Elphege from St. Paul's, London, to Canterbury;[2] this was done in the year 1023.[3] Canute took up the body of St. Elphege with his own hands[2] from its first resting place; and, afterwards, in company with Emma, "the Lady,"[3] and their son Hardicanute, and Archbishop Ethelnoth, earls, bishops, and crowds of lay and clergymen, he saw the body borne with "songs of praise" into Canterbury. His participation in this ceremonial gave token of the lively interest he took in Church affairs, and was also evidence of the penitence

---

Flor. of Worcester.   [2] Will. of Malmesbury.

[3] *Saxon Chronicle.* Elphege was murdered in 1012; and this account of the removal of his body goes to prove that the events recorded in this chronicle were written about the time of their occurrence; were it not so, it would not have stated that his body was *first* buried in London, 1012.

of the representative of those Danes who had so cruelly treated the martyr of Canterbury.

Canute was fond of display at home and abroad. This characteristic was shown in connection with the removal of the body of St. Elphege, and his pilgrimage to Rome. It has also been stated[1] that the marriage of his daughter Gunhilda to Henry III., Emperor of Germany, was celebrated with such extraordinary pomp that minstrels and actors were unable to describe it at banquets and in taverns with sufficient force.[2]

Canute at the sea-side. When at the summit of his power he placed his seat by the sea side,[1] and addressed the approaching tide thus :—" You, also, are subject to my authority, as the land upon which I am seated is mine ; and no one has withstood my command with impunity. I, therefore, order you not to flow over my land, nor to presume to wet my royal robes." But on came the waves and dashed against the feet and legs of the king : then he leaped backwards, and explained—" Let all men know how empty and worthless is the power of kings, for there is none worthy of the name, but He, whom heaven and earth and sea obey by everlasting laws.'[3] For the last few months of his life the king declined to wear the crown, but placed it, in token of his humility, on an image of the Saviour.[3]

Canute's influence. No king of England exercised so wide-spread an influence over European affairs as Canute : on the

---

[1] Henry of Huntingdon.

[2] Matt. of Westminster and Will. of Malmesbury state that she was married during the reign of her brother, Hardicanute.

[3] Henry of Huntingdon : this writer states that when he was a boy he heard some very old people give an account of the massacres on St. Brice's Day in 1002 ; and he places Canute's encounter with the sea in 1035, consequently he was now approaching his own days, and must have conversed with persons familiar with this interesting incident.

continent he ruled Denmark, Norway, and Sweden, and enjoyed the confidence and support of the Pope and the Emperor; in Great Britain he ruled the whole of England in an absolute manner, for while he lived Siward, Leofric, and Godwin, dared not disturb the public peace, or act over their respective Earldoms in an independent manner; moreover, Scotland acknowledged his lordship, and Wales was quiet upon his Borders.

The character of Canute is an interesting study. It has three distinct features, that of an insatiable tyrant and crafty and jealous monarch, that of the humane and considerate man, and that of the religious reformer. As a tyrant, no ties of kith or kin, no regard for human life, no religious obstacle, was allowed to stand between him and the object upon which he had set his heart. As a crafty and jealous monarch, he removed every member of the stock of Cerdic, and afterwards banished or murdered his puppet lieutenants, Edric of Mercia, Eric of Northumbria, and Thurkill of East Anglia; caused the exile and death of Olave of Norway, and of his own nephew, "the doughty jarl"[1] Haco, who had married his niece Gunhilda, for he feared he would take away his life or his kingdoms.[2] As a humane and considerate man he framed laws that favoured the poor, the penitent, and the widow; he made roads[3] and considered the hardships of unknown pilgrims. As a religious reformer he built churches, restored and endowed monasteries, considered the souls of those whose bodies he had slain, made provision for the needs of all classes of his subjects at Rome,[4] freed

---

[1] *Saxon Chronicle.*   [2] Flor. of Worcester.
[3] Matthew of Westminster.
[4] He granted for all time the alms called "Romscot."—Henry of Huntingdon.

I

Canute's
character.
his bishops from papal extortions, and promised to amend[1] himself. Whatever Canute did, he did it with all his might: his character might be epitomised and rightly expressed by one word—thorough.

When we take into consideration his temptations, his difficulties, his conquests, and his various words and deeds, we may express sympathy with the sentiment[2] that he was—"Canute the Magnificent."[3]

LEADING EVENTS.

[1] Flor. of Worcester.   [2] *Saxon Chronicle.*
[3] Matthew of Westminster.

HOUSE OF CANUTE.

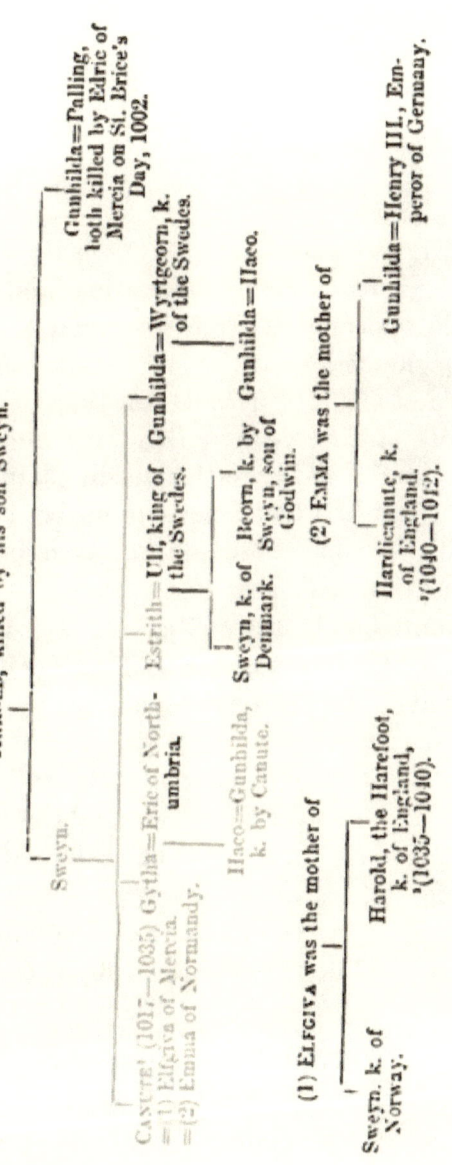

Harold, killed by his son Sweyn.

Sweyn.

Canute¹ (1017—1035) Gytha=Eric of North-   Estrith=Ulf, king of   Gunhilda=Wyrtgeorn, k.   Gunhilda=Palling,
=(1) Elfgiva of Mercia.   umbria.   the Swedes.   of the Swedes.   both killed by Edric of
=(2) Emma of Normandy.   Mercia on St. Brice's
Day, 1002.

Haco=Gunhilda,   Sweyn, k. of   Beorn, k. by   Gunhilda=Haco.
k. by Canute.   Denmark.   Sweyn, son of
Godwin.

(1) Elfgiva was the mother of   (2) Emma was the mother of

Sweyn, k. of   Harold, the Harefoot,   Hardicanute, k.   Gunhilda=Henry III, Em-
Norway.   k. of England,   of England,   peror of Germany.
¹(1035—1040).   ¹(1040—1042).

¹ Saxon Chronicle.

CHAPTER XIV.

HAROLD, THE HAREFOOT.

Harold,
son of
Canute,
1035 to
1040.

As long as Canute lived his extensive territories enjoyed freedom from foreign invasion and civil strife. It would appear that from his royal seat at Winchester his eagle eye quelled every foe, and that his iron hand was felt from Cornwall to the Orkneys, from the islands of the west to Denmark, and from the frozen regions of Norway to the sun-lit plains of Italy. But the breath had no sooner left his body than his mighty empire became as disunited as a bundle of faggots deprived of its encircling band.

Canute had bestowed the kingdom of Denmark[1] upon his son Hardicanute during his life-time; and that of Norway[2] upon his son Sweyn. They were their father's representatives.

For the throne of England the following were now eligible: Edward, son of Edmund the Ironside; Alfred, and Edward, the sons of Ethelred the Unready; Harold, and Hardicanute, the sons of Canute. A strong party were in favour of Godwin, son of "Child" Wulfnoth,[3] but the wary and loyal earl[4] rejected their

---

[1] Flor. of Worcester.   [2] Matt. of Westminster.

[3] Vita Æduardi Regis qui apud Westmonasterium requiescit: according to this Biography certain nobles tried to persuade Godwin to seize the crown whilst Canute was absent from England.

[4] The Danish kings appeared to have changed the term "*caldorman*" to that of "*earl*:" thus, in the first year of Canute's reign, Edric is termed "the caldorman;" but in 1036 we read of Godwin "the earl."—*Saxon Chronicle.*

flattering suggestion. The popular candidates were Harold and Hardicanute, as, in consequence of their long absence from England, Alfred and the two Edwards were looked upon as strangers and aliens.

A Witan was held at Oxford. The Danes and the citizens of London,[1] headed by Leofric, earl of Mercia, **Leofric.** took the part of Harold; the Saxons, headed by Godwin, **Godwin.** earl of Wessex, desired to elect Hardicanute,[2] or one of the sons of Ethelred. After much discussion it was decreed that Harold should rule as "chief of all England,"[2] and that Emma should dwell at Winchester and hold all Wessex in the name of her son Hardicanute: Godwin was the commander[3] of her army.

This division of England was made in the year 1035. In the following year[4] Alfred, the eldest son of Emma of **Alfred,** Normandy, made an attempt to gain the throne of his **son of** **Ethelred.** ancestors. With the help of a small fleet[5] he conducted many Norman knights[6] into England. It was given out that he wished to consult his mother[6] at Winchester, and also the king[5] in London : perhaps he expected that Emma would espouse his cause, as his half-brother continued to stay in Denmark, and that Harold would permit him to rule Wessex in the place of Hardicanute. Whatever his expectations were they were not realized.

By Godwin and the Saxons Alfred was looked upon as a perfect stranger. During a sojourn of twenty years

---

[1] Will. of Malmesbury. [2] *Saxon Chronicle.* [3] Henry of Huntingdon.

[4] *Saxon Chronicle*, Flor. of Worcester, &c.; Will. of Malmesbury states that Alfred entered England after the death of Harold. Henry of Huntingdon affirms that he landed upon our shores after the death of Hardicanute. Matthew of Westminster affirms that Alfred came to England in 1036, with 25 picked ships full of armed men, and that his intention was to take possession of his father's kingdom, which was his right, in a peaceable manner if possible, but by *force of arms* if necessary.

[5] Flor. of Worcester.

in Normandy he had forgotten the Saxon, and had
adopted the Norman language and customs. By the
Danes he was contemned, as a member of that royal
family that had been overcome by their rulers. It is
not surprising, therefore, that his arrival was viewed
with distrust and suspicion by all parties in England;
more especially as the force that accompanied him was
too numerous to afford him the excuse that he had come
upon a friendly errand. This force was calculated to
inspire alarm, and its appearance caused both Saxon
and Dane to conclude that the Atheling was determined
to acquire by *might*[1] what was his by *right*.[2]

Murder of
Alfred,
1036,

Alfred was seized. Godwin was accused[1] of betraying the Atheling. The same accusation was brought
against Living, Bishop of Crediton.[3] One writer[4] states
that Godwin determined upon the destruction of Alfred,
because he wished to marry his daughter to his brother
Edward, as he thought that Alfred would scorn such a
union, and that he prevailed upon the Saxons to fall
upon the Normans, by whispering in their ears that
Alfred had brought too many foreign followers, that he
had promised them the lands of the Saxons, that it
was not safe to allow so bold and crafty a race to take
root among them, and that these foreigners should be
punished so as to prevent others at some future time
intruding among the Saxons, on the ground that they
were related to the royal race of England.

Guildford[1] was the scene of Alfred's capture. The
Saxon Atheling was received by Godwin with the kiss
of Judas,[1] who provided him and his followers with a

---

[1] Matt. of Westminster.   [2] As the eldest son of Ethelred the Unready.

[3] Will. of Malmesbury.   [4] Henry of Huntingdon.

banquet. That night they were seized and decimated[1] twice[2] over, and the survivors with Alfred were sent to Harold, who[3] caused the former to be killed and the latter to be blinded. The *Saxon Chronicle* comments upon this massacre and mutilation as follows :— *Murder of Alfred, 1036.*

> " But Godwin him[3] in bonds set ;
> and his companions he dispersed
> and some divers-ways slew ;
> some they for money sold,
> some cruelly slaughtered,
> some did they bind,
> some did they blind,
> some did they scalp.
> It was decreed
> that he should be led
> To Elybury.
> Soon as he came to land
> in the ship he was blinded ;
> and him thus blind
> they brought to the monks :
> and he there abode
> the while that he lived."[4]

In the following year, 1037, as Hardicanute continued to live in Denmark, Harold was chosen king of all England.[5] He hastened to Winchester and seized upon the treasures which had been left to his step-mother by his father. Emma was banished,[5] and took refuge with Baldwin of Flanders.

With the death of Alfred, the disappearance of the queen-mother, and the absence of her sons Edward and Hardicanute, Harold looked forward to quietness and ease ; but he died in three years' time.[5] *Death of Harold, 1040.*

---

[1] Nine out of every ten were killed.

[2] Matthew of Westminster. [3] Alfred.

[4] No mention is made by this chronicler of the date of Alfred's death ; but Florence of Worcester states that he died *shortly after* he was placed in the custody of the monks of Ely.

[5] *Saxon Chronicle.*

This king was very fond of hunting on foot: he was renowned for his speed, hence his name—Harold, "The Harefoot."

LEADING EVENTS.

CHAPTER XV.

HARDICANUTE, KING OF ENGLAND.

BEFORE the death of his half-brother Harold, Hardicanute had, at the earnest advice of his mother, determined to make an attempt to seize the crown of England. With this object in view he engaged the services
of a considerable body of men, whom he conveyed from
his kingdom of Denmark in sixty ships.[1] Instead of
directing his course to England, he made sail for
Flanders in order to consult his mother, who resided at
Bruges.[2] Whilst he was there Harold died; and both
Saxons and Danes[2] sent messengers to invite him to
come to England and ascend the throne. He did so,
and was received with universal[3] satisfaction.

The joy of the nation at the accession of Hardicanute
soon ceased. He showed his new subjects that he had
a bad heart, for as soon as he was crowned and established in his kingdom, he sent Elfric, Archbishop of
York, Godwin, and others, to dig up the body of his
predecessor, to cut off the head, and to throw both body
and head into the river Thames.[2] A fisherman dragged
up the body in his net,[4] and the Danes buried it in
their cemetery at London.

This savage and senseless act[5] was done in childish
revenge for his exclusion from the throne of England,

---

[1] *Saxon Chronicle;* Flor. of Worcester gives 50 as the number of ships.
[2] Matt. of Westminster.   [3] Flor. of Worcester.   [4] Will. of Malmesbury.
[5] Charles II. appears to have studied this portion of history, as shown by his treatment of Cromwell's dead body.

his mother's banishment from its shores, and his half-brother's cruel treatment and death.

Accusation of Godwin.

Shortly after his arrival, Elfric accused Godwin, and Living, Bishop of Worcester,[1] of the murder of the Atheling Alfred. Living was deprived of his bishopric, which was bestowed upon Elfric, a suspicious exchange, who only held it one year, as at the end of that time Living was reinstated. Godwin was very indignant at the charge brought against him. He made an oath, and all the chief men and thanes of the country stated that he told the truth, to the effect that it was not at his advice or with his consent that the king's brother's eyes had been put out, but that Harold had given orders for what had been done.[2]

Godwin's gift to Hardicanute.

In order to remove the impression of the foul accusation brought against him, and to gain the king's favour, Godwin made him a rich and beautiful present—a ship of admirable workmanship, with a figure-head of gold,[3] rigged with the best materials, and manned with eighty chosen soldiers magnificently armed: on each arm they had two[3] gold bracelets weighing 16oz. a-piece: they wore a triple coat of mail, and a helmet partly gilt;[2] a sword with gilded hilt was girt by their sides; a Danish battle-axe, inlaid with gold and silver, hung from their left shoulders; in their left hands they held a shield with boss and studs of gilt, and in their right hands a lance.

In the year 1041, Hardicanute imposed a heavy tax upon his subjects in order to pay eight marks[4] to each

---

[1] William of Malmesbury terms him Bishop of Crediton.

[2] Flor. of Worcester; Matt. of Westminster, &c.

[3] Will. of Malmesbury.

[4] A mark, a Danish coin, varied in value from 8s. 4d. to 13s. 4d.

oarsman and ten marks to each pilot of his fleet. His father, Canute, had reduced his fleet to sixteen[1] vessels : Harold maintained the same number. The total amount of money he compelled his subjects to raise for the support of his Danish army and fleet was upwards of 32,000[1] pounds of silver. This tax caused those who had longed for him before it was levied to hate him[2] after its imposition. The king sent the huscarls, his body guard, to collect the money. Two of them, Fleader and Thurstan,[3] went to Worcester. Their presence caused a tumult. The citizens rose up against them. The tax collectors fled for safety to an upper chamber of the abbey tower; there they were found, and there they were killed.

Revolt of Worcester 1041.

Hardicanute determined to avenge the death of his servants. So he sent Godwin of Wessex, Leofric of Mercia, Siward of Northumbria, with their forces, together with those of other Saxon nobles, and almost all his huscarls, to Worcester, with orders to kill all its people, to burn down the city, and to lay waste the province. For four days this large force burnt and destroyed. The number captured and slain was small, as the people heard of their approach and fled in all directions.

A considerable number of the citizens determined to stand up for their lives. They took refuge in a small island called Beverege, which was situated in the middle of the river Severn. They fortified it, and fought so well against their enemies that they obtained

---

[1] Henry of Huntingdon ; Will. of Malmesbury states that this tax was levied in order to pay twenty marks to each soldier who had followed Hardicanute from Denmark.

[2] *Saxon Chronicle.*   [3] Flor. of Worcester.

terms of peace, and were allowed to return to their homes.[1] This is one of the very few instances recorded in history of citizens repelling the attacks of a large and disciplined force, and of overcoming a confederation of king, nobles, and army.

Hardicanute did "nothing royal"[2] during his reign, except that his mother was well treated by him, and that he also received his half-brother Edward with honour, and entertained him at his court. The Atheling arrived in England from Normandy in the year 1041. His presence in England familiarised him with its people, and helped him to the throne.

In addition to his kindness to the members of his own family, the King appeared to have studied the tastes of the eating and drinking nobles of his day, for we are informed that he excelled as an entertainer of guests; four times[3] a day the royal tables were set with generous hospitality for the refreshment and entertainment of his whole court. After the Norman Conquest princes only provided one meal a day for guests.[3]

With his companions he was familiar,[3] and the manner of his death in the flower[3] of his age gives evidence of this familiarity, and of the habits of his Danish followers, for at the feast given in honour of the marriage of Gytha, daughter of Osgod Clappa, a man of great power,[4] Hardicanute caroused, full of health and spirits,[1] with the *bride* and others. And "as he stood at his drink,"[2] he suddenly fell to the earth in an awful spasm, and "lost his life amidst his cups."[5]

Death of
Hardi-
canute,
1042.

---

[1] Flor. of Worcester.   [2] *Saxon Chronicle.*   [3] Henry of Huntingdon.
[4] Matt. of Westminster.   [5] William of Malmesbury.

Thus ended the Danish rule in England, 1042: it began with blood; it ended with drink!

LEADING EVENTS.

THE DESCENT OF EDWARD THE CONFESSOR FROM CERDIC.

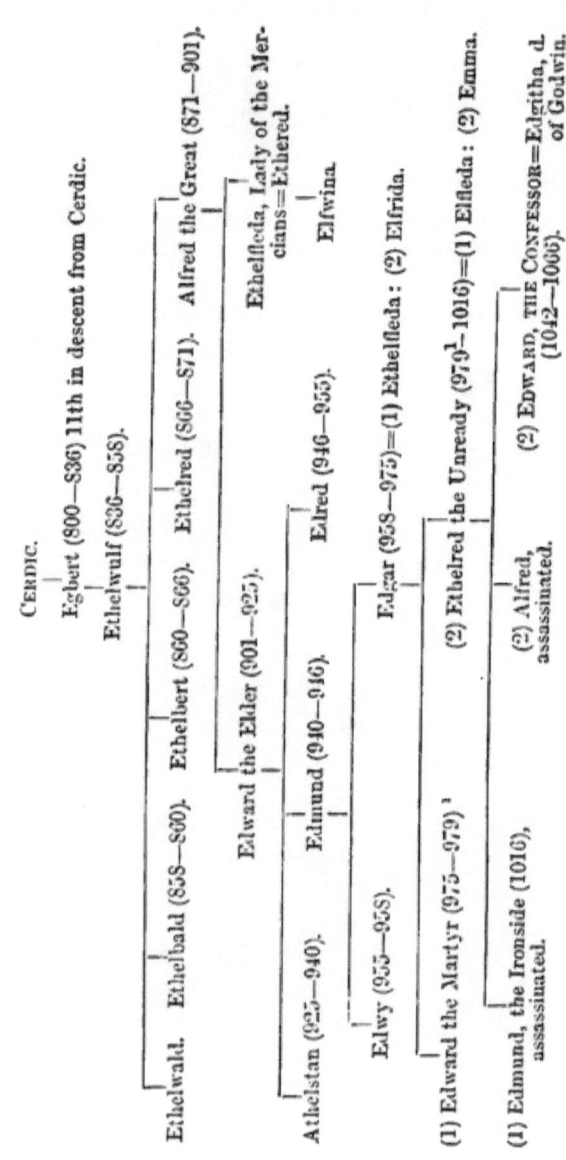

Cerdic.

Egbert (800—836) 11th in descent from Cerdic.

Ethelwulf (836—858).

Ethelwald. Ethelbald (858—860). Ethelbert (860—866). Ethelred (866—871). Alfred the Great (871—901).

Ethelfleda, Lady of the Mercians=Ethered.

Elfwina

Edward the Elder (901—925).

Elred (946—955).

Athelstan (925—940). Edmund (940—946). Edgar (958—975)=(1) Ethelfleda : (2) Elfrida.

Elwy (955—958).

(1) Edward the Martyr (975—979) [1]

(2) Ethelred the Unready (979[1]—1016)=(1) Elfleda : (2) Emma.

(1) Edmund, the Ironside (1016), assassinated.

(2) Alfred, assassinated.

(2) Edward, the Confessor=Edgitha, d. (1042—1066). of Godwin.

[1] Or 978—Florence of Worcester, &c.

CHAPTER XVI.

EDWARD THE CONFESSOR, OR, ENGLAND UNDER THE RULE OF GODWIN, 1042—1053.

UPON the death of Hardicanute, the heir, *by descent,* to the English throne, was Edward, son of Edmund the Ironside, but the heir by *conquest* was Sweyn, King of Norway,[1] son of Canute.

Edward the Confessor, 1042 to 1066.

But the Saxons, at the advice of Godwin,[2] with one voice,[3] clergy and people,[4] acknowledged Edward, son of Ethelred the Unready and Emma, as king.

The Normans ignored the influence of Godwin in bringing about the restoration of the stock of Cerdic to the throne of England. In their opinion Edward ascended the throne of his father through the influence of the Norman duke. Robert of Poitiers, the Conqueror's chaplain, states that Edward made William of Normandy his heir out of gratitude for the kind treatment he had received in Normandy, and for his restoration, and that he handed over to him the son, Wulfnoth, and the grandson, Haco,[5] of Godwin, as pledges of his heirship: as William was only fifteen years of age at that time, he could not have had any voice in Edward's restoration.

According to our first historian,[6] Edward, upon the death of Hardicanute, sent messengers to Godwin to request an interview with him. When they met, the Atheling would have fallen at the feet of the powerful

Godwin.

---

[1] He was driven out of Norway by Magnus, St. Olave's son.
[2] Florence of Worcester; Vita Æduardi.   [3] Saxon Chronicle.
[4] Matthew of Westminster.   [5] Haco was not born at this time.
[6] William of Malmesbury.

carl, but he raised him up; and, reminding him that he was the son of Ethelred and the grandson of Edgar, stated that the kingdom was his right; that his age, and his acquaintance with difficulties and poverty would enable him to rule well; if, therefore, he would rely upon him, every obstacle would disappear: all he had to do was to become his friend, to honour his sons, and to marry his daughter. Edward readily agreed to Godwin's proposals. A meeting was held at Gillingham: Godwin addressed the assembled nobles in the Saxon tongue: his powerful speech, his ready wit, his authority, and his presents, caused all present to receive the Atheling as King, and to pay him homage.

Godwin helps Edward.

Henry III., Emperor of Germany, and Henry I., King of France, rejoiced with Edward upon his becoming King of England; and, at his coronation, friendly messages were delivered to him by their ambassadors.

The following year Edward was consecrated King at Winchester[1] by the Archbishops of Canterbury and York. In this year he married Edgitha, Godwin's daughter, in accordance with an agreement that he had made with the powerful Saxon.[2] In the same year he went to Winchester in company[3] with Godwin, Leofric and Siward, and deprived his mother of her treasures, because she had not been so kind to him as she should have been.[4] Godwin, Leofric, and Siward were the real rulers of the land.

Emma.

---

[1] The Biographer of Edward states that he was consecrated at Canterbury.

[2] Henry of Huntingdon.   [3] *Saxon Chronicle.*

[4] Upon the death of Canute, Edward came to England with 40 ships and a body of soldiers, in order to try to secure the crown for himself. He landed in Hampshire. No doubt, he expected his mother would assist him: but, instead of meeting with allies, he was opposed by a great number of the Saxons; thereupon, he returned to Normandy.

Siward[1] was a great warrior. He was a giant[2] of a Siward. man, and very brave. When he heard that his son had been killed by the Scots, he was most anxious to know whether his death-wound pierced the front or the back part of his body: when he was told, "the front," he replied—"I am very glad, no other death suited him or me."[2] He afterwards invaded Scotland and defeated Macbeth, who had killed Siward's son-in-law, Duncan, King of Scotland, and usurped the throne.[2] When, in 1055, Siward felt he was dying, he was very sorry that he had not been killed in one of his many battles, and so have escaped the disgrace of dying like a *sick cow*."[2] He ordered his men to dress[2] him in his well-tried armour, to gird his sword by his side, to place his helmet upon his head, his shield in his left hand, and his battle-axe inlaid with gold in his right hand, so that he might die "in a soldier's garb": when he was fully dressed he gave up the ghost.[3]

Siward and Leofric always opposed Godwin. They Leofric. were leaders of the Danish subjects of the king, while Godwin was the head of the Saxon portion of the people of England. At the commencement of Edward's reign these Earls and their followers cordially united in obedience to the king. Afterwards, his safety lay in their jealousies of one another, for, had they joined together, they could have removed him at will.

---

[1] By the Danes Siward was called "*the brave man.*" Vita Æduardi; Shakespeare alludes to him in his play called Macbeth.

[2] Henry of Huntingdon: this writer states that Siward ruled Scotland, whereas he placed Malcolm upon its throne.

[3] These particulars of Siward are given in order to show the character of one of the leading men of that time; in those days the great earls were the heads and hearts of the country; their deeds and their words were the deeds and words of their numerous adherents and dependents, from the powerful noble to the humble serf.

K

Famine,
1044.
Severe
winter,&c.
1046.

The Saxon chroniclers tell us that a very great famine took place in 1044; and that the severity of the winter of 1046, with its frost, snow, tempest, mortality of mankind, murrain of cattle, and death of birds and fish, were beyond the recollection of man. They also mention the occurrence of an earthquake, and the appearance of a comet. But, in the main, they simply record the doings and sayings of the king, of bishops, earls, thanes, and abbots. Concerning the welfare and every-day life of the *people*, they are wordless.

Leofric.

Leofric[1] built monasteries:[2] he was, therefore, in favour with the church, and he is known as "the man of virtuous memory."[3] With the help of his son Algar he opposed the Godwin family upon every favourable opportunity. In the year 1046, Sweyn, the firstborn of Godwin, sailed to Denmark, because he was not allowed to marry the abbess of Leominster. His property was divided between his brother Harold and his cousin Beorn.

Sweyn,
son of
Godwin,
1046.

Upon Sweyn's return to England, the king was willing to restore his former possessions to him, but Harold and Beorn declined to give them up. Thereupon Sweyn enticed Beorn on board his vessel and killed him. The Witan pronounced him to be a "nithing,"[4] that is, a vagabond upon the face of the earth, and an exile from England. He was reconciled to the king by Aldred,[5] Bishop of Worcester; or by his father.[6]

---

[1] Matt. of Westminster gives an account of the ride through Coventry of his wife, Godiva, in order to obtain a charter for its people.

[2] William of Malmesbury.   [3] Matt. of Westminster.

[4] *Saxon Chronicle.*   [5] Flor. of Worcester.   [6] Henry of Huntingdon.

On two occasions King Edward assembled a fleet at Saxon fleet, 1045, 1049.
Sandwich, in the years 1045[1] and 1049.[2] In 1045 the
fleet was assembled against Magnus,[3] King of Norway,
who had threatened to invade England, which he declared was his through an agreement with Sweyn,
Canute's son. Sweyn, Ulf's son,[4] who was at this time
King of Denmark, declared war against Magnus, and
obliged him to give up his expedition against England.
In 1049 the Saxon King was once more with his fleet
at Sandwich. He had been requested by Henry III.,
Emperor of Germany, who had attacked Baldwin of
Flanders by land, to cut off his escape by sea. In
return for this service Baldwin became the sworn
friend of the Godwin family, and the uncompromising
enemy of Edward.

Not long afterwards the king and Godwin became
bad friends. Various reasons have been given for their
quarrel. He and his sons were banished, because they Godwin's defence of Dover, 1051.
ruined the monasteries, encouraged false judgment, and
laughed at the easiness of the king ;[5] because Godwin,
Sweyn, and Harold were conspiring against Edward ;[6]
because Godwin refused to punish the citizens of Dover
who had defended themselves against the assaults[2] of
Eustace II. of Boulogne, who had married the king's Eustace.
sister ; because Edward feared[7] Godwin ; because[8] the
Welsh accused them of coming to betray the King ;
because[9] Godwin desired Eustace to be given up to him.

<hr/>

[1] Flor. of Worcester.   [2] *Saxon Chronicle.*
[3] Magnus was the half-brother of Harold Hardrada, on the mother's side.
[4] See page 131.   [5] Will. of Malmesbury   [6] Henry of Huntingdon.
[7] Wace's Roman de Rou.   [8] *Saxon Chronicle ;* Will. of Malmesbury.
[9] Matt. of Westminster. From Florence of Worcester we gather that
Eustace paid a visit to Edward. At Dover his soldiers, while enquiring for
lodgings, killed a townsman : in revenge, a neighbour killed a soldier. In
their rage the count and his followers put many men and women to the

Robert,
Arch-
bishop of
Canter-
bury.

The most likely cause of the quarrel was Robert, once abbot of Jumieges, who had accompanied Edward to England. Robert was appointed Bishop of London, and afterwards Archbishop of Canterbury, in preference to a relative of Godwin, one of the monks of Christ Church. Godwin was angered at the rejection of his relative, and attacked Robert before the king's council. Whereupon Robert accused him of taking possession of church lands, and also persuaded Edward that Godwin meant to take the king's life by stratagem, as he had before taken that of his brother, and that he wanted his son Harold to be king.[1] The king believed these reports. He called a meeting of nobles at Gloucester, where Godwin was accused of murdering his brother. Godwin, having been informed of these proceedings, sent ambassadors to the king, and implored his peace, and sought the aid of the law to declare him innocent of so great a crime. But Edward had made up his mind not to listen to any word of explanation or excuse.

Siward,[1] Leofric,[1] Algar,[1] and Ralph[2] and their forces were with the king at Gloucester. It was decided to enquire into the accusation against Godwin in London.[1][2]

sword, and trampled babes and children under their horses' hoofs. As soon as they saw the townsmen flocking together they fled to King Edward, who was at Gloucester. Godwin was enraged when he heard the news, and raised an immense army from his own earldom and the earldoms of his sons, Sweyn and Harold, and demanded the surrender of Eustace and his men.

The King, in great alarm, sent in haste for Leofric and Siward and their forces. Upon their arrival, at the suggestion of Leofric, the King and Godwin were advised to settle their quarrel in a legal way at London. When the day of settlement came Godwin's army had dwindled away; thereupon the King and Witan banished him and his sons; so Godwin and part of his family went to Flanders: Harold and Gurth sailed from Bristol for Ireland in a ship provided for Sweyn. Queen Edgitha was divorced by the King, and sent with one maid to Wherwell Abbey.

[1] Vita Æduardi.   [2] Flor. of Worcester.

Stigand, afterwards Archbishop of Canterbury, tried to **Stigand.**
reconcile the king and Godwin, but failed to do so.
Meanwhile Archbishop Robert continued to influence
the king against the Earl of Wessex. The sentence of
the court was—that Godwin should obtain peace after
he had returned the Atheling Alfred and his followers,
alive, to the king, together with the property of the
living and the dead.[1]

When Stigand delivered this message to Godwin, he
shed a few tears; then, dashing aside the table which **Flight of**
was at his side, he rushed out of the room, mounted **Godwin,**
his horse, and rode off in haste to the sea-shore at **1051.**
Bosham,[2] where his ships awaited him. It was well

[1] According to William of Malmesbury, Eustace had a secret audience
with the King, and made the most of his own story, and excited his anger
against the English. Godwin was summoned to the palace; upon his arrival
Eustace's story was repeated to him; whereupon the King ordered him to
proceed at once with an army into Kent, and to take signal vengeance upon
the people of Dover (William calls it Canterbury). Godwin refused to do so
for three reasons—(1) because he saw with displeasure the hold all foreigners
were getting upon the King; (2) because he was wishful to show his regard
for his fellow-countrymen; (3) because *it was not just to pass sentence on
those people unheard*, as they had a particular right to protection. He therefore advised the King to summon in a gentle manner the principal townsmen
of Dover into his presence : if they could give a satisfactory account of the
tumult, they were to be allowed to return home unhurt; but if they could
not, they should give satisfaction to the King and to the Country by fine or
bodily punishment. He then left the King's presence, thinking that the
King's anger was only temporary. Then followed the Council of Gloucester,
where the Welsh so inflamed the passions of the King and his court that an
immediate battle between the forces of the King and those of Godwin was
imminent. Friendly advice prevailed, and the Council was postponed to
London. It was then announced that Sweyn was not to accompany Godwin
and Harold to it, and that the latter were to attend it (1) unarmed ; (2)
with twelve men only ; (3) to deliver up to the King the command of their
troops. To this demand Godwin observed (1) that they could not go to a
party meeting without sureties and pledges ; (2) that they were willing to
give up their soldiers and everything else to their King, *except risking their
lives and reputation ;* if they went unarmed, their lives might be in danger ;
if with few followers, their glory would be diminished. The King would
not listen to intercessions on behalf of the bold Earl, and so an edict was
published that he and his family should leave England in five days.

[2] Vita Æduardi.

that he did so, for that night he was followed by armed men, who tried, but in vain, to overtake the earl, in order to put him to death.

Godwin, his wife, Gytha, and their sons, Sweyn, Tosti, Wulfnoth, and Gurth, sailed to Flanders, where they met with a hearty reception from Count Baldwin. Harold and Leofwine sailed to Ireland, and received protection, hospitality, and help from Dermot,[1] King[2] of Leinster.

Feeling of
the
country
upon
Godwin's
banish-
ment.

Their banishment took the country by storm. The *Saxon Chronicle*,[3] contrary to its wont, expresses its astonishment in a lengthy passage, and explains: "It would have seemed wonderful to every man that was in England, if any man before that had said that it would so happen: for he (Godwin) had been before exalted to that degree, as if he ruled the king and all England; and his sons were earls and the king's darlings, and his daughter was wedded and married to the king."

The Biographer[4] of the Confessor and of the Godwin family thus describes the opinion of the Saxon public concerning the earl's exile: "His absence they considered the destruction of the English race, the ruin of the whole country. So that he considered himself happy who had it in his power to go into exile after him. Some went to him, some sent messengers to say they were ready, if he wished to return, to receive him, even with violence, into his native country, to fight for him; and for him, if it were necessary, they

---

[1] Vita Æduardi.   [2] Ailfred.

[3] MS. "D": this MS. is the only one that gives an account of the battle of Hastings. The seven Saxon Chronicles are called by the letters—A, B, C, D, E, F, G.

[4] Vita Æduardi Regisqui apud Westmonasterium requiescit.

were willing even to die.   And this was brought about, not secretly or privately, but openly and in public, and not by some particular party, but by almost every native of the country."   Can it therefore be surprising that each individual member of this illustrious family, the queen excepted, risked their all on behalf of a people who loved them and theirs so intensely?

The king[1] of France and Count Baldwin sent ambassadors to Edward, beseeching him to recall Godwin. But even these, with all their endeavours, failed.

Godwin, mindful of his old valour, and of the deeds of his youth, seeing himself thus wrongly treated, and that, too, by the machinations of the wicked,[1] determined to recover his former greatness by force of arms. This determination was quickly made known to Harold, who, first landing in the west, utterly put to rout the forces that opposed him, leaving thirty thanes dead upon the field of battle.   He then set sail for the Isle of Wight.   There the united forces of father and brothers made an imposing appearance.   Their joy at their safe reunion was unbounded.   They spoke of their past dangers and their future hopes.   They set out at once for London.   As they slowly advanced they were joined by ships from the south, east, and even the west of England.   The chronicler asserts that the people ran as children to meet a father long desired.   The sea was covered with ships: their arms sparkled in the bright sunshine of a summer's day.   The monk king was forced by the Normans to embark in the fleet sent to oppose Godwin.   But after a mock trial, the outlawed family, Sweyn excepted, was restored to all its former possessions and influence.

Harold, son of Godwin.

Return of the Godwin family, 1052.

---

[1] Vita Æduardi Regisqui apud Westmonasterium requiescit.

Upon the return of Godwin, the Normans, bishops and nobles, fled away for their very lives. The queen was removed from the cloister to the court: and the voice of the Saxon earl, outspoken and free, was heard once more in the council chamber that had oft-times echoed with his wit and eloquence, but which of late had resounded with the wily tones of the plotting Norman prelate, Robert of Canterbury. Thus Godwin and Harold rid the country from foreign influence for the second[1] time.

Death of Godwin, 1053. The end of the mighty earl was at hand. At Eastertide of 1053,[2] on the second day of the feast, he sat with his sons Harold and Tosti at the king's table in the royal town of Winchester,[3] when at once he sank down speechless by his footstool. He was carried into the king's chamber,[2] as they thought his illness would soon pass away. But he continued speechless and powerless[4] for three[4] days, and then he "resigned his life."[4]

Such is the simple and touching account given by the Saxon writers of the death of Godwin. But the Norman[5] writers would have us believe that his death was the visitation of God on the murder of the Atheling Alfred. The king's cupbearer made a false step, but recovered himself with his other foot. Godwin saw the occurrence, and observed—"One brother brought

---

[1] Thierry gives them the credit of freeing England from the Danes upon the death of Harold, the Harefoot.   [2] *Saxon Chronicle.*

[3] The king held his court in Gloucester at Christmastide ; at Winchester at Eastertide ; and in London at Whitsuntide.

[4] *Saxon Chronicle.* Flor. of Worcester says *five* days : and he states that Gurth was also at the feast.

[5] Matt. of Westminster ; he places his death in 1054, and so does Henry of Huntingdon, &c.

assistance to the other." "Yes," retorted the king, "my brother might have assisted me lately, had it not been for the treachery[1] of Godwin." The earl protested his innocence, and hoped he would be choked with the piece of bread he held in his hand if he were guilty : the bread stuck in his throat, so that he died on the spot !

The events and stirring incidents connected with Godwin's life for about half a century were of insular and continental repute. With a glance of the mind's eye his whole career is laid bare before us. We behold him as a youth, stalwart and strong, with mellow laugh and joyous song, tending his father's cattle[2] in the county of Worcester. Next he comes before us as the guide of the jarl Ulf,[2] as they sought Canute's ship after the battle of Sherston. We then hear him address[3] his followers before the night attack upon the Swedes ; and then we see him charge and overcome[4] the foe. The herdsman and the warrior disappear and give place to the statesman, who is admitted to the secret and

---

[1] Godwin could not have been guilty of Alfred's death ; (I.) as no Saxon writer accuses him of it ; (II.) Norman writers contradict one another concerning (a) the *place*, Gillingham (William of Malmesbury), or Guildford (Matthew of Westminster), where his followers were murdered ; (b) the *place* where Alfred's eyes were torn out, Ely (Henry of Huntingdon), or Gillingham (William of Malmesbury) ; (c) the *date* of Alfred's expedition, during the reign of Harold the Harefoot (Matthew of Westminster), or after his death (William of Malmesbury), or after the death of Hardicanute (Henry of Huntingdon) ; (d) the circumstances that attended the massacre and mutilation. Most probably the whole story was invented by the Conqueror, in order to excite popular prejudice against his heroic rival Harold.

We have to bear in mind that the Saxon writers were in England, and that they wrote at the time of Godwin's death, — that the Norman writers were not in England, that they gave an account of his death years after its occurrence, and they hated Godwin and his family with a bitter hatred.

[2] Knythinga Saga.   [3] William of Malmesbury.

[4] Henry of Huntingdon.

most confidential councils of his king.[1]   The statesman
decides the fate of kings—Harold, the Harefoot, and
Hardicanute acknowledge his supremacy: whilst the
half-brother of the latter kneels at the feet of the son
of the "king's servant;"[2] and afterwards listens in
amazement to his ready wit and eloquent voice as he
prevails upon the listening throng to proclaim the
suppliant king of England.[3]   Time rolls on, and in the
next scene we see the herdsman's daughter wedded to
the last stem of the stock of Cerdic, and listen to the
shouts that welcome the union of a damsel, whose great
grandfather's name is unknown, with the representative
not merely of the kings, but of the very gods[4] of the
Saxons.   Again the scene shifts, and the lion-hearted
earl starts up in majestic magnificence between his
king and wanton and unjustifiable massacre.[5]   Yet a
little while and he is informed that the man who
"preferred death rather than commit any disgraceful
act," has been pronounced a vagabond and an outlaw.[6]

That night the old man was flying for his very life;
woe betide him should his horse stumble or fall, for the
churchman's[7] armed troops are in his rear, riding fast
and furious to take his life.[1]   Then he grasps the hand
of a friend.[8]   Next he witnesses a nation's gratitude,
and hears the loud shouts of welcome, as the huge

---

[1] Vita Ædnardi.   [2] Matt. of Westminster.   [3] Will. of Malmesbury.

[4] Woden and Frea—Matt. of Westminster: this writer states that Alfred
the Great was the 21st in descent from Woden, and remarks that after death
Woden was translated to the gods!

[5] The king was very wrath with the townsmen of Dover, and bade Godwin
the earl go in hostile manner against Dover: the earl would not consent
to the inroad, as he was loath to injure his own people.—Saxon Chronicle.

[6] Godwin was allowed a safe conduct for five nights to go out of the land.
—Saxon Chronicle.   [7] Robert, Archbishop of Canterbury.

[8] Count Baldwin of Flanders.

multitude surges around him, like children, welcoming Life of a well-beloved father. Once more his eloquent tongue[1] Godwin. goes home to the hearts of his listeners. He recovers his children's and his own honours; and he has the gratification of seeing the Normans driven with ignominy[1] from the land, and of hearing his old enemy pronounced a public disturber, and also a poisoner of the royal mind.

Though his son and his daughter sat upon the throne of England, Godwin declined[2] the tempting seat; yet he was enthroned in the hearts of the people; and while they, with constant tears,[2] remembered him as the father and supporter of the realm, we may cast aside the epithets of "dog"[3] and "traitor,"[4] and incline to think of him as a man of—"glorious fame."[4]

LEADING EVENTS.

[1] William of Malmesbury.   [2] Vita Æduardi.
[3] Matt. of Westminster.   [4] Henry of Huntingdon.

CHAPTER XVII.

THE AFFAIRS OF WALES, FROM THE REIGN OF HYWEL DDRWG TO THAT OF GRIFFITH AP LLEWELYN.

We have read that in the year 974, Iago, son of Idwal Voel, was expelled from his kingdom by his nephew Hywel Ddrwg. Iago is supposed to have fled to the court of Edgar,[1] who is said[1] to have reconciled him to Hywel, and to have prevailed upon the two Princes to divide the sovereignty of Gwynedd between them. But in the year 980 Iago was captured[2] by Hywel : afterwards, Hywel ruled as sole king of Gwynedd, for in 981 he not only defeated, but also slew with his own hand his cousin, Iago's son, Cystenyn Ddu—Constantine the Black, who, with the help of the Danes, had ravaged Anglesey and part of Carnarvonshire. With his own hand, in the same year, he is supposed to have killed[3] his uncle, Idwal Vychan—Idwal the Little.

In 986 Hywel was killed by the Saxons. Some time after his death, Meredith, grandson of Hywel Dda, became the Pendragon. He laid claim to the princedom of Powys through his mother ; to that of Gwynedd by the murder of his cousins, brothers to Hywel Ddrwg; and to that of Deheubarth, because of the youth of his nephews, the sons of his brother Einion.[4]

Hywel Ddrwg.

Cystenyn Ddu, 981.

Idwal Vychan, 981.

Meredith.

[1] Powell, &c.

[2] According to the *Annales Cambriæ*, Iago was blinded by Hywel

[3] The desperate character of the Welsh Princes is strikingly evidenced by the fact that out of 60 who lived between the years 877 and 1077, 45 died a violent death.

[4] Einion was torn to pieces by the men of Gwent, 983.

In 989 Wales was ravaged by the Danes, who were eventually bought off. This year was distinguished by mortality amongst cattle, and also by a famine, consequently the sufferings of the people were of a very severe character. In the same year the Pendragon's father, Owain ap Hywel Dda, and Ieuaf ap Idwal died. **Owain. Ieuaf.** They had not taken an active part in public affairs for some time. For three years Wales enjoyed comparative rest; at the end of that period of time Edwyn ap **Edwyn.** Einion tried to wrest the sovereignty of Deheubarth, to which he was the rightful heir, from his uncle. He was helped by the Saxons, with whom he plundered part of the country. No engagement took place between the hostile parties, and Meredith succeeded in reconciling his nephew.

In 995 Meredith was defeated at the battle of Llan- **Idwal.** gwm by Idwal, the grandson of Idwal Voel; Tudor ap **Tudor.** Einion was killed at this battle. After this victory Idwal was acknowledged as sovereign of Gwynedd, over which district his ancestors had ruled. Two years afterwards Idwal was killed by Sweyn; and Meredith followed him to the grave in the year 1000. Meredith's daughter, Angharad, married Llewelyn ap **Llewelyn** Seisyllt. This Llewelyn was, on his mother's side, the **ap Seisyllt** fourth in descent from Rhodri Mawr. He became Pendragon, and ruled Wales well and peaceably for some time.

Llewelyn overcame a Scot,[1] who, pretending to be his wife's brother, had been acknowledged by the South Walians as their prince. Llewelyn was killed in 1023 by the sons of Edwyn ap Einion, his wife's cousin, thereupon Iago, great-grandson of Idwal Voel, became **Iago.**

[1] Brut.

King of Gwynedd. Griffith, the son of Llewelyn and Angharad, revenged the defeat of Meredith, his mother's father, by killing Iago ap Idwal in 1039; and the murderers of his father soon felt the power of his arm.

Griffith ap Llewelyn, 1039 to 1063

Griffith ap Llewelyn was among Welshmen what Harold, son of Godwin, was among Saxons. His exploits, heroism, and patriotism are particularised in the next chapter.

LEADING EVENTS.

The Capture of Iago ap Idwal Voel............................. 980 A.D.
The Death of Cystenyn Ddu and Idwal Vychan 981
The Death of Hywel Ddrwg 986
The Death of Meredith, Pendragon 1000
The Death of Llewelyn ap Seisyllt, and the Accession
  of Iago ap Idwal... 1023
The Death of Iago, and the Accession of Griffith ap
  Llewelyn, Pendragon.. 1039

THE DESCENT OF GRIFFITH AP LLEWELYN.

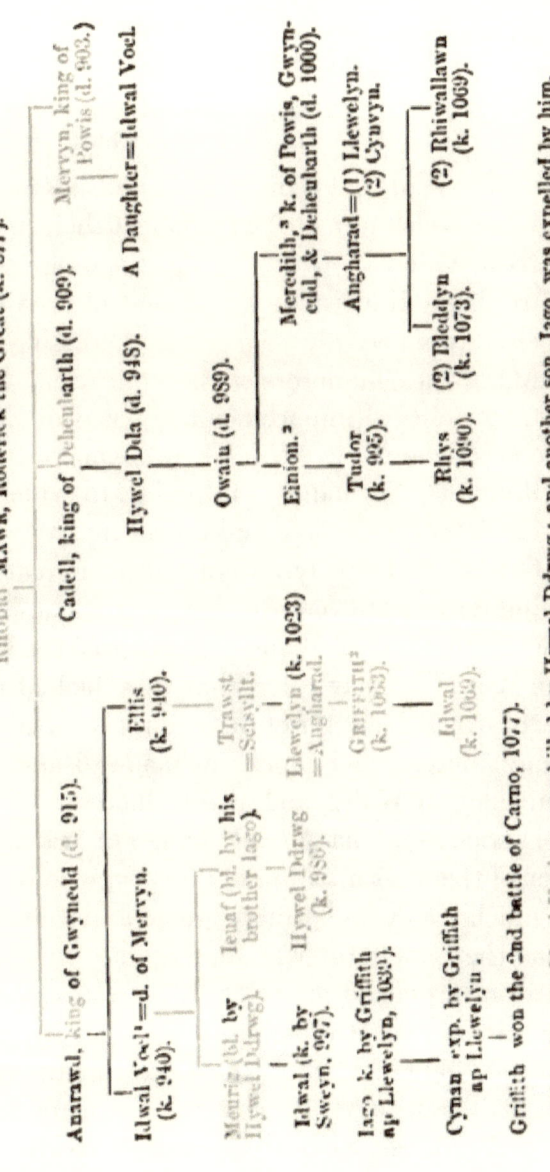

RHODRI MAWR, Roderick the Great (k. 877).

Anarawd, king of Gwynedd (d. 915).

Cadell, king of Deheubarth (d. 909).

Merryn, king of Powis (d. 903.)

Elfis (k. 940).

Idwal Voel[1] = d. of Merryn.

Hywel Dda (d. 945).

A Daughter = Idwal Voel

Meurig (bl. by Hywel Ddrwg).

Ienaf (bl. by his brother Iago).

Trawst = Sehyllt.

Owain (d. 989).

Meredith,[3] k. of Powis, Gwyneddd, & Deheubarth (d. 1000).

Hywel Ddrwg (k. 986).

Llewelyn (k. 1023) = Angharad.

Einion.[3]

Angharad = (1) Llewelyn.
         (2) Cynvyn.

Idwal (k. by Sweyn. 997).

GRIFFITH[3] (k. 1063).

Tudor (k. 925).

(2) Bleddyn (k. 1073).

(2) Rhiwallawn (k. 1069).

Iago k. by Griffith ap Llewelyn, 1039).

Idwal (k. 1069).

Rhys (k. 1040).

Cynan exp. by Griffith ap Llewelyn.

Griffith won the 2nd battle of Carno, 1077.

[1] Idwal's son, Idwal Vychan, was killed by Hywel Ddrwg; and another son, Iago, was expelled by him.

[2] Griffith's daughter, Nesta, married Hywel ap Edwyn ap Einion: Hywel was killed by his father-in-law.

[3] Meredith was also the father of Caradog, whose son, Trahaiarn, was killed in the second battle of Carno (1077).

CHAPTER XVIII.

GRIFFITH AP LLEWELYN, PENDRAGON; OR, WELSH INFLUENCE UPON THE DOWNFALL OF SAXONDOM.

Griffith ap
Llewelyn.
1039 to
1063.

WE have read that Canute, the Danish King of England, left the Welsh unmolested amongst their mountains and narrow valleys. But during the reigns of his sons, Harold and Hardicanute, and that of the Confessor, the Welsh were actively engaged in harassing the descendants of the conquerors of their ancestors; and no event of any political importance happened in England, from the accession of Griffith as Pendragon to the victory of William of Normandy at Senlac, in which the Welsh did not take an active and a leading part.

Griffith ap Llewelyn was a prince of great courage and indomitable perseverance. He was the King of Gwynedd, and Pendragon of Wales. Such was the confidence of the Welsh in their ruler, that they looked upon him as the destined deliverer of their country. During his reign a most determined effort was made to assert the independency of Wales, and also to increase its limits.

It was, as we have read, an age of warlike heroes, of men of the most undaunted bravery, who were possessed of much policy and of unbounded ambition. About this time the Conqueror was undergoing all the bitterness of an unprotected minority in the midst of a turbulent, rapacious, and stubborn nobility. Now, too, Harold, son of Godwin, was about to exhibit the first-fruits of his skill as a ruler by his successful management of the East Anglians. Siward was earl of Northumbria, Leofric of Mercia, and Godwin of Wessex.

Giraldus Cambrensis[1] thus describes the Welsh of Character of the Welsh. his day, and what he says of them would be true of his countrymen in the time of Prince Griffith :—"This people is light and active, hardy rather than strong, and entirely bred up to the use of arms; for not only the nobles but all the people are trained to war, and when the trumpet sounds the alarm, the husbandman rushes as eagerly from his plough as the courtier from his court. They anxiously study the defence of their country and their liberty; for these they fight; for these they undergo hardships ; for these they willingly sacrifice their lives. They esteem it a disgrace to die in bed; an honour to die in the field of battle."

It required, therefore, but little persuasion to induce such a people to go out to battle against their neighbours. Everything tended to a rupture between the two nations. Griffith was young, fiery, and enthusiastic. Griffith. His memory was overflowing with the glory of the deeds of his ancestors. His ambitious and revengeful longing was further incited by the burning words which seemed to flow in a continuous torrent from the impassioned lips of the hoary bards of his country, who reminded him of the days when the heads of his house held sway over the whole of England. The listening throng were also goaded almost to madness by the recitals of the cruelties and injuries which had been inflicted upon their forefathers by the hated Saxon, but above all by the recollection that these abhorred invaders had deprived them of the fair plains and vales of England, and had cooped them up among the hills of Wales.

The Saxons had taken the precaution to fortify that

[1] *Descriptio Cambriæ*, chap. viii.

L

part of England adjoining Wales. In addition to Offa's Dyke, the Welsh March was lined by a series of camps, forts, and ditches. The protection they afforded was but a feeble one; yet it tended somewhat to raise the confidence of the English and to intimidate the Welsh. Moreover, beacon fires were sometimes kept prepared upon the topmost heights of the chain of hills or isolated summits which run along the Borders from Cheshire, through Salop, into Herefordshire and Worcestershire. Whenever a rupture into England was expected, the beacon on the nearest hill was lit, and in a short space of time the whole March was thrown into consternation by the huge fires which seemed to leap from hill top to hill top, spreading alarm and dismay into the hearts of those who were in sight of their lurid glare, for well they knew, if not from sad experience, at least from hearsay, that that fire was but the prelude to the firing of huts, hamlets, villages, and towns, as the Welsh seldom returned without devastating the border counties with fire and the sword, nor did they return to their mountain fastnesses without herds of kine, and the crops and goods of their hated neighbours.

The most conspicuous of the isolated peaks which skirt the counties of Montgomery and Salop is that of Corndon. From its summit, now, a most fair and pleasing sight meets the eye of the spectator. In the far distance can be seen glimpses of misty Plinlimmon, cloud-topped Cader Idris, and the lowering summits of the Berwyn Range; while at its base, facing the Severn, and stretching as far as that river, lies an undulating tract of land, through which the waters of the Camlad slowly flow in a zig-zag course. Turning slightly to the left, the town of Montgomery forces itself upon one's view, with its ruined castle frowning down upon it from a rocky eminence at its back; a memento of the conquest, of feudalism, and of Roger de Montgomery, who advised William to invade England, and afterwards led the Norman right wing[1] at Senlac. Still turning towards the left, we perceive an offshoot of the vale of the Camlad running up between the hills of Montgomery and of Kerry. Following the Camlad towards its source, we enter another vale, which is hemmed in on one side by the Long Mynd. This vale leads us into Herefordshire, by way of Stokesay Castle and Ludlow. Turning to the right, we perceive Forden Hill, between which and Corndon lie the villages of Churchstoke and Chirbury. From the last village the country is comparatively level to Shrewsbury.

To the east of Corndon the country is even now both rugged and wild. But eight hundred and fifty years ago the aspect of the surrounding country from this hill was of a totally different nature. A huge forest extended almost to the mountain top, and clothed the vale beneath and the opposite hills, on one of which a large fort, defended by four great ditches, had been erected by the Welsh. In winter the Camlad, swollen by rain and the rivulets from the neighbouring hills, spread its sluggish waters far and wide, which gave birth to the reed, the sedge, and the bulrush; which, in their turn, sheltered the heron, wild duck, the otter, and the solitary beaver; while in the surrounding thickets abode the badger, stoat, fox, and wild cat. But if the objects beneath the feet of the spectator were then of so wild a nature, much more so were those across the banks of the Severn. It was with a feeling

[1] Wace's *Roman de Rou.*

The Welsh Borders. of dread and of mystery that he looked beyond that river, and lifted up his eyes to the dark hills which rose, ridge upon ridge, as far as the eye could see, and then ended in a dark mass against the sky, shrouded by mists and clouds, the home of the gaunt wolf, and of men not less active or ferocious, and imbued with an equal spirit of dash, temerity, and of freedom.[1]

This portion of the Marchland has been particularised because there was fought one of the most decisive and eventful of the many battles which took place between the Saxons and the Welsh.

Rhyd y Groes. The scene of this battle was Rhyd y Groes, in the Vale of the Camlad. This vale may be aptly termed the war path of the Welsh, as through it Griffith and others of his kin frequently led their wild followers to meet, defeat, and spoil the enemy. It afforded a safe ingress into the March country in two directions—the one opening towards Shrewsbury; the other towards Hereford and Worcester. The latter was probably the more frequented route.

Griffith had not been long upon the throne before he began his warlike preparations against Saxondom. Over hill and through vale, over mountain and through forest, across rivers, morass, and fenny lake, spread the welcome news that a foray, under the leadership of their young king, was about to be made into the rich border land. Swiftly each warrior sped to the place of meeting, and motley was the throng when the whole force had arrived.

The time chosen was most favourable for the designs of the Welsh king, as the Saxon monarch, Hardicanute,

---

[1] This description of this particular locality is typical of that of the rest of the country.

allowed his foreign freebooters to harry the country
from end to end.   In order to satisfy these ferocious
pests, he imposed, as we have read, an exorbitant tax
upon his subjects.   Worcester resisted the impost, and
in consequence was besieged by earls Godwin, Siward,
and Leofric, and after a stubborn resistance, sacked and
burnt.   This was a terrible example of the unsettled
state of the country, and enacted, too, before the very eyes
of the Welsh.   To add to the confusion, Hardicanute
died in a sudden manner.   Moreover, the great earls
Godwin, Leofric, and Siward were jealous of one
another, and divided the country into rival factions.
A foreigner, in the person of the Confessor, was raised
to the throne, chiefly through the influence of Godwin.

State of England.

A large force was collected by the Mercians to oppose
and punish the Welsh king.   At its head was Edwin,
brother of Leofric.   Next in command were Thurkill
and Elfgeat, two noble king's thanes.[1]

Edwin and his force advanced towards the Burgh
which had been erected by the Lady of the Mercians at
Chirbury.[1]   We are not informed whether this Burgh
continued to be held by Saxons; most probably it
had been destroyed, and its inhabitants slain, by the
Welsh long before the year 1039.

Edwin and his followers evidently expected to secure
an easy victory over the ill-clad and light armed
mountaineers.   But the latter were acquainted with
the country, and well knew the nature of its deceitful
marshes.   They took the further precaution of laying
an ambuscade, into which Edwin fell.   All at once his
army was assailed on all sides by Griffith and the

Edwin, Leofric's brother.

---

[1] Florence of Worcester's *Chronicon ex Chronicis*, under the years 1039 and 1052.

Battle of Rhyd y Groes, 1039 choicest of the Britons, who hurled a perfect shower of darts and arrows upon the astounded Mercians, and then rushed upon them. The thanes endeavoured, but in vain, to stem such a current of human beings. Their followers were soon beyond their control, and scattered in every direction. The enthusiastic valour and the extraordinary activity of the Welsh won the day. They pursued the flying enemy, shouting and pouring in flights of arrows. Many "very good men"[1] were left dead upon the marshy level of Rhyd y Groes.[2] Among the number were Edwin, Thurkill, and Elfgeat. Many, too, were drowned in the Camlad, or swallowed up in the bogs which lay between them and their homes.

Griffith was fully aware of the importance of his victory, and this battle may be considered the turning point in his life, as was that at the bridge of Lodi in the life of Napoleon I. He now began to occupy himself in settling the internal affairs of his kingdom, and in consolidating his power in the north. For three years he remained comparatively quiet, and refrained from carrying out his ambitious designs.

Hywel, 1044. Griffith was forced to fight several battles before his sway was acknowledged throughout Wales. He expelled his father's murderer, Hywel ap Edwyn, from South Wales. Hywel, with the help of the Danes[3] of Ireland, returned in 1044, but he was defeated and slain by Griffith and his men of Gwynedd. This Hywel had married Griffith's daughter, Nesta, and had killed his father. Griffith also expelled Cynan ap Iago from

---

[1] *Saxon Chronicle*, 1039.   [2] The ford of the cross.

[3] The Danes had established themselves in Dublin; thence they made occasional expeditions against England and Wales.

his dominions, and forced him to remain in Ireland. So bitter was the enmity between the North and South Walians, that the former destroyed everything they could in the territory of the latter, so that Deheubarth[1] became a waste.

By the year 1048 the Pendragon's successes along the Borders enabled him to establish himself in Hereford-shire, which was under the control of Sweyn, son of Godwin. In that district Griffith built a castle, and did every kind of disgrace and harm to the king's forces.[2] Earl Godwin determined to punish the invaders. With this object in view he summoned to his presence his sons Sweyn and Harold, and his own and their forces, and proceeded towards Gloucester, to seek the help and council[2] of the king.

At this juncture of events, Eustace II. of Boulogne came flying to Gloucester, after his discomfiture at Dover. Apparently Griffith had spies at the king's court, who informed him of the rupture between the king and Godwin, consequent upon the refusal of the latter to take the part of Eustace against the men of Dover. Griffith and Godwin proceeded to Gloucester, but the Welshmen were the first to arrive in the king's presence. They accused Godwin and his sons of conspiracy against their sovereign, and assured him that their coming was for the purpose of betraying the king.[2] Edward believed them. According to William of Malmesbury, the charges brought against the Godwin faction caused its members to become hateful to the whole Court. Indeed, so successful were the Welsh in inflaming the minds of their listeners, that a rumour went forth that the king's army would

Griffith in Herefordshire, 1048

Griffith conspiring against Godwin

_____

[1] *Brut.*   [2] *Saxon Chronicle.*

attack the Earl of Wessex and his men there and then. When Godwin heard this rumour he prepared his forces, and told them that if they were attacked they were not to retreat without avenging themselves. Griffith must have anxiously desired a conflict between the rival parties, as the results of such an engagement would weaken England and strengthen Wales. But the chronicler tells us that his desires were not gratified, as better counsels prevailed, and averted a dreadful scene of misery, and a worse than civil war. Then followed the banishment of the Godwin family. In all this fortune favoured the Welsh king, who was even at that time the ally of Algar, earl Leofric's son. Algar obtained possession of the estates and dignities of Harold the earl, and Griffith was left unmolested in his designs of aggrandisement and spoil. Little did they think that their successful conspiracy at Gloucester would be followed by years of untold toils and troubles, that the grave alone would put an end to.

Griffith's victory at Leominster, 1052.

In 1052, Griffith plundered[1] Herefordshire, and marched against the castle of Leominster, which was garrisoned by Saxons and Normans.[2] The Welshmen gained the victory, and killed a great number[1] of the enemy, including very many knights.[3] This battle took place on the anniversary[4] of the battle of Rhyd y Groes. Griffith returned to his country with much plunder.[1]

[1] Flor. of Worcester.

[2] These Normans very probably were left behind by their duke when he visited England during the banishment of the Godwin family.

[3] The *Saxon Chronicle* terms them "goodmen."

[4] The *Saxon Chronicle* remarks that this battle took place on the same day on which, thirteen years before, Edwin was killed; this comment shows the importance the Saxons attached to Griffith's victory against Edwin in 1039; perhaps the same writer recorded both victories.

In the year 1053 the Welsh made another inroad into England, when they attacked Westbury: here they killed a great many Saxons.[1]

Griffith's victory at Westbury, 1053.

Upon Harold's return he did not forget the fact that Algar had held his earldom of East Anglia during his absence, and that he was arrayed against his father and himself before their banishment. Accordingly, in 1055, Algar was himself banished. He took refuge for a short time in Ireland, thence he made his way to Griffith of Wales, whom he implored[2] to help him. The Welsh king promised him his protection;[3] and immediately assembled a large army[2] from every part of Wales.

Banishment of Algar, 1055.

Algar's forces joined those of the Welsh king. The combined army marched upon Hereford. To oppose their progress, Ralph, the king's nephew,[3] who was the earl of this district, took up his position two[2] miles out of the city with a great force.[1] Ralph appears to have tried to teach the Saxons the military tactics of the Normans, for he ordered them not to fight on foot, as they had been accustomed to do, but to act as cavalry. A panic seized upon his forces: they fled without striking a blow;[1] and Ralph, with his French[2] and Normans,[2] were the first to take to flight. But notwithstanding the fact that the Saxon army was on horseback, and the Welsh on foot, the latter pursued the former, overtook them in their fright and confusion, and killed between four and five hundred of the fugitives,[1] and wounded many[2] more. Astonishing to relate, not a single[1] Welshman or Irishman was killed in this battle! Griffith and Algar entered the city, killed the canons[2] who defended the chief church, plundered[1] the monas-

Griffith and Algar attack Hereford, and sack it.

---

[1] *Saxon Chronicle.*   [2] *Flor. of Worcester.*   [3] See page 103.

tery, killed some of the citizens,[1] took others captive,[1] and then burnt the town[2] and the monastery,[1] and departed with the spoil.

The news of this victory was soon made known. The king gave orders that a large army[1] should be levied from every part of the country: it was placed
Harold pursues Griffith and Algar.
under the charge of Harold, who pursued[1] Griffith and Algar to the heights of Snowdon.[3] The Welsh king seemed determined to weary out the brave Saxon, for, instead of meeting him in battle array, he proceeded into South Wales.[1] His tactics were successful. Harold, leaving part of his army behind him, hurried back to Hereford, which he surrounded with a wide and deep trench, and protected with gates and bars.[1]

The result of Griffith's victory was a conference between him and Algar and Harold: thereat terms of peace were drawn up and accepted:[1] and Algar was restored to all his possessions and dignities.[4]

Griffith attacks Hereford, 1056.
Hereford did not enjoy peace for any length of time: the following year, 1056,[2] Griffith made another expedition into England. On this occasion he was not opposed by Ralph, the cowardly son of King Edward's sister,[5] but by Leofgar, Bishop of Hereford. Leofgar was a muscular christian: he, doubtless, owed his preferment to the see of Hereford to Harold, as he had been his domestic chaplain.[6] He could ride on horseback[6] before he was a bishop, and accompanied Harold in his various journeys; and, after his consecration, he armed himself

---

[1] Flor. of Worcester.   [2] *Saxon Chronicle.*

[3] According to the *Saxon Chronicle* Harold did not penetrate Wales upon this occasion, but contented himself with fortifying Hereford.

[4] The *Saxon Chronicle* states that he was inlawed.

[5] "Timidus dux Radulfus;" Flor. of Worcester.

[6] Mass priest: he wore his *knapsack* before he was a bishop.

with spear and sword, and went forth to fight the ruth- Griffith's
less Welshmen. But his generalship and strength were victory.
not on a par with his temerity, for he was killed, and
so were his priests, together with the sheriff and many
others,[1] while the rest of his forces ran away. Hereford
was burnt down a second time.[2]

Then the chronicler[1] wails forth—"It is difficult to Hardships
describe the hardship, the marching, the camping, the of Saxon
sore distress, and the slaughter of men and horses which army.
the whole of the Saxon army endured." From this out
burst of lamentation and woe we gather that the Welsh
king and his men gave no quarter, and that their movements were stealthy and expeditious.

The Saxon king wished to gain the good-will of his
Celtic contemporary, so he sent Leofric, Harold, and
Aldred,[3] Bishop of Winchester, to him; and Griffith
declared upon oath that he would become Edward's
"under-king," and that he would be faithful and no Second
traitor.[4] But in two years' time Algar was banished banish-
ment of
for the second time, and deprived of his father's earl- Algar,
1058.
dom, to which he had succeeded in 1057.

For the second time he sought the aid of the Welsh
king, to whom he gave his daughter, Elgitha, in marriage. Griffith triumphantly reinstated his father-in-law
by force of arms,[1] to his earldom, 1058.

Griffith had now reached the zenith of his power.
Within Wales he had asserted his supremacy by the
death of Griffith[4] ap Rhydderch, king of South Wales,

---

[1] *Saxon Chronicle.*   [2] Matt. of Westminster.

[3] When Harold proceeded to Bristol, after the banishment of himself
and family, the king sent Aldred to capture him, but he "would not, or
could not" overtake him.—*Saxon Chronicle.*

[4] This Griffith defeated Bishop Aldred in 1049; his brother Rhys was
captured by the Saxons in 1053, and was put to death by King Edward's
orders; his head was brought to the king's court at Gloucester.

1054: along the Borders there was none to withstand his expeditions into England: at the Saxon court he had a powerful ally in Algar, who kept him informed of its intrigues: so far fortune had smiled upon him, and no defeat had thrown a shadow upon his path. With the death of Algar his power and influence began to decline.

Edwin and Morcar, sons of Algar.

Algar's sons, Edwin and Morcar, received from their brother-in-law the support their father had received from him. Harold determined to undermine their influence, and, in order to do so, he deemed it necessary to bring about the overthrow and death of the Welsh king,[1] and thus cut them off from refuge and succour in the hour of sore distress. Accordingly, in the year 1063, just after Christmas time,[2] when Griffith, in fanciful security, was at his royal residence of Rhuddlan, Harold, at the order of the king, advanced into Wales at the head of a small troop of cavalry to take the Pendragon's life.[2]

Harold's second invasion of Wales.

He almost effected his purpose; an enemy was not expected by Griffith. The Welsh, however, heard of the approach of the Saxon earl, and rushed off to inform their ruler. It was a race for the king's life between the Welshmen on foot and the Saxons on horseback:

---

[1] Dr. Lingard was of the opinion that "the Welsh prince and his subjects had long deserved the *name* and *punishment* of *robbers* and *assassins*"—that is, extirpation! This humane historian forgot that Griffith and his subjects were the representatives of the people who owned the greater part of Britain long before the Saxons sought its shores. Such being the case, if Griffith and his men were "*robbers* and *assassins*," because they fought against and defeated the Saxons of their day, and deprived them of part of the lands and goods which their forefathers had unjustly seized from the Celts, what name should be applied to those Saxons who robbed and assassinated wholesale? For "robbers" and "assassins," Dr. Lingard should have written—"patriots" and "revengers."

[2] Florence of Worcester.

topographical knowledge, no doubt, saved the king and frustrated the earl. Griffith rode off to the mouth of the river Clwyd,[1] where his fleet lay at anchor, and was just in time to get on board one of his ships ere the Saxons reached the spot. Harold had the mortification of seeing the fugitive sail away into the Irish Sea; in his rage he set fire to his palace and also to his ships, and then, before the enemy could have time to assemble in force, he began to ride back *the same day.* The fact that he was able to ride from Gloucester through Wales as far as Rhuddlan and back again with a "small troop of horse," without molestation, shows that the half-brothers of the Welsh king had already agreed to help the Saxons against their sovereign, in return for his position and territories after his removal.

Griffith's extremity 1063.

In the month of May of that year Harold made another attack upon Wales with a land and a sea force. He placed himself at the head of the fleet, while his brother Tosti, at the king's command,[2] took charge of the cavalry. The one sailed round Wales, the other rode through it. Their combined forces struck terror into the hearts of the Welsh, who submitted to the Saxon earls, delivered hostages to them, and deposed and banished their king. In August of that year Griffith was killed by his own men.[3]

Harold's third invasion of Wales.

Assassination of Griffith.

Thus fell—the lion of the north, the head and shield of the Britons, the inflexible defender of their homes, the faithful ally, the ferocious enemy, the last king

---

[1] The Voryd, close to the town of Rhyl.   [2] Flor. of Worcester.

[3] *Saxon Chronicle;* thus Wales was defeated, not from without, but from within; it was not the arm of the invader that deprived Griffith of his li e's blood, but it was that of the traitor. As it was in the days of Cæsar and of Griffith, so it afterwards was in the days of Llewelyn—the Welshman plotted against his king, his country and his race.

who held sway over Wales in a manner becoming a royal rival of the houses of Cerdic and of Godwin—the staunch and true-hearted Griffith ap Llewelyn.

Griffith's head was brought to Harold, who carried it to the king.[1] Thus, for the second time, the Confessor had an opportunity of looking upon the gory remains of a contemporary prince; the sight caused him to contemn[2] the Welsh. But the ghastly relic must have given him satisfaction, for it was proof positive of the death of his dauntless foe, who had been removed from his path through the treachery of his own subjects,[1] by the valour of earl Harold,[3] or in revenge for the death of his father by Caradog.[4] Griffith was succeeded by his half-brothers Bleddyn and Rhiwallawn, who swore allegiance, and delivered hostages as pledges of their good faith, to Edward and to Harold.[5]

The influence of Griffith over the affairs of England.

Griffith of Wales exercised an undoubted influence over the destiny of the Saxons: (i.) From 1039 to 1063 he had waged an almost incessant war against the Saxons, and had won battles at Rhyd y Groes, Leominster, Hereford, and other places: in his many

---

[1] *Saxon Chronicle.*   [2] Geoffrey Gaimar.   [3] Will. of Malmesbury.

[4] Flor. of Worcester: if so, Caradog ap Griffith ap Rhydderch killed Griffith ap Llewelyn because he had killed his father in 1054. Caradog also killed the three sons of Owain ap Edwyn ap Hywel Dda, and was himself killed in the second battle of Carno.

[5] *Saxon Chronicle.*—The fate of Griffith in the days of Harold was somewhat similar to that of Llewelyn in the days of Edward I. : both were betrayed by Welshmen—both were opposed by their nearest relatives ; but here the parallel ends, for Prince David appears to have repented of his unbrotherly and unpatriotic conduct—conduct more than expiated by his unfurling the standard of independence, and by his barbarous assassination: whereas, though both died a violent death, Bleddyn and Rhiwallawn enjoyed, for 19 and 6 years respectively, the fruits of their non-adhesion to, and betrayal of, the cause of their magnificently patriotic half-brother, Griffith ap Llewelyn.

expeditions into England he had killed multitudes of the foe, had carried off everything he could, and had utterly destroyed what he was not able to remove; thus he weakened the power, and overthrew the confidence, of the Saxons at a time when they stood in urgent need of every man and of every confidence. (ii.) Griffith helped to split up England into hostile camps: at Gloucester he took the part of Siward and Leofric against the Godwin faction, and accused the latter of conspiring against their sovereign; in consequence of this accusation Godwin and his sons "might not come within his (Edward's) eyes' sight."[1] (iii.) Upon the return of the Godwin family from banishment, Griffith continued to support their rivals of the family of Leofric; and, on two occasions, as we have read, he compelled the Saxon king and the Saxon Witan to "inlaw" Algar, son of Leofric, and to restore to him all his territories and offices. (iv.) The disunion in England and the continual successes of Griffith, must have encouraged the crafty and lion-hearted Duke of Normandy in his designs upon the throne of England, the duke would naturally conclude that he could overcome in battle the people who had been routed by the Welsh king and his small forces; thus Griffith fanned the hopes of one whose heart and eye were fixed upon the Saxon throne long before the year 1063. (v.) The Red Dragon of Cambria had indeed paled before the White Dragon of Wessex, and the Pendragon of the Welsh had succumbed to the representatives of the Saxon Bretwalda; but, though dead in the body, Griffith's spirit still lived and influenced his brave

The influence of Griffith over the affairs of England.

---

[1] *Saxon Chronicle.*

followers, who continued to support the cause of the earls Morcar and Edwin, the brothers-in-law of their heroic king; and this support encouraged those earls to demand at Northampton,[1] the banishment of Tosti; and when his banishment was pronounced, then was rung out the death-knell of the Saxon dynasty.[2]

LEADING EVENTS.

---

[1] *Saxon Chronicle*, Henry of Huntingdon, Iolo MSS., &c., informs us that *many Welsh* supported Edwin and Morcar at Northampton: doubtless, had they failed in their designs against Tosti, they would have found a safe refuge in Wales.

[2] Lord Lytton, in his " *Harold,*" gives a splendid description of Griffith's undying patriotism.

THE DESCENT OF WILLIAM THE CONQUEROR.

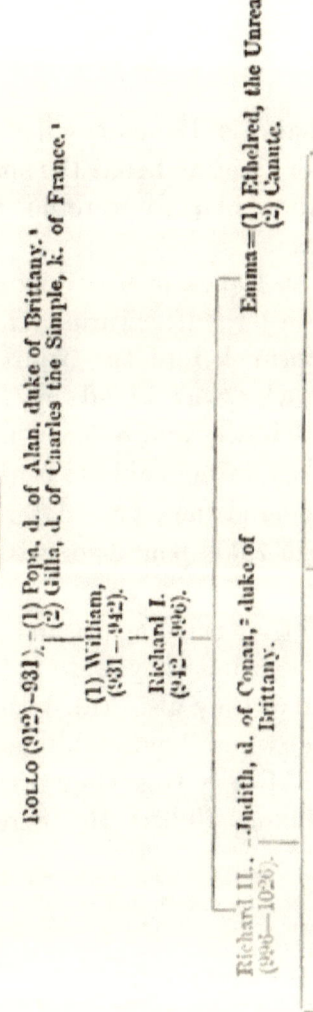

ROLLO (912)–931, –(1) Popa, d. of Alan, duke of Brittany.[1]
(2) Gisla, d. of Charles the Simple, k. of France.[1]

(1) William,
(931—942).

Richard I.
(942—996).

Richard II. –Judith, d. of Conan,[2] duke of
(996—1026).   Brittany.

Richard III.,
(1026—1028),
[2]poisoned by
Robert.

Robert,
(1028—1035).

WILLIAM=Matilda, d. of Baldwin
(Duke: 1035—1066),   of Flanders.
(King: 1066—1087).

Emma=(1) Ethelred, the Unready.
(2) Canute.

A Daughter=Guy of Bur-
gundy.[2]

Guy, who tried to take the
duchy of Normandy from
William.

[1] Matt. of Westminster.   [2] Will. of Malmesbury.

M

CHAPTER XIX.

THE NORMANS.

The Normans. WE have read that the Danes assailed the coasts of England time after time, and that the shores of France, Spain, and even those of Italy were not free from their ruthless depredations.

The first of these Danes, or Northmen as they were called in France—a term afterwards changed to that of Normans,—to appear before the walls of Paris was **Regner Lodbrog. 845.** Regner Lodbrog, who was killed by Ella[1] of Northumbria. This was in the year 845. Charles the Bald,[2] King of France, was quite unable to beat off the Northmen, so they plundered the city. After this was done the king paid them 7,000 pounds of silver to leave the land.

Paris captured 857. In the year 857 they came again, and again captured Paris: upon this occasion they were not satisfied with plundering the city, they also killed thousands of the defenceless people, whose bones whitened the banks of the river Seine. After a time they were successfully opposed by a Saxon, Robert the Strong,[3] Count of

---

[1] Matthew of Westminster states that Regner was killed by the huntsmen of Edmund, king of East Anglia, and that Regner's sons, from mistaken revenge, tied Edmund naked to a tree, riddled his body with arrows, and then cut off his head: a chapel was erected on the spot, and a Burgh grew up around it : see p. 38, and p. 107.

[2] He was grandson of Charlemagne ; his daughter Judith was the second wife of King Ethelwulf.—*Henry of Huntingdon.*

[3] He was related to King Charles of France, as they were both descended from Pepin, the great-grandfather of Charlemagne. Robert, as the great grandfather of Hugh Capet, was the founder of the Capetian dynasty of France.

Anjou: but he was killed by Hastings, the terrible sea-king.[1]

During the reign of Alfred the Great, the Northmen appear to have plundered England and France alternately. During the winter of 885 they besieged Paris for the third time. The Northmen were under the leadership of Rollo, one of the most daring and successful of their sea-kings. The French king, like Ethelred the Unready, thought of removing the Northmen who had settled in the land by treachery; one of their leaders was killed and another blinded. Then their fellow-countrymen, to the number of 30,000, marched against Paris, and besieged it for upwards of eighteen months. Odo, Count of Paris, headed the besieged; while the King of France, who was also Emperor of Germany, neglected for a long time to come to the help of his brave subjects, and, when he did come, he gave Rollo and his men 800 pounds of silver to go away. The Danes afterwards visited England; but Alfred defeated them in every direction. We have read[2] of the success of Hastings in France. After he had made peace with its king,[3] the country had rest for some time.

Rollo, the Northman, had been obliged to leave Denmark in accordance with a decree[4] of that country, which enacted that, whenever the land was too full of men, a number of the bravest should be obliged to seek their fortunes in other lands. He sailed to England. He dreamed a dream: and in his dream he heard and saw a swarm of bees flying over him and his army: he

Paris besieged a third time by Danes, 885.

Rollo.

---

[1] Henry of Huntingdon; see pp. 40-42.   [2] See p. 52.

[3] Charles the Fat: Flor. of Worcester says that the city of Paris was saved in 886 by the merciful help of God.

[4] Matt. of Westminster

watched their progress, until he saw that they crossed the sea, and that, after examining flowers of different colours, they settled down upon a particular spot.[1] When Rollo awoke, he considered the dream, and came to the conclusion that he should find a resting place for himself and his companions in the land to which the bees had flown.

Chartres besieged, 910. In the year 910, Rollo besieged the city of Chartres; he failed to take it by surprise or direct attack. Its citizens had chosen as their standard what was supposed to be a garment of the Virgin Mary: Rollo and his men were provoked to laughter at its appearance, whereupon a panic seized them, and they took to flight: the men of Chartres pursued and killed thousands[1] of them.

In two years' time the Northmen renewed their attacks upon the Frenchmen, and captured Bayeux, Paris, and Evreux. In their desperation the people went to their king, Charles the Simple, and complained of his inactivity. Whereupon he sent the Archbishop of Rouen to the Danish leader to promise him all the sea **Rollo swears fealty to Charles and marries his daughter, 912.** coast from the river Epte to the confines of Brittany, together with the hand of his daughter Gilla,[1] if he would become a Christian. With the advice of his council Rollo agreed to the Archbishop's proposal. Upon a fixed day he swore fealty to Charles, and also married his daughter: and Brittany was added to his domains: its duke, Alan, swore fealty to him. Rollo was asked to kiss the king's foot, in token of vassalage. He did so; but scorning to bend his knee, he took up his foot roughly, and, lifting it to his mouth, threw the king on his back upon the ground, to the intense delight

[1] Matthew of Westminster

of his followers, who laughed[1] heartily at the sight of the sprawling monarch. Upon his return to Rouen, Rollo was baptized, named Robert, after his godfather, Robert,[1] Duke of France, son of Count Robert the Strong.

Upon the death of Gilla, Robert re-married his first wife, Popa, daughter of Alan of Brittany, whom he had divorced, in order to marry Gilla.

In his treatment of the Northman Rollo, Charles followed the example of Alfred's treatment of Guthrum. Rollo, Count of Rouen, died in 931: he had greatly improved his dominions and subjects. He was succeeded as Count by his son William, who took the part of Hugh the Great, son of Robert, Duke of France, in his political intrigues. At first both William and Hugh espoused the cause of Louis the Foreigner, Athelstan's nephew, and recalled[1] him to France; but they afterwards rebelled against him. William extended his dominions to the sea by adding to it the Contentin. He was treacherously killed by Arnulf,[1] Count of Flanders in 942. Under him the Northmen who frequented his court forgot their own and adopted the French language and habits; but those residing along the sea shore continued to cling to the Norse language and superstitions.

William was anxious that his son Richard should learn the language of his ancestors: he was therefore educated at Bayeux, which was the chief town of those Northmen who had not forgotten the speech and ways of their forefathers. Richard married the daughter of Hugh the Great, Duke of France, and helped his son, Hugh Capet, to the throne of France. Richard married

Death of Rollo, 931

William, his son.

Richard, son of William.

---

[1] Matthew of Westminster.

his daughter Emma to Ethelred the Unready. The Saxon king and his wife did not agree over well;[1] and, in consequence of his daughter's representations, Richard seized[2] every Saxon, whether clergy or lay, in his dominions; he killed some of them, and others he imprisoned; Pope John XV. made peace between them. Emma's steward of Exeter, the "French churl,"[3] was the first Norman to betray the land of his adoption.

Death of Richard, 996. Richard of Normandy died in 996, and was succeeded by his son Richard, a minor: the peasants now rose in rebellion, but they were quelled in a merciless manner.

In the eleventh century the Counts of Rouen became Dukes of Normandy, and their soldiers were among the most renowned in Europe; whilst architecture, literature and agriculture made steady progress amongst

Richard II. 996 to 1026. them. Richard II. of Normandy afforded protection to his sister Emma, to his brother-in-law Ethelred, and to their sons Edward and Alfred; his influence in England, prior to the time of Canute, may aptly be termed its moral conquest, as, in the hour of distress, his was the hand stretched out to comfort and succour the royal and other fugitives.

Richard III., 1026 to 1028. Richard II. of Normandy was succeeded by his son Richard III., who was poisoned by his brother Robert: a woman,[1] skilled in poisons, is reported to have been engaged by him to do this dreadful deed.

Robert II. He defends Henry I. of France. Henry I., King of France, in the day of disaster, took refuge in Normandy, and called upon Robert to defend his cause. Robert defeated the rebel nobles and the queen mother in three battles; and, having overcome all the king's foes, he obtained, as a reward

---

[1] William of Malmesbury.   [2] Matthew of Westminster.
[3] *Saxon Chronicle :* Hugh betrayed Exeter to the Danes.

for his loyal exertions, an extent of land that brought his dukedom within twenty miles of Paris.

This Norman Duke boasted that he would set the crown of England upon the heads of his cousins, the Athelings Alfred and Edward. With this meritorious object in view, he assembled a fleet and filled it with soldiers. But he was doomed to be disappointed, for the elements, which have not unfrequently protected the shores of England, persistently fought against his ships, so that he was obliged to disband his forces; and his vessels were allowed to decay in the harbour of Rouen.[1]

Robert never married, but he had a son whom he named William; he was born in the year 1027. In 1035, when his boy was seven years of age, Robert recommended him to his barons as his heir[2] at a public meeting: he then departed for Jerusalem,[2] as he was wishful to atone for the death of his brother; while returning, he was poisoned by his servant. As long as he lived his barons honoured his son, but, upon his death, they began to look after their own affairs, and revolted from their boy duke. But after a time William became too powerful for his revolted subjects, whom he defeated time after time, and finally routed them at Valesdune,[3] 1047.

William was able to afford protection to his father's cousin, Edward the Atheling; and when, in 1052, his throne was threatened by the power of Godwin, he landed in England to give him both succour and advice:

William, son of Robert II.

---

[1] William of Malmesbury attributes the adversity of the wind to the hidden counsels of God; he states that the remains of the fleet were to be seen in his days.

[2] Guy of Amiens; Matt. of Westminster, &c.   [3] Will. of Malmesbury.

he was accompanied by "a great body of Frenchmen."[1] When he returned to Normandy he left his chaplain, William, at Edward's court; he became bishop of London. Other Normans, military and clerical, also remained in England; and, while ostensibly engaged in the service of its King, they were quietly and patiently paving the way for the triumphant return of their Duke in 1066.

LEADING EVENTS.

---

[1] *Saxon Chronicle:* Florence of Worcester terms them "a vast retinue of Normans."

CHAPTER XX.

EDWARD THE CONFESSOR: OR, ENGLAND UNDER THE RULE
OF HAROLD THE EARL, FROM 1053 TO 1066.

UPON the death of Godwin his son Harold succeeded to **Edward** his position at the king's court and in the hearts of the **the Confessor's** people. **personal appearance and** It may not be uninteresting to read that Edward the **habits.** Confessor was of a moderate height. His personal appearance was of a pleasing description: his hair and beard were milk white; his face was full and ruddy; his hands were thin and white; his figure was perfect and kinglike. He was of a cheerful, though quiet, disposition. To every one he was affable and condescending; and when he refused a request he did so in such a courteous manner that he seemed to confer a favour. In public he conducted himself as king and ruler: in private he was as a companion to his friends. He counselled the bishops and other religious men to act up to their professions; and he caused the judicial chiefs and lawyers to administer justice with equity, and to condemn crime. He did away with evil laws, and made just ones to take their place. He delighted in hawks and other birds of prey; and also in dogs. He passed most of his time in hunting, in religious devotions, in conversation with abbots and monks, and in acts of hospitality.[1]

With such a character it was altogether impossible that Edward should rule the land without the help of

[1] Vita Æduardi.

men able to conduct campaigns, and to influence the
Witan. He was simply the head of a confederation of
nobles, who succeeded to their fathers' positions and
estates as a matter of course; consequently, upon the
death of Godwin his son Harold succeeded him as earl
of Wessex, and Algar took his place as earl of East
Anglia.[1] The influence of the Godwin family was thus
much lessened; for whilst Godwin lived England was
divided into five parts—Northumbria under Siward,
Mercia under Leofric and Sweyn, East Anglia under
Harold, and Wessex under Godwin. But upon the
death of Siward in 1055, as his son Waltheof[2] was too
young[3] to rule the turbulent Northumbrians, Tosti,
through the influence of his brother Harold and his
sister,[4] succeeded him. He was the king's and queen's
favourite;[4] but notwithstanding his frequent attendance
at court, he ruled his subjects well for ten years.

The family biographer[4] draws a comparison between
Harold and Tosti. They were distinguished by fine
forms, and were possessed of equal strength and boldness. But Harold the elder was the taller, better able
to bear watching and want, of a more gentle turn of
mind, and more ready wit: he never took vengeance
upon any one, and whom he considered faithful he
consulted: he surpassed all people in strength of body
and mind, and, like a second Judas Maccabæus, he was
the friend of his own people and country: he was distinguished for his patience, and for his sympathetic
and friendly manner. Tosti was of a more serious turn

---

[1] *Saxon Chronicle.*
[2] Waltheof was put to death by William I. It is stated that his head
was cut off whilst he was repeating the Lord's prayer, and that he continued
to repeat it *after* his head was severed from his body.—*Ordericus Vitalis.*
[3] Henry of Huntingdon.   [4] Vita Æduardi.

of mind, and more unrelenting in punishing guilt; he was endowed with manly firmness: it was difficult to see through his plans, and he seldom communicated them to others: he presented gifts with the greatest liberality. Each carried on in a steady manner their respective duties, Tosti bravely, Harold with more wisdom than his brother. The writer concludes with the statement that "*no age and no country ever produced two such men,*"[1] and that, by their means, the king dwelt in peace and security, and was able to enjoy himself with dogs and birds, and religious conversations and exercises. *Harold and Tosti.*

Another writer[2] states that Harold was brave in arms, of great stature and incomparable strength, and excelled in personal beauty all the great leaders of the world; that he was the right hand of the king; and that, endowed with wisdom, and skilled in all accomplishments which became a soldier, he showed himself an illustrious man in everything.

Harold paid a visit to Rome.[1] On his way he carefully studied the habits of the chiefs and people with whom he came in contact. After a course of prayer and confession[1] he returned to England, and escaped the plots of those whose enmity he had aroused. *Harold visits Rome.*

Harold is reported to have paid a special visit to William of Normandy: but it is highly probable that he did not do so, as (i.) no Saxon writer alludes to such a visit; (ii.) it is mentioned by only one contemporary writer,[3] whose biography contains statements[4] which

[1] Vita Eduardi.   [2] De Inventione Sanctæ Crucis.
[3] William of Poitiers, the Conqueror's chaplain.
[4] He states (a) that Edward made William of Normandy his heir in 1012, whereas Florence of Worcester and other writers state that Edward summoned Edward the Atheling and his family from Hungary to England

are contradicted by a consensus of authority; (iii.) succeeding Norman writers contradict one another concerning the particulars of Harold's visit.[1]

Various explanations have been given for Harold's visit to William of Normandy in 1063—(i.) he was crossing the sea to Flanders, and was driven by a storm

in 1057, as he wished to make him his heir : *(b)* he states that Edward gave William in 1042 Wulfnoth and Haco, the son and grandson of Godwin, as pledges of his succession ; whereas the *Saxon Chronicle*, Vita Æduardi, Henry of Huntingdon, Matthew of Westminster, do not mention these hostages.

[1] Matthew of Westminster states that Harold bound himself by an oath to deliver up to William the castle of *Canterbury*, and the kingdom upon the death of Edward ; in return, William betrothed him to his *little girl*, and gave him her inheritance and his intimate friendship : but he does not mention the expedition into Brittany, nor the oath *upon the relics*.

Henry of Huntingdon states that Harold swore *upon the relics* to marry William's daughter, and to help him to become King of England after the death of Edward ; he says not a word about the expedition into Brittany.

William of Malmesbury says that Harold, of his own accord, promised William the castle of *Dover*, and the kingdom of England when Edward died ; in return, William betrothed his *child* to Harold, promised that he should continue to hold his possessions in England, and received him into his strictest intimacy. William took Harold with him on an expedition into Brittany, as he wished *(a)* to learn his disposition, *(b)* to try his courage and strength, and *(c)* to show him that the Norman sword was better than the Saxon battle-axe : but he does not mention the oath *upon the relics*.

The Bayeux Tapestry shows that Guy of Ponthieu took Harold to Beaurain ; Wace states that he took him first to Abbeville, and then to Beaurain.

Wace says that William gave Guy lands in exchange for Harold ; Benoit states that threats and military preparations occasioned his release.

Wace says that Harold swore on the relics at Bayeux ; Ordericus Vitalis says at Rouen ; and William of Poitiers at Bonneville ; and we are informed that the oath was taken *(a)* in the palace, *(b)* under an oak tree near Rouen.

Guy of Amiens states that Harold did homage, promised allegiance, and swore *three* oaths to William. The Tapestry shows that Harold was knighted by William *after* the campaign into Brittany, but Wace says *before* it.

Wace states that he took the oath *after* the expedition into Brittany ; William of Poitiers states *before* that expedition. Wace mentions three or four expeditions into Brittany ; the other writers record only one.

upon the coast of Ponthieu[1]; the statement that Harold Harold visits William of Normandy crossed the sea coincides with plate iv. of the Bayeux Tapestry—" Hic Harold : Mare : Navigavit "—here Harold has put to sea; and that he encountered a storm is corroborated by plate v.—" Et velis : Vento : Plenis Venit : In Terra : Widonis Comitis "—and his sails, being *filled with wind*, he comes to the land of Count Wido, that is, Guy : (ii.) that, while Harold was amusing himself in a fishing boat,[2] a storm drove him upon the shores of France : (iii.) that he was ordered by the king to go to William and assure him that he should have the realm after his death[3] : (iv.) that Harold pitied the hostages, and was anxious to bring them home;[4] but when he went to take leave of the king, Edward, by entreaty and command, desired him not to go to Normandy, lest William, who was very shrewd, should draw him into some snare; and he suggested the despatch of a messenger in his place : (v.) that, being bound hand and foot[5] and cast into prison by Guy, Harold, in order to obtain freedom through William, *pretended* he had been sent by Edward to confirm the promise he had made to him by inferior persons concerning his succession to the throne of England : (vi.) that, having been cast into prison and bound with chains on suspicion of being a spy,[6] in order to obtain his release, Harold informed William that he was prevented by the Count of Ponthieu from delivering to him certain messages from King Edward; and the same authority also states

---

[1] Henry of Huntingdon   this writer places Harold's visit to Normandy in 1063, before his last expedition into Wales.

[2] Will. of Malmesbury; Matt. of Westminster.

[3] Wace : this idea is portrayed in the Bayeux Tapestry.

[4] Wace : this writer asserts that Harold swore upon the relics.

[5] Will. of Malmesbury.   [6] Matt. of Westminster.

that Harold was sent into Normandy to conduct William to England, as Edward was thinking of making him his heir: (vii.) Harold was sent by the king to

Harold's oath.

confirm upon oath[1] the promise that Edward had made William when he ascended the throne ; and that Harold was chosen to do this particular service for three reasons—(1) he was the first of Edward's subjects in wealth, honour, and power; (2) the hostages that Edward had given William as pledges of his succession to the Saxon throne were Harold's brother and nephew; (3) should the Saxons object to William's succession, and make some new arrangements in accordance with their customary perfidiousness, Harold, by his wealth and influence, would be able to overcome their objections. The same writer states that Harold swore fealty to William, and promised to be his representative in the Saxon senate, to do all he could to establish William upon the throne after the death of Edward, and, meanwhile, to permit him to garrison Dover Castle and other places.

Bearing, therefore, in mind the silence of Saxon writers upon so important a matter, the incredible statements of the Conqueror's chaplain concerning it,

---

[1] William of Poitiers: this writer states that Harold's brother Wulfnoth and his nephew Haco were delivered up by Edward to William of Normandy as early as 1042: this statement is incredible for two reasons—(a) at that time William was a boy, and (b) Godwin was the most powerful man in England. And Godwin would not have given up his son and grandson in 1052, as some writers suppose, for at that time England was at his feet. Again, if Harold went to Normandy in 1065 to redeem the hostages, he would have brought back with him his brother, and not his nephew: and yet William of Poitiers states that he returned with his nephew only ; and in this statement he is indirectly backed up by William of Malmesbury, who has it that Wulfnoth spent his life in captivity, and died as an old man in confinement at Salisbury : Florence of Worcester states that Wulfnoth was released by the Conqueror on his deathbed, but that the Rufus confined him in Winchester.

and the conflicting explanations given by succeeding
writers as to the manner in which Harold got to
Normandy, and the object that took him there, together
with their irreconcileable records of his words and acts
whilst there, we cannot but conclude that it is more
than probable that Harold did not swear allegiance to
William, and that he did not visit Normandy, unless he
did so on his way to or from Rome.

In the previous chapter we read of Harold's successful campaigns in Wales. By the death of Griffith he
removed a dangerous neighbour, and an encourager of
sedition in the land. Moreover, by marrying his widow,
Elgitha, daughter of Algar, Earl of Mercia,[1] he put an
end to the hostility of the adherents of her house, if
he did not secure the friendship and co-operation of her
brothers Edwin and Morcar.

In 1065 Tosti was outlawed by the thanes of his earl- Outlaw of
Tosti, 1065
dom, because he robbed God,[2] and had ill-used those
under his rule;[2] because the thane Cospatric had been
treacherously killed at court by the queen for Tosti's
sake,[3] and the thanes Gamel and Ulf in Tosti's chamber
at York;[3] because his subjects had heard that he had
assaulted his brother Harold in the king's presence, as
he was jealous of his favour with the king,[4] and that
Harold had dashed him upon the floor,[5] and that in
revenge Tosti killed and mutilated Harold's servants at
Hereford; because of his austere manners.[6]

Another writer[7] praises Tosti, and refers to his
devotion and magnificence whilst on a pilgrimage to
Rome in the company of his wife Judith, and his

---

[1] See next page.   [2] Saxon Chronicle.   [3] Flor. of Worcester.
[4] Henry of Huntingdon: he states that Tosti was older than Harold.
[5] Matt. of Westminster.   [6] Will. of Malmesbury.   [7] Vita Æduardi.

HOUSE OF LEOFRIC OF MERCIA.

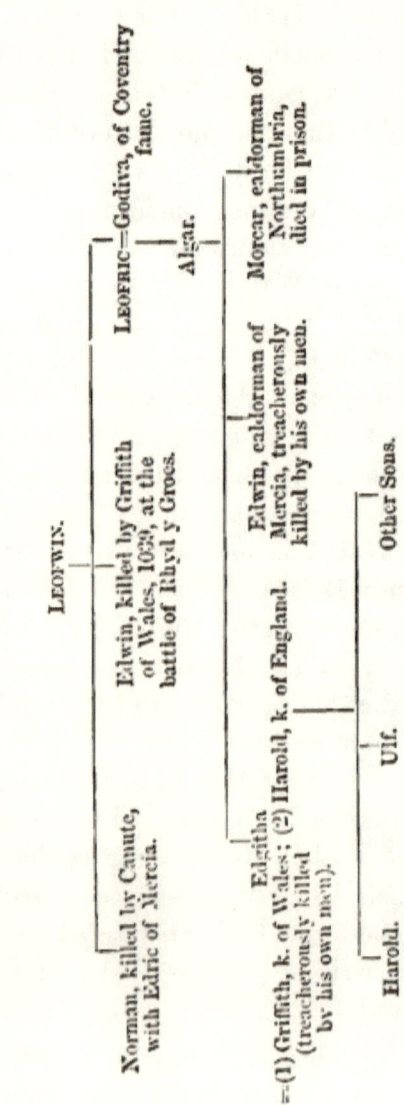

LEOFWIN.

LEOFRIC=Godiva, of Coventry fame.

Algar.

Norman, killed by Canute, with Edric of Mercia.

Elwin, killed by Griffith of Wales, 1039, at the battle of Rhyd y Groes.

Morcar, ealdorman of Northumbria, died in prison.

Edgitha
=(1) Griffith, k. of Wales; (2) Harold, k. of England. (treacherously killed by his own men).

Elwin, ealdorman of Mercia, treacherously killed by his own men.

Harold.   Ulf.   Other Sons.

brother Gurth. When Northumbria came under his rule, highway robbery and murder were very frequent in the land: this portion of England had always been noted for its wild character; out of fourteen of its rulers only one had died in possession of the earldom, the others had been killed, banished, or had become monks. It was no easy matter, therefore, for Tosti to rule such a people. He put down robbery and murder with impartiality. His strictness was hateful to his subjects; so a faction of the nobles formed a conspiracy against him, and they invited to their aid Edwin and, Morcar, as these nobles had hated Tosti[1] for a long time. They were successful in every direction: they seized Tosti's treasures,[2] killed his huscarls and adherents, and banishing him, made Morcar their earl.[3] Morcar led them to Northampton, where he was joined by his brother Edwin, and many Welshmen.[4]

The king was anxious that the rising should be put down by force of arms,[1] and Harold set out to avenge[5] his brother's expulsion. But when he came to Northampton he tried to reconcile[4] the contending parties, but he failed to do so; the Northumbrians informed him that they were a free people, and unable to put up with the cruelty of any prince, and that they had been taught by their ancestors to be free, or to die.[5]

Great Councils were held at Northampton and Oxford,[6] and ambassadors[5] were sent between the king's court and the rebel's camp, and Tosti called God to witness[6] that he was innocent of the charges laid against him, but to no purpose; and, while negociations were being carried on, the Northumbrians, Mercians, and Welsh

Tosti.

Council at Northampton.

---

[1] Vita Eduardi.   [2] Flor. of Worcester.   [3] Henry of Huntingdon.
[4] Saxon Chronicle.   [5] Will. of Malmesbury.   [6] Matt. of Westminster.

N

killed men, and burnt houses and corn.[1] At last the
king was persuaded, much against his will, to give his
consent to the banishment of Tosti. It is stated that
Harold influenced the king in favour of Morcar, as he
regarded the quiet of the country more than the
advantage of his brother;[2] but it was whispered that
he had, by deceitful plans,[3] excited the revolt of the
Northumbrians.

Edward gave pledges that he had granted the
demand of the Northumbrians to have Morcar to rule
over them, and he renewed Canute's law;[4] so they
departed northwards, taking with them thousands of
cattle,[4] and hundreds[4] or thousands[5] of captives.
Northampton and the bordering counties suffered for
many years[4] after their visit.

Departure of Tosti. Tosti, enraged against everyone,[2] departed with his
wife and children to Flanders, to seek the protection
and aid of his father-in-law, Baldwin, its Count. We
may here pause to consider the intimate and sincere
ties of relationship and of friendship that united the
county of Flanders with the country of England.
We have read that the founder of the family of
Baldwin married Judith, the widow of Ethelwulf, and
the divorced wife of his son Ethelbald; and that their
son Baldwin married Ethelswitha, the daughter of
King Alfred. After this marriage Flanders became
the house of refuge of the rulers of Wessex. In 1037,
when Queen Emma was banished from Wessex, which
she held in the name of her son Hardicanute, she sailed
to Bruges, and there dwelt in safety. In 1040, when
Hardicanute determined to seize England by force of

---

[1] Matt. of Westminster.   [2] Will. of Malmesbury.   [3] Vita Æduardi.
[4] Saxon Chronicle.   [5] Henry of Huntingdon.

arms, it was to Bruges that he sailed for aid and advice.
In 1046, when Sweyn, Godwin's son, was pronounced
a "nithing," it was to the Count of Baldwin that he
fled for refuge. In 1049, Edward of England leagued
with the foes of Baldwin : from henceforth this "ancient
friend of the English race"[1] attached himself more
closely to the party of Godwin, so much so that when
the latter was exiled, Baldwin treated him nobly whilst
he abode within his domains, and aided him when he
sought to recover his lands and his honours. And again,
when Gytha, the noble wife of such a noble man as
Godwin, and the excellent mother of such excellent
sons as Harold, Gurth, and Leofwine, widowed, desolate
and alone, but not heart-brokened, sought the house of
Baldwin, she was consoled by him and his, and also
aided by them in her heroic efforts to avenge the
slaughter of her offspring. Verily Baldwin was a
friend of the English race!

The king was stricken to the heart with grief at the
forced absence of his favourite, so that he sickened
and continued sick to the day of his death, complain- Death of
ing that he was deserted by those who should have The
Confessor,
protected him.[1] At his deathbed stood the queen, 1066.
Harold, and Stigand : to his wife he said—"May God
grant favour to you, my wife, for the kind way in
which you have done your duty to me;" and to Harold
he said—"*I commend this realm to you to be guarded
by you;*" and asked him to defend those Normans
who, out of love for him, had come to England, or
to send them back to their own land.

Edward endeared himself to his subjects by relieving The
them of the tax called Danegelt, which was first Danegelt.

[1] Vita Eduardi.

imposed by his father, Ethelred the Unready, for the
payment of his Danish huscarls,[1] and which the Saxons
had paid their kings for thirty-eight years.[2] This heavy
impost of 38,000[1] pounds of silver distressed the people
very much;[3] it was paid before all other taxes.[3]
Edward was also sparing in the exactions of other
taxes, and abominated the insolence of their collectors.[4]

When an exile at the court of the Norman dukes,[5]
Edward had made a vow that he would visit Rome if
he obtained his father's kingdom : when king, Pope Leo
absolved him from his vow on condition that he either
built or restored a monastery ; thereupon he restored

**West-
minster
Abbey.**

the Abbey of Westminster, and, with the consent of
the Witan, he endowed it with estates, revenues, and
privileges.[1] This noble erection was completed just
before his death, and his was the first body that was
entombed within its walls.[3]

The king appears to have been fond of ships. On
four occasions he took part in a naval demonstration,
in 1046 when England was threatened by Magnus of
Norway, in 1048 after Sandwich had been ravaged, in
1049 when he took the part of the Emperor of Germany
against Baldwin of Flanders, and in 1052 when Godwin
returned from banishment.

**The Con-
fessor's
habits.**

He led an active life, for in the morning he attended
divine service, and then enjoyed himself with fleet dogs
and in falconry ;[4] the rest of the day was spent in conversations with men of religious orders,[1] and with
supplying the poor with the necessaries[2] of life, and in
entertaining the stranger and the foreigner.[1]

But, notwithstanding the fact that he advised his

---

[1] Matt. of Westminster.   [2] Flor. of Worcester.   [3] *Saxon Chronicle.*
[4] Will. of Malmesbury.   [5] Richard II., Richard III., Robert.

bishops and abbots to act up to their calling,[1] and the administrators of the law to decide justly, and punish vice,[1] and that he pitied the poor and feeble,[1] yet he ordered Godwin to fall upon the citizens of Dover,[2] and Harold to destroy the rebels at Northampton,[1] and thus he showed that at times he was endowed with the ruthless spirit of his father.

Though jealous of his kingly prerogatives, he rarely wore the regal ornaments.[1] And such sanctity was attached to his person, that he has the credit of having cured skin disease with his fingers dipped in water; and the water in which he washed his hands restored the blind to sight.[3] But his simplicity and sanctity did not increase his filial love, for he seized his mother's treasures and lands, and afterwards banished her,[4] because she had mocked[3] his needy state and never assisted him during the many years that he lived upon the bounty of strangers and foreigners; nor did these excellent traits of character prevent him swearing St. Dunstan's oath[5] at a peasant, and threatening him because he had interfered with his arrangements whilst hunting deer.[3] He was also credited with the gift of prophecy; and it is stated that he foretold the evils that should befall England after his death, and announced their cessation in the words—" When a green tree shall be cut through the middle, and the part cut off, after having been carried a distance of three acres from the stem, shall unite itself to the stem without any assistance, bud out with leaves and stretch forth its fruit as before from the sap uniting once more."[6]

[1] Vita Æduardi.   [2] Saxon Chronicle.   [3] Will. of Malmesbury.
[4] Henry of Huntingdon.   [5] "By God and his mother."
[6] Will. of Malmesbury: The green tree means the Saxon dynasty; the severing of the trunk means the cessation of the house of Cerdic ; the three

Edward was liked by Saxons and Normans, so that when he died one and all united in lamenting his departure, and in expressing the sorrows of the people. We read that he was buried "amidst the tears of the crowds who flocked to his funeral;"[1] that his body was washed "with the tears of his countrymen;"[2] that he surrendered "his pure spirit to heaven;"[3] that he exchanged "his temporal kingdom for an eternal one;"[4] that—

> "This noble, from earth
> angels carried,
> Steadfast soul,
> into heaven's light,"[5]

and that his last words to his wife[2] were: *"I do not die, but grow strong in my God."*

LEADING EVENTS.

acres signify Harold, William I., William II. ; the two parts of the trunk indicate the Saxon and Norman dynasties ; the union of the two parts of the trunk indicate the marriage of Henry I. and Matilda of Scotland ; the leaves refer to their daughter Matilda, and the fruit is her son Henry II.

[1] Flor. of Worcester.   [2] Vita Æduardi.   [3] Will. of Malmesbury.
[4] Matt. of Westminster.   [5] *Saxon Chronicle.*

CHAPTER XXI.

WILLIAM, DUKE OF NORMANDY.

WE have read that William was opposed by his nobles, William of Normandy who were headed by Guy of Burgundy. Guy fancied that he had a better right to the duchy of Normandy than William, as he was the legitimate grandson of Richard II. He attacked William by night, and had it not been for his jester, the Norman duke would have been killed in his bed; as it was he escaped in a half naked state, with his breeches, shirt, and cloak.[1] Guy and his confederates were defeated at the battle of Valesdune, 1047.

Henry,[2] King of France, took the part of William at the battle of Valesdune. He did so from a deep sense of duty, as he remembered that he owed his throne to the Norman duke's father. In return for his help against his rebel nobles, William assisted the French king in his encounter with Geoffrey of Anjou.[2] William was now, though only twenty years old, full of manly vigour,[2] and so recklessly brave that when alone he would attack numbers, and, in the hour of battle, would rush into the thickest ranks of the foe.

By his exploits against Geoffrey he gained Henry's greatest regard, who styled him the ornament of the French and the safeguard of the Normans.[2]

Geoffrey[3] was the son of Fulk, Count of Anjou. His

---

[1] Wace's *Roman de Rou*.   [2] Will. of Malmesbury.

[3] Geoffrey's sister was the mother of Fulk, who was the grandfather of Geoffrey, the husband of Matilda of England, and the father of Henry II.

Geoffrey of Anjou. father, when old, entrusted his dominions to him. Geoffrey treated his subjects very badly, and was also insolent to his father, and took up arms against him, whereupon the old man defended himself, and compelled his son to carry a saddle[1] upon his back for some miles, in token of submission and in acknowledgment of his bad conduct: when they met, Fulk spurned his son with his foot, exclaiming, "You are conquered." "Yes," retorted Geoffrey, "by you, as you are my father; to others I am altogether invincible." This spirit of invincibility led Geoffrey to contend in battle with many of his neighbours. He attacked and defeated the earls of Poitou and of Blois, and took possession of their territories. And he also seized the castle of Alencon,[1] which belonged to Normandy. As soon as William heard of its capture he marched into Anjou: and though Geoffry[1] boasted that he would show the world that an Angevin could beat a Norman in battle, yet he retreated without striking a blow.

William of Arches. The Norman duke had next to fight against William, earl of Arches, and Guy of Ponthieu. Such was the terror his appearance inspired that more than three hundred soldiers, who had left the castle of Arches to plunder, fled as soon as they saw him, though he had only a few followers[1] with him at the time. The earl William was helped by the king of France, who, doubtless, had become jealous of the reputation of the duke of Normandy.

And now William had to struggle against the overwhelming forces of France, which over-ran Normandy in two armies: the one was led by the king in person: the other was under the command of his brother.

[1] Will. of Malmesbury.

William also divided his army into two divisions: with the one he followed the marches of Henry, watching for an opportunity to attack him with advantage: the other division was victorious at Mortemar,[1] as the king's brother, with his forces, fled after a slight engagement. Guy of Ponthieu was captured[1] at this battle. When William heard of the victory at Mortemar he sent a messenger to proclaim it, in the dead of night, close to the king's tent.[1] When Henry heard the news he fled back to France and made peace with William, 1054.

In the year 1058 Henry entered Normandy for the second time, boasting that the sea[1] alone should put a stop to his advance. On this occasion William exhibited the skill of a great general. He did not oppose the march of the French army before they came to the river Dive.[1] Part of Henry's forces had crossed the river, and then William fell upon that part that had not crossed, and completely overwhelmed it: the tide prevented their fellows re-crossing to their aid; and Henry, having witnessed the destruction of his forces, returned home and died.

Before the death of Edward the Confessor, William had obtained the goodwill of Baldwin of Flanders, and had married his daughter Matilda:[2] he was at peace with Philip, King of France; and he had added, by conquest, Maine and Brittany to his domains. One of his admirers[3] states that he was at that time " vigorous, and full of wisdom in all things." And another[4] asserts that he heard and judged in his own person " the cause

---

[1] William of Malmesbury.

[2] Matilda was the fifth in descent from Ethelswitha, one of the daughters of Alfred the Great; her sister was Judith, Tosti's wife.

[3] Guy, in his " Carmen de Bello Hastingensi."   [4] William of Poitiers.

william of of the poor, the fatherless, and the widow;" and that
Normandy his justice "kept back his courtiers and favourites from
deeds of wrong;" and that so impartial and strict was
he, that in his days "the mighty man durst not remove
the landmark of his poor neighbour."

And while Harold was protecting churches and
monasteries,[1] and building and endowing his abbey at
Waltham[2] for the Seculars; William, under the guidance
of Lanfranc, was building churches and fostering the
cause of the Regulars. While Harold was victorious
over Wales, and beloved in England, William was the
model ruler upon the continent. Such were the two
men who stood forth as giants in ability, strength,
bravery, generalship, and undaunted determination
amongst their contemporaries.

LEADING EVENTS.

The Battle of Valesdune .... 1047 A.D.
The Battle of Mortemar 1054
William's Victory upon the Dive 1058

[1] Flor. of Worcester.   [2] De Inventione Sanctæ Crucis.

CHAPTER XXII.

HAROLD, THE KING.

UPON the death of Edward, there were three claimants Harold, to the throne of England, Harold, son of Godwin, Edgar son of Godwin. the Atheling, and William of Normandy.

The Confessor, being fully aware of the rivalry that existed between Harold and William of Normandy, was wishful to make Edward,[1] the son of his half-brother, Edmund the Ironside, his heir. Edward the Atheling, Edward, who was neither valiant nor a man of ability,[2] lived in the Outlaw. Hungary, where he had married the sister of the queen of that country. He came to England, at his uncle's request, in 1057, but he had scarcely landed, and had not seen Edward's face before he died[3] of illness, leaving a son and two daughters dependent upon the king's bounty.

His son was Edgar the Atheling. He had nothing Edgar, to recommend him: he was a mere boy, and was foreign the Atheling. born and bred; and though some[4] of the Saxons sought to make him king, as the Confessor had recommended him as nearest to the throne in point of birth,[5] his claims were disallowed.

William, duke of Normandy, claimed the throne of England upon three grounds, (1) Edward's promise,[5] (2) Harold's oath,[6] (3) relationship[4] to the Saxon king

---

[1] See page 103.　　[2] Will. of Malmesbury.

[3] Harold, and also the Normans, are suspected of having killed him.

[4] Henry of Huntingdon.　　[5] William of Poitiers.　　[6] Wace.

William's
claims to
the throne
of England (1) As regards Edward's promise,[1] the throne of England was not an hereditary one, consequently this promise, unless it had been made with the full knowledge and consent of the Witan and the Saxon people, was of no avail. And it is evident that even William's chaplain looked upon it in this light, for he states that Harold declared, after he had taken the oath, that he would be "duke William's *representative*[2] in the *Senate* (that is, the Witan) of his master King Edward as long as he lived."

(2) As regards the oath, we have given our reasons for concluding that it is more than probable that it was never taken. If Harold took the oath of allegiance to William, he must have taken it with the full knowledge that he would not be able to be true to his oath, therefore he stands forth as a self-convicted perjurer. If he promised to do all that he could to raise William to the Saxon throne, he did so without consulting the Saxon Witan, therefore, he was a traitor to his country. If he promised to admit a Norman garrison into Dover or Canterbury Castle without his sovereign's knowledge and express sanction, he was a rebel; but contemporary writers, who knew him well, write of him as no false swearer, traitor, or rebel.

(3) As regards William's claim to the throne of England upon the grounds of relationship to its king, he was simply the illegitimate son of Edward's cousin.

As to the claims of Harold, son of Godwin, they were universally acknowledged—(i.) by the king, who addressed him, within the hour of his death, with the

---

[1] Will. of Malmesbury states that Edward gave the succession of England to William of Normandy upon the death of Edward of Hungary.

[2] William of Poitiers.

words—"*I commend this realm to you to be guarded*
by you."[1] (ii.) By the Saxon nobility and people[2]—

> "*And the sage*[3] (that is the Witan)
> *the realm committed to a high born man,*
> *Harold's self,*
> the noble earl.
> He in all time
> his rightful lord
> obeyed faithfully
> by words and deeds,
> nor aught neglected
> that needful was
> to his sovereign king."

(iii.) By consecration and coronation: upon the day of King Edward's burial Harold was consecrated[4] and crowned as king by Aldred,[5] Archbishop of York.

When Harold ascended the throne of England it had been occupied for 571 years by the descendants of Cerdic. Unlike his predecessors, he held it, not through

---

[1] Vita Eduardi.

[2] *Saxon Chronicle:* the Norman writers unite in denying Harold's claims to the throne. Guy of Amiens states that he "*took* the crown contrary to all right;" William of Malmesbury says "Harold *seized* the crown and *extorted* from the nobles their consent;" Henry of Huntingdon has it that "Harold, relying on his power and his pretensions by birth, *seized* the crown;" William of Poitiers observes, "Harold, the *mad* Englishman, did not wait to find out the wishes of the people, but on the very day of Edward's burial *assumed* the crown;" Matthew of Westminster states that "Harold *extorted* an oath of fealty from the nobles, and *placed the crown on his own head;*" Wace says that Edward, being pressed by Harold and his friends to name him his successor, said—"Let the English make the Duke or Harold king, as they please."

[3] Florence of Worcester states that Harold was *chosen* his successor by Edward, and also *elected* by the nobility as king.

[4] Harold having succeeded to the kingdom as the king had *granted* it to him, and had also *chosen* him thereto, *was blessed as king.—Saxon Chronicle.*

[5] Florence of Worcester: In order to throw discredit upon Harold's succession, certain Norman writers state that he was crowned by Stigand, who had been excommunicated because (*a*) he had become archbishop during the absence of Robert, Godwin's foe, and (*b*) he had received the pallium from Benedict X. who had usurped the Papal See. Most probably both Stigand and Aldred were present at Harold's coronation.

divine or hereditary right, but because, by continued
integrity, industry, and bravery, he had become more
prudent in council, more powerful in arms, more skilled
in the laws of the land than any one of his contemporaries.[1]

Harold's
conduct.

And as soon as Harold held the reins of government
he began to abolish unjust laws and frame good ones.
He favoured the churches, monasteries, and the clergy
of every degree.   He showed himself kind and considerate to those who observed the laws; but to the
evil-doer he was most strict, for he ordered everyone
who was responsible for the order and quietness of the
land, from the earl down to the humblest officer of
peace, to arrest thieves, robbers, and public disturbers,
while the navy and army were constantly kept at work
to secure the safety of the country by land and by sea.[2]
Meanwhile the Norman duke and the exiled earl were
plotting the destruction of Harold, and the overthrow
of the Saxon dynasty.

William
hears of
Harold's
accession.

William was in his park at Rouen when he heard the
news of the change of kings in England. "In[3] his hand
he held a bow which he had strung and bent, making
it ready for the arrow, when a soldier, who had
journeyed from England, went straight to the duke,
and told him that King Edward was dead, and that
Harold was raised to be king."   When the duke heard
this, "he became as a man enraged.   Oft did he tie his
mantle, and oft he untied it again.   He spoke to no
man, and no man dare speak to him.   Then he crossed
the river Seine in a boat, and came to his hall and
entered therein.   He sat down at the end of a bench,

[1] De Inventione Sanctæ Crucis.
[2] Flor. of Worcester.   [3] Wace.

shifting his place from time to time, covering his face with a mantle and resting his head against a pillar. Thus he remained long in deep thought; for no ono dare speak to him; but many asked aside, 'What ails the duke? why makes he such bad cheer?'"

William of Normandy made up his mind to invade England. He sent a special messenger to Pope Alexander III., who gave him his blessing, and also a standard[1] as an auspicious presentiment of the conquest of England. He afterwards summoned a council of his nobles in order to obtain their advice and help in his great undertaking. It is very probable that more than one meeting was summoned before the nobles of Normandy could be prevailed upon to help their duke in his designs against England. It appears that William was not present at the first meeting of his barons and retainers: on this occasion the debate lasted a long time, as the assembly could not come to a conclusion as to what answer they should give him; some complained of grievances, others said they feared the sea and were not obliged to serve beyond it, some expressed their willingness to supply ships and to cross the sea with their duke, others said they would not go as they were poor.[2] At another meeting William was present: several barons tried to persuade him not to invade England; they said that Harold had great riches with which he could gain over powerful kings to his cause, that his navy was large, and manned by experienced sailors, and that he had more soldiers than he had.[3] But tho Norman duke was not to be moved from his purpose; he dispelled the fears of his listeners by assuring them that they would soon be supplied with a navy, and by

William's preparations for the invasion of England

---

[1] Will. of Malmesbury.　　[2] Wace.　　[3] William of Poitiers.

William's
prepara-
tions for
the inva-
sion of
England.
reminding them of the good fortune and valour of the
Normans; and he excited their cupidity by promising
them the lands of the Saxons: after this speech they
were eager[1] for the expedition.[2]

The mouth of the river Dive,[1] in Normandy, was the
final place of meeting. The nobles were expected to
supply ships for the invasion of England, in proportion
to the extent[1] of their possessions. Odo, bishop of
Bayeaux, and Roger de Beaumont each furnished one
hundred vessels; Roger de Montgomery and William
Fitz Osbern each supplied sixty: while Walter Giffard
brought with him thirty vessels and one hundred armed
men.[3] The total number of ships were 700; in addition
to these there were about 2,300 skiffs and boats.[4]

Great numbers flocked to William's standard. Fifty
thousand soldiers were in his own pay.[5] An unfavour-
able wind detained them for a month; yet, through the
duke's foresight, all had sufficient to eat without
plundering.[5]

From the mouth of the Dive they proceeded to the

---

[1] Will. of Malmesbury.

[2] Henry of Huntingdon states that William Fitz Osbern, duke William's
steward, met the chief barons, who had been called together to consult
with the duke upon the conquest of England, as they were about to enter
the council room, and, pretending that he was against the undertaking on
the ground that the Saxons were a most warlike people, he succeeded in
securing their pledges that they would abide by his speech at the approaching consultation; upon which he presented himself at their head before the
duke, and assured him that both he and they were ready to follow him
with devotion in his proposed expedition.

Guy of Amiens writes that William, having assembled his barons together
told them that Harold had taken the crown of England, to which hi
relative Edward had made him heir, and that this Harold had perjured
himself as regards the oaths he had taken to him in Normandy: whereupon they advised him *with one voice* to take revenge upon Harold, and
to secure the crown of England by war, if it could not be got by any
other means.

[3] Guy of Amiens.   [4] Wace.   [5] William of Poitiers.

harbour of St. Valery.[1]   A storm destroyed some of the vessels; but the bodies of the drowned were buried privately, and the drooping spirits of the survivors were animated by the exhortations of the duke.[1]

While the Norman duke and his allies were busily engaged in the construction of the vessels which were to carry the invading army across the English Channel, Tosti, sailing from Flanders, landed in the Humber with sixty ships.   He was met and defeated by the Earls Edwin and Morcar.   This was the first of the four battles which were fought in England during the year 1066; it took place in the spring[2] of that year. In Scotland Tosti joined Harold[3] Hardrada,[4] King of Norway, whom he had persuaded to invade England with three[3] hundred ships.[2]

Harold was one of the most renowned warriors of his age, and his exploits were sung by minstrels in many lands, for he was well known in Sicily, Turkey, Palestine, and Russia: at Constantinople, where he served the emperor, he was condemned, for an act of lawlessness, to fight a lion without any weapon: he met the huge beast, and strangled it by the mere strength of his arms.[5]   Harold and Tosti attacked and defeated Edwin and Morcar at Fulford Bridge, near York, with great loss, this battle was fought on 20th September.[2]

Harold, the king, was upon the shores of the South of England when he heard of the landing of his namesake and his brother Tosti, and of their victory over his brothers-in-law.   And when he heard the news he started northwards "by day and by night."[3]   He took the foe unawares, and, having slain both Harold of

Tosti and
Harold of
Norway.

---

[1] William of Poitiers.   [2] Flor. of Worcester says 500 ships.
[3] Saxon Chronicle.   [4] Harold, the Fair Haired.   [5] Will. of Malmesbury

Norway and his brother Tosti, he gained the victory, and made a great slaughter of the men of Flanders[1] and **The Battle of Stamford.** of Norway at Stamford Bridge,[2] 25th September. This battle is distinguished for two things—(i.) the bravery of a Norwegian who stood upon the bridge that spanned the river and kept the whole Saxon army at bay: forty[3] of the bravest fell by his hand, and, while he was taunting the Saxons with cowardice, he was pierced from beneath the bridge and slain: (ii.) for Harold's kindness to Olave, the son of the Norwegian king, whom he sent back[4] to Norway with honours and in perfect safety. In return for this humane treatment, in after years Olave hospitably received his son Harold, and took him with him on an expedition against the Orkneys, and the islands of Man and Anglesey.[5]

At this critical juncture of events Harold was helped by his brother Gurth, "a youth on the verge of man- **Gurth, son of Godwin** hood, and possessed of knowledge and valour surpassing his years."[5]

The hearts of the two brothers, though grieved for the untimely end of the vainglorious Tosti, beat high with hope. Fortune seemed to smile upon all their efforts: their foes were crushed. They laughed at the long delayed threat of the Norman. But the same gloomy night that shrouded in darkness the hideous carnage at Stamford Bridge, separated the duke's ship Mona[6] from the rest of his fleet. According to one writer,[3] Harold was at the banquet, refreshing himself after the fatigues of the march and battle, when he

---

[1] *Saxon Chronicle.*   [2] Flor. of Worcester.   [3] Henry of Huntingdon.
[4] Florence of Worcester: Henry of Huntingdon states that Harold of England *burnt* the prisoners taken by him after the battle of Stamford Bridge.
[5] Will. of Malmesbury.   [6] Guy of Amiens.

heard of William's arrival upon the shores of England.
Another writer[1] states that he was on his way south
with the trophies of war when he was met by a Saxon,
who, having witnessed the arrival of the Normans, had
hastened on horseback to inform his king of their landing, and assured him that the Norman cavalry were as
many as the fish of the sea, and their forces as countless as the stars of heaven.

The Saxon ships, which numbered seven hundred,[2]
were not upon the southern shores to oppose the
duke's landing, for they had separated to procure
provisions, and the strong winds that had damaged
William's fleet prevented their return.   William's ship, The
the Mona, was distinguished by a crimson[3] sail: its fleet. Norman
prow was adorned with a brazen[4] child bearing an
arrow and a bended bow.   Each vessel was provided
with a light, as the days were short, and twilight was
approaching when the Norman fleet left the shores of
Normandy.   The duke placed a lantern upon the mast
of his ship, in order that the other ships might see it
and steer in its course ;[*] but during the night the Mona
outsailed the rest of the fleet, and, when the morning
broke, it was alone upon the waters of the English
channel.   What an opportunity was this for Harold's
fleet, had it not ceased to keep watch, to frustrate the
patiently executed and costly prepared plans of the
Normans with one blow !

Harold expressed his regret that he had not been at
Pevensey to repel the Norman: he declared that had
he been there he would have conquered William on
land, or driven him into the sea.   But he spent no time

[1] Guy of Amiens.
[2] William of Poitiers: Guy of Amiens said he had 500 ships.
[3] William of Malmesbury.   [4] Wace.

Harold hastens southwards. in vain regrets; he hastened southward with his mounted warriors and the most able of his now wearied troops. Only five days[1] separated the battles of Stamford Bridge and of Hastings. Gurth followed after, picking up stragglers, collecting fresh troops, and cheering the hearts of all with the prospects of another victory and great booty.

Council at London and Gurth's speech thereat. The final place of meeting was London.[2] There a council met in all haste. Gurth was the chief speaker. He showed at once that he possessed in an eminent degree the well-known eloquence of his father, and that like him he was also wise and prudent in council, and had great influence over his hearers. Wace gives a lengthy account of this council, and also of the battle that followed. Gurth thus addressed Harold:[3] "Fair brother, remain here, but give me your troops. I will take the adventure upon me, and will fight William. I have no covenant with him by oath or pledge. I am in no fealty to him, nor do I owe him my faith. It may chance that there will be no need to come to blows. But I fear if you fight you will pay the penalty of your perjury, seeing you must forswear yourself: and he who has the right will win. But if I am conquered, and taken prisoner, you, if God please, being alive, may still assemble your troops, and fight, or come to such an arrangement with the duke, that you may hold your kingdom in peace. Whilst I go and fight the Normans,

---

[1] *Saxon Chronicle.* Florence of Worcester states that the Battle of Stamford Bridge was fought on 25th September, and that of Hastings upon 22nd October; therefore, according to him, 27 days separated these battles.

[2] According to Guy of Amiens Harold held a meeting of his nobles at Stamford Bridge, when they all shouted, in reply to his speech, that they would "fight, or even die, rather than be subject to another king."

[3] Wace.

do you scour the country, burn the houses, destroy the villages, and carry off all stores and provisions, swine, goats, and cattle: that they may find no food, nor anything whatever to subsist upon. Thus you may alarm and drive them back, for the duke must return to his own country if provisions for his army shall fail him."[1] This sage advice shows that Gurth was perfectly collected at this critical period. It also exhibits his brotherly love and patriotism in the most brilliant colours, offering himself, as he thus did, as the victim of Divine vengeance for his brother's *seeming* sacrilege in violating his oath. Other chiefs, and also Gytha,[2] urged Harold to abide by the advice of Gurth, but he impetuously replied, "How[3] can I injure the people I should govern ? I cannot destroy or harass those who ought to prosper under me. Men will hold me a coward, and blame me for sending my best friends where I dare not go myself." No more was said between Harold and Gurth till the evening before the battle. They then rode out of their camp alone to view the Norman host.

The king felt alarmed at their formidable array, and timidly suggested that they should fall back upon London, but the earl rejected this untimely wavering with great scorn, and cried out fiercely, "Thou base coward! this council has come too late. It is of no use now to flinch, we must move onward. Base coward! When I advised you, and got the nobles also to beseech you, to remain at London and let me fight, you would

Gurth and Harold spy out the Norman forces.

[1] William of Malmesbury states that this speech was delivered by Gurth after the return of the spies whom Harold had sent to the camp of William. William of Poitiers gives an account of some Saxon spies who visited William's fleet before it started for England.

[2] Ordericus Vitalis.   [3] Wace.

not listen to us, and now you must take the consequence.
You would take no heed of anything we could say.
You believed not me or anyone else. Now you are
willing, but I will not. You have lost your pride too
soon. Quickly indeed has what you have seen abated
your courage. If you should turn back now, everyone
would say that you ran away. If men see you flee,
who is to keep your people together? And if they
once disperse, they will never be brought to assemble
together again." From words Gurth proceeded to
blows; he lifted his battle axe, but Harold spurred his
horse on, so that the blow missed its object, and struck
the horse behind the saddle, glancing along Harold's
shield. Thus Harold narrowly escaped being felled to
the ground. Leofwine, a mere stripling, was in despair
when he discovered their absence: he imagined they
had either been slain or betrayed.

In his grief he rushed forth out of the camp, crying
and shouting like a madman. We may easily picture
to ourselves his intense delight when he beheld his
brothers galloping amicably towards him and his
followers. All signs of their recent dispute had now
disappeared.

Messages between William and Harold. Several messages[1] had been exchanged between the
duke and Harold, and even during the 13th of October,
the day before the battle, William attempted in person
and by messenger to come to terms with the king.

---

[1] According to William of Malmesbury, the first messenger was sent by
the Norman duke to Harold shortly after the death of Edward the Confessor:
this messenger upbraided Harold for not keeping his oath; Harold is
reported to have replied that he was hasty in confirming to William the
kingdom of England without the *consent* and *demand* of the Witan and of
the people; and that a rash oath, taken under compulsion, ought not to
be kept.

His design was to cast the odium[1] of the coming contest on his rival, and to shake the confidence of the Saxons in their chief; but his attempts, whatever might have been their ultimate object, were frustrated by the daring eloquence and presence of mind of Gurth, who seemed at this stage of the proceedings to take the lead. He evidently dreaded Harold's rashness, a trait in his character which the writers favourable to him acknowledge and bewail; one[2] asserts that he was headstrong and too confident in his own valour. Therefore when William proposed a personal encounter between himself and Harold, and when he approached the position of the enemy to speak with the king, Gurth, dreading that Harold would accept the challenge, sprang upon his feet, and said to the messenger,[3] "Harold will not go. Tell your lord to send his messenger to us hither, and let us know what he will take, and what he will leave, or what other arrangement he is willing to make."[3] The duke then offered Harold Northumbria and whatever belonged to that kingdom beyond the Humber, and Gurth the lands of his father Godwin.

[1] It was to arouse the ill feeling and prejudice of the continent against Harold that the Bayeux Tapestry was designed and executed: there is little doubt that, while William was securing men and ships and the aid of the Pope, his wife Matilda and her ladies were engaged upon the Tapestry as far as it refers to Harold's supposed oath, and the other incidents connected with his supposed visit to Normandy. The Bayeux Tapestry is an historical representation of the Norman conquest: it contains 1,512 figures of men, horses, dogs, ships, trees, buildings, &c.; it is 227 feet long, and 20 inches broad. It represents fifty-eight distinct scenes, beginning with the figure of king Edward and finishing with the figures of the Saxons fleeing from the battle of Hastings: a Latin inscription of an explanatory character is fixed to each scene. The figures and letters are stitched in worsted.

[2] De Inventione Sanctæ Crucis.

[3] Wace: William of Malmesbury states that Harold, when challenged to meet William in single combat, replied, "God will decide between me and the duke."

These offers were indignantly refused. His messenger
then declared that all who accompanied or supported
Harold were excommunicated by the Pope and his
clergy.

This dreadful announcement had its desired effect:
the Saxons were much alarmed. But Gurth soon removed the feelings of dismay which were beginning to
damp the enthusiasm of his fellow-countrymen. He
said that, if they went beyond the Humber, William
would take the land from them too, and also that he
had already given away their lands to his followers.

The dauntless youth proceeded as follows:[1] "They
will chase you from your lands, and, still worse, will
kill you. They will pillage your vassals, and ruin your
sons and daughters. They do not come merely for
your goods, but utterly to ruin you and your heirs
Defend yourselves, then, and your children, and all that
belongs to you, while you may. My brother has never
given away, nor agreed to give away, the great fiefs,
the honours or lands of your ancestors: but earls have
remained earls, and nobles enjoyed their rights. The
sons have had their lands and fiefs after their father's
death; and you know this to be true which I tell you,
that peace was never disturbed. We may let things
remain thus if we will, and it is best for us so to
determine. But if you lose your houses, your manors,
and other possessions, where you have been nourished
all your lives, what will you become, and what will you
do? Into what land will you flee, and what will become of your kindred, your wives and children? Into
what country will they go begging, and where shall they
seek an abode? When they thus lose their own hon-

our, how shall they seek it of others?" In reply to this speech the Saxons cried out that the Normans had come on an evil day, and had embarked on a foolish matter, and then rushed off to make ready for to-morrow's fight, or the night's carousal.

The numbers of the contending forces have been vari- **Number ously estimated by the chroniclers. William and Harold of con- are said[1] to have had 60,000 troops each, but that the forces at Norman duke had more barons and better men than Hastings. the Saxon king;[1] the same writer states that Harold boasted he had 400,000 followers. Another writer states that William had 50,000 troops *in his own pay*,[2] and that Harold's army was a more numerous one. A Norman contemporary[3] says that Harold had 1,200,000 followers, and William 150,000. A Saxon contempo- rary[4] emphatically asserts that the Normans were *four times* more numerous than the Saxons. Other writers state that Harold fought with "a very small army,"[5] "before *all* his army had come up,"[6] "before a *third* of his army was in fighting order,"[7] and that he had "very few forces."[8]

Though his forces were fewer than those of his power- ful antagonist, Harold was so confident of victory that he sent a fleet of 700 vessels[9] to cut off the escape of the Normans by sea. He also determined to attack the enemy suddenly;[10] but he was unable to carry out his intentions.

[1] Wace.
[1] William of Poitiers: from the above assertion we should conclude that William had other forces in the pay of his barons.   [3] Guy of Amiens.
[4] De Inventione Sanctæ Crucis.   [6] Matt. of Westminster.
[4] *Saxon Chronicle*.   [7] Flor. of Worcester.   [8] Will. of Malmesbury.
[9] William of Poitiers; Wace gives the number as 500.
[10] De Inventione Sanctæ Crucis: William of Poitiers states that Harold in- tended to attack the Normans suddenly by night: Guy states that, instead of surprising the Normans, he was himself surprised: and the *Saxon Chronicle* has it that William came against Harold "*unawares*."

The night before the battle.   It has been stated that the Saxons passed the night before the battle of Hastings without sleep, and that they whiled away the time in singing and drinking; but that the Normans, religiously disposed, spent the whole night in confessing their sins, and that, in the early morning, they received the Sacrament.[1] On the day before the battle Harold retired to the abbey of Waltham: there he vowed a vow unto the Lord, and said that if victory attended his arms he would enrich the church and supply it with clerks to serve Him, and that he himself would serve his God; then, stretching himself upon the earth in the form of a cross, he prayed, lying on his face [2]

LEADING EVENTS.

The unanimous election of Harold, son of Godwin,
    to the throne of England ....
The Defeat of Tosti ....   } 1066 A.D.
The Battles of Fulford Bridge, and of Stamford Bridge
The Landing of William of Normandy ....

---

[1] Will. of Malmesbury.   [2] De Inventione Sanctæ Crucis.

CHAPTER XXIII.

THE BATTLE OF HASTINGS.

AT length the day—the fourteenth[1] of October, 1066— The Battle
on which the fate of England, and that of Europe, was of
to be decided, dawned. Hastings.

Before the battle began the hearts of the Saxons
beat quick in anticipation of victory and of immense
spoil: they recollected that their king had been successful in every undertaking, and that his head had planned
and his arm had accomplished the complete overthrow
of every foe—Celt, Norman, Norwegian, Fleming, and
traitorous Saxon. The Normans had also every confidence in the skill and daring of their duke; moreover,
his mother's dream,[2] the blessing of the Head of the
Church, omens,[2] and the appearance of a comet,[3] increased their confidence in him; and their enthusiasm
was aroused by the spirited address of their leader,
who said—"if I conquer, you will conquer; if I win
lands, you shall have lands:" he concluded with the
words—"strike hard at the beginning; stay not to take

[1] On the festival of St. Calixtus—Sanctæ Crucis, and Henry of Huntingdon, &c.; Wace states that this Battle was fought upon Harold's birthday,
the 1st of October—other days are mentioned by various writers.

[2] William of Malmesbury: at the duke's birth he grasped the rushes
that strewed his mother's chamber, whereupon the midwife declared the
boy would become a king; William fell, as he stepped upon the soil of
England, whereupon a soldier exclaimed, "My lord, you grasp England,
its future king;" when he was being armed for battle the hind part of his
hauberk was placed upon his breast, this incident was looked upon as a
sign that his "dukedom would be changed into a kingdom."

[3] *Saxon Chronicle:*

spoil, all booty shall be in common, and there will be plenty for everyone. There will be no safety in peace or flight: the English will neither love nor spare Normans; villians they were and are, false they were, and false they will be."[1] We are assured that the Duke's words so aroused his listeners that they rushed[2] upon the foe, and left him speaking to himself!

The last command given by Harold was that no one was to move from his post under any pretence or provocation whatsoever. The Saxons occupied a rising ground, and a valley separated them from the Norman camp. On all sides save one they were defended by barricades: a fosse guarded one side of their army. The Saxon army has been likened to a boar baited by dogs foaming at the mouth.[3]

The position of the Saxons.

The men of Kent were entitled, according to an ancient custom, to strike the first blow, and to compose the van; the men of London to guard the king's body, to place themselves around him, and to guard his Standard. All were on foot,[4] and carried themselves right boldly. Had they remained steady behind their barricades they would not have been conquered that day. From 9 a.m.[5] till 3 p.m. the majority obeyed the

---

[1] Wace.

[2] Henry of Huntingdon: this chronicler puts a very long speech into William's mouth, in which he alluded to that "most valiant of men, my predecessor, Hastings," to Rollo, to Richard II., to his own victories, to Harold's (supposed) perjury, to the death of Alfred the Atheling, and concluded thus—"Let the lightning of your glory flash, and the thunders of your charge be heard from east to west, and be ye the avengers of the noble blood which has been spilt!"

[3] Guy of Amiens.

[4] William of Malmesbury: Sir F. Palgrave placed Harold on horseback: Florence of Worcester says that the Saxons were *not* in the habit of fighting on horseback: William of Poitiers states that the Saxons left their horses *behind* them: and Guy says that they *despised* the use of cavalry.

[5] Wace.

earnest command of the king to fight at their posts; and to repel the oft repeated attacks of the Normans. In vain did their heavy armed knights rush up to the Saxon defences: they fell like corn before the glittering and ponderous battle-axes of the sturdy islanders: the horse and its rider fell crushed, once and for ever. Their arrows were received upon the shield. The Saxons fought in so close order that their dead bodies were left standing as though alive.[1] Three times[1] did the Normans retreat: on the first occasion they pretended to run away, in order to entice the Saxons from their vantage ground. This stratagem caused a body of the Saxons to pursue the foe, whereupon the Normans faced about and compelled them to fly; but the Saxons made a stand upon a rising ground, and hurling darts and rolling down stones upon their pursuers, they destroyed such as were beneath them to a man; they then made their way to the main body of their countrymen by means of a short cut, and thus they avoided a deep ditch; here they trod under foot such a number of their enemies that they made the hollow level with the plain with their dead bodies.[2] The Saxons now pressed the contest with greater alacrity, and thought nothing of those who were taken from them: whereupon the invaders began to flee in reality, and the pursuing Saxons shouted after them in derision—"Cowards, it is of little use to run back, unless you can cross the sea at a leap, or drink it dry."[3] The duke, when he saw the flight of his men, made great efforts to stop them. He asked them where they would flee to. He entreated them to stop, pointed out their difficulties, reminded them of their valour, and

Flight of the Normans.

[1] Guy of Amiens: William of Poitiers. [2] William of Malmesbury. [3] Wace.

called the English sheep:[1] at last he succeeded in inspiring his terror-stricken followers with confidence, and renewed the attack. The Norman arrows were now, at 3 p.m., ordered[2] to be shot into the air, so as to strike the enemies' heads and faces. This order won the day for the Normans, for up to that time the Saxons, covered with their shields and barricades, were able to wield their battle-axes and use their bills with irresistible force and murderous effect; but now, whilst repelling the direct attack, showers[3] of arrows fell upon their heads and faces, and put out the eyes of many, and all were afraid to open their eyes while their faces were unguarded : still, their hearts did not quail, for they struggled on under the inspiriting influence of their leaders.

Harold, Gurth, and Leofwine continued to fight on, side by side. The king made constant attacks upon the brave Normans; with one blow he cut[3] into two, or levelled[4] with the ground, both horse and rider. Anxiously he looked for the arrival of the earls, Edwin and Morcar, with their forces: had they arrived upon the battle-field at this juncture of events, most probably, with their aid, and the enthusiasm caused by their appearance, the Saxons would have utterly routed their foes; but it was not to be, as they tarried behind in London, and plotted for the crown.[5] It was now twilight,[6] and the approaching darkness was welcomed by the wearied Saxons. At this period of the day an arrow pierced the right eye of Harold. He broke its shaft

Non-arrival of Edwin and Morcar.

---

[1] Guy of Amiens : William of Poitiers.   [2] Wace : Henry of Huntingdon.
[3] William of Malmesbury.   [4] Matthew of Westminster.
[5] Will. of Malmesbury states that Edwin and Morcar, hearing in London of Harold's death, asked the citizens to make one of them king.
[6] Flor. of Worcester.

with his hands, and threw it away; the pain was so Harold's agony.
great that he leaned upon his shield.[1] He continued
to struggle on. No character in history comes before
us in such a striking manner as the tall and strong
Harold rushing upon the enemy with the cruel barb
just seen above his right eye, and blood and water
coursing down his cheek: verily he was a perfect
martyr for his country's liberties! Gurth's heart must
have bled in sympathy with his brother's bleeding eye
and ebbing strength. He now felt that he was the
leader of the nobles and peasants,[2] who continued firm
around him, as Leofwine was now dead—whilst in the
very act of dashing his terrible battle-axe against a
horseman he had been pierced through by the lance of
his assailant—and Harold was sinking fast.

Already the Conqueror had had two horses killed under him. The death of the second was speedily revenged,
as its slayer[3] was embowelled by the duke's weapon.

Another[4] false retreat was made with the same success as the previous one; the Normans wheeled round
upon their pursuers, surrounded them, and cut them
off to a man.[4] And now the duke determined to make
a desperate and final effort to crush that gallant band
that still fought on around the Dragon of Wessex—the
Standard[5] of the English king—which, glittering with
pearls, diamonds, and other precious stones, floated

---

[1] Wace: Bayeux Tapestry, plate XVI.

[2] In the Bayeux Tapestry they are called "peures" boys, and they are
described as armed with clubs, and other rude weapons.

[3] Guy of Amiens.   [4] William of Poitiers.

[5] According to Henry of Huntingdon, the Saxon standard was captured
about the time Harold's eye was pierced by the arrow; a band of twenty
knights pledged themselves to take it, the greater number of them were
killed, the rest hewed a way with their swords and took it; no doubt it
was seized by the Normans *after* the death of Gurth.

proudly and mockingly in the soft autumn breeze. Onward he rushed, attended by 1,000[1] chosen warriors.
His course was checked by a wrestler,[1] who wounded
him, but not severely; this obstacle soon lay shattered
among the dead and dying. Then William saw Harold[2]
slaying the Normans; and he called upon four Norman
knights, namely, the son of Guy of Ponthieu, Eustace
of Boulogne, Gillard, and Montford, to make a determined and simultaneous attack upon the dying hero.

The one pierced his shield and breast, the other struck
off his head, the third laid bare his body and scattered
his bowels along the gory soil, the fourth gashed his
thigh.

Thus fell—"The glory of his kingdom, the honour
of his church, the fortitude of the soldiers, the buckler
of the unarmed, the strength of the warriors, the
protection of the weak, the consolation of the desolate,
the restorer of the poor, the pride of the nobles."[3]

The battle was not over, as Gurth still lived, and so
long as he lived the Normans could not claim the
victory.

The earl of Sussex determined to aim at no common
foe, but to direct his remaining strength against the
chief cause of all that havoc. He therefore took a
javelin, and hurled it with all his might against
William. It was a critical moment: the duke was
saved by his steed,[2] into whose body the terrible javelin
had entered: this was the third[1] horse he had lost that
day. And now the only surviving member of the
Godwin family "saw[1] the English falling around him,
and there was no remedy. He saw his race hastening

[1] Wace.   [2] Guy of Amiens.   [3] Sanctæ Crucis.
[4] William of Poitiers; Will. of Malmesbury.

to ruin, and despaired of any aid. He would have fled, but could not, for the throng continually increased. And the duke pushed on till he reached him, and struck him with great force: it is said that he fell under that blow, and rose no more." From one source[1] we learn that William followed Gurth like a raging lion, and that he hacked him limb from limb, saying that he gave him the *crown that he deserved.*

Gurth well knew the value of his life, and how much depended upon his individual exertions; hence, after he had done all that mortal man could do, he endeavoured to escape in order that he might raise another army. William also fully comprehended the importance attached to Gurth's life, for he knew that if he succeeded in escaping from the battle-field he would have to oppose one as brave as Harold, and his superior in cool determination. With Gurth at their head the Saxons would have rallied, the subtle traitors, Edwin and Morcar, would have been over-awed, and the risings in the west, east, and north would have resulted in the overthrow of the Normans, and in the continuation of the dynasty of the House of Godwin.

Explanation of Gurth's conduct.

Even after the death of Gurth, the Saxon nobles disdained to flee;[2] they continued to fight on, and some of them died from sheer exhaustion:[2] they were all,[3] or nearly[4] all, killed in that terrible battle. The ordinary[2] soldiers and the light armed[1] fled, some on foot and some on the horses which had carried the fallen leaders[5] to battle. The Normans, although ignorant of the country, eagerly pursued the fugitives: even the hoofs of their horses lacerated the dead bodies

Flight of the Saxons.

Guy of Amiens. [2] Matt. of Westminster. [3] Ingulphus. [4] Florence of Worcester [5] William of Poitiers.

P

as they scoured over the top of the slain. The Saxons
in their flight, came to a steep ravine: here they made
a stand and killed several Norman nobles, and compelled Eustace of Boulogne and fifty knights to retreat.[1]
But the Norman duke, although he thought that the
foe had been reinforced, neither stopped nor altered
his course: he checked the flight of Eustace and his
followers. The count advised him to go back, saying
that if he advanced he would be killed. While Eustace
was speaking he received a dreadful blow from an
unknown hand, and was carried away in a half-dead
state by his attendants. William, despising fear and
dreading disgrace, continued to advance, and trampled

The
Normans
pursue
the
Saxons.

all who resisted him under foot. Having overcome all
resistance he returned to the battle-field, where he found
such slaughter that even his iron heart was touched
with pity[1] when he looked upon the dead and dying.
Far and near the flower of the Saxon nobility and
youth strewed the ground[1]; and on every hand nothing
was to be seen but the red hue of blood.[2] The Normans
held "the place of carnage,"[3] and all that night they
watched upon the hill top.[4] William pitched his tent
and fixed the Pope's banner upon the spot where
Harold's Standard had stood; and there he ate his
supper and passed the night.

The
number
of the
slain at
Hastings

It is not known how many Saxons fell at the battle
of Hastings: but it is stated that the Norman duke, at
the lowest computation, lost more than 10,000 men.[3]
After the battle the Conqueror buried the bodies of his
own men, but the bodies of the Saxons were left unburied, to be eaten by worms and wolves.[4] The body

---

[1] William of Poitiers.   [2] The Chronicle of Battle Abbey.
[3] *Saxon Chronicle.*   [4] Guy of Amiens.

of Harold was recognised by certain marks upon it,[1] and was placed in a purple cloth.[2] Ten marks of gold,[3] or its weight in gold,[4] were offered for it, and refused.[3]

William the Conqueror refused[1] Gytha[5] the melancholy satisfaction of burying the mangled remains of her three sons; so that even in death he was jealous of those who so manfully opposed him while living. It is generally believed that Harold was buried in mockery[4] upon the sea shore.[6] William's treatment of the Godwin family deserves every censure. We are informed[7] that he was at all times a very stern and wrathful man, and that whoever thwarted his will he deprived of life. Harold had, no doubt, excited his envy by his martial successes, and had, without doubt, aroused his hate and cupidity by his unanimous election to the throne of England—hence his conduct towards him and his.

Burial of Harold.

When oppressed by the tyrant Norman lords, the Saxons patiently and with child-like faith awaited the re-appearance of their darling, who for fourteen years had successfully maintained against all foes the honour and the rights of his countrymen, but they waited in vain: neither the recluse of Salop nor the hermit of

The supposed escape of Harold,

---

[1] William of Poitiers: the writer of the discovery of the Holy Cross states that Harold's body was discovered by Edith, "the Swan's neck."

[2] Guy of Amiens.

[3] De Inventione Sanctæ Crucis: this writer states that William gave up Harold's body to the monks of Waltham.

[4] William of Poitiers.

[5] Mr. Freeman, in his magnificent History of the Norman Conquest, gives an eloquent and pathetic account of Gytha.

[6] William of Poitiers; Benoit; Guy of Amiens; Ordericus Vitalis. According to the writer of De Inventione Sanctæ Crucis, William of Malmesbury, and Wace, he was buried at Waltham Abbey.

[7] *Saxon Chronicle.*

and of

Chester could be identified[1] with the martyred Harold the Second—the first king of his line, and the last of his race.

Gurth.

Gurth, too—like Richard II. from Pomfret, like the young Duke of York from the murderous clutches of his tyrant uncle, like Lovel from the spies of Bacon's model king,[2] like James IV. after Flodden Field—was fondly supposed to have escaped from the carnage at Sanquelac—the Lake of Blood.

LEADING EVENTS.

The Battle of Hastings—the Position of the Saxon Forces; the Flight and feigned Retreats of the Normans; the Death of Leofwine, Harold, and Gurth; the complete Overthrow of the Saxons; the Normans sleep upon "the place of carnage." } 1066 A.D.

[1] Giraldus Cambrensis mentions Harold's escape from battle; and the author of Vita Haroldi appears to be convinced of his escape.
[2] Henry VII.

THE END.

INDEX.

INDEX.

GEORGE PHILIP AND SON, PRINTERS, LIVERPOOL.

THE OPINIONS OF THE PRESS

ON

A HISTORY OF ENGLAND AND WALES,

FROM THE ROMAN TO THE NORMAN CONQUEST.

By T. MORGAN OWEN, M.A.,
ONE OF H.M. INSPECTORS OF SCHOOLS.

"This is a period about which more should be popularly known, and this volume should meet with a hearty welcome. When treating of the early history of England, the Welsh—the pure descendants of the Celts that opposed the Romans—have been slightingly by other writers passed over. This was a mistake, for the Welsh played an important part in many a trying period of history. Mr. Morgan Owen, a Welshman and a scholar, devotes much time to show how his countrymen were connected with events that happened out of their own territory. Not the least successful of Mr. Owen's investigations is his examination of historic myths. The lives of eminent men—as Hastings, Dunstan, Edgar, Canute, Edric, Edward the Confessor, and Harold—are concisely yet strikingly depicted.

"The relation of events one to the other is clearly traced. The history is not one of disjointed parts, but of a symmetrical whole. One occurrence overlaps another, and the flood of time is nevertheless shown to be one, and the way it glides along, carrying all, high and low, with its waters, is vividly pointed out. To the modern Celt and Saxon the book may be cordially commended as a readable and instructive account of England and Wales before the arrival of the iron-heeled Norman."—*The Liverpool Daily Courier, 30th May,* 1882.

"A 'History of England and Wales,' from the Roman to the Norman Conquest, the work of Mr. Morgan Owen, follows with accuracy the accounts handed down to us from the original authorities. In nearly every incident which might form the subject of controversy, or which is differently given by other historians, the source from which the author derives his information is added in a note: useful genealogical tables are also given."—*Daily Telegraph, 8th June,* 1882.

"Historiography has become a science. There has been much blundering and devising of untruths amongst the old illiterate historians, who subsisted ' on their own resources.' But by this time a real scholar who understands the profession is demanded. By-the-bye, the author of this book is a scholar. He knows many languages, and how far in this direction and in that direction it is possible to tread with safety. He recognizes his men. With certain reservations, he is ready to follow the *Saxon Chronicle*; to tread in the footsteps of William of Malmesbury ; and to walk step by step with our old friend Owen Williams of Waenfawr, in the peregrinations of the ancient Cymry.

"We hail Mr. Morgan Owen's *History of England and Wales* with delight for many reasons : amongst others, because he does not show partiality towards one nation more than another, and because he has written a cheap popular book of very charming reading. It consists of twenty-three chapters, beginning with the landing of Cæsar, in the year B.C. 55, and terminating with the Battle of Hastings in 1066. During this extended period—over eleven hundred years—many stirring events took place which it would be well that all our readers should become conversant with ; and we know of no better opportunity of becoming acquainted with these facts than by studying this work of Mr. Morgan Owen. It contains also eight Genealogical Tables, which, we are confident, will be valuable to many. The library of no Welshman who understands English will be complete without this volume. We wish every success to the work amongst Welshmen and Englishmen."—*Baner ac Amserau Cymru*, 26th April, 1882.

"This volume bears evidence of striving after a simplicity of language, so as to be comprehended by the young, and by Welshmen endeavouring to master the English tongue.

"But while Mr. Morgan Owen strives after simplicity, he never degenerates into a puerile style. The language of the book is characterised by short and strong sentences.

"The glory of the historian is to seek after the truth diligently, and to be sufficiently unbiased to publish it freely when found : in this Mr. Morgan Owen far excels. He brings in much of the history of the Celts or Welsh—and gives them perfect justice. Yet, while he brings out the best characteristics, and chronicles the doughty deeds of his nation, he never allows his feelings to have the better of his judgment, and so lead him to make unwarrantable assertions on their behalf.

" Again, the same even-handed justice is dealt out to the English race. Their valiant deeds are recorded, and justice is done to their character. The history is free from beginning to end of *false* colouring, and, in our opinion, of *over* colouring also.

" The contents of this volume will incline the reader to be proud of the Briton race, in its Celtic root, and in the grafting upon it the Saxon tribes. The history makes the Welshman a better Welshman, and the Englishman a better Englishman, and leads them to magnify each other.

" The author pays special attention to some of the leading events of this long, dark, and stormy period. On these occasions he enters into details—he gives a microscopic view of the events : giving the reader an opportunity, in mind and thought, to approach the different parties, and to get a firm grasp of the leading thread of the history. This adds much to the worth of the book.

" We can but give this volume a hearty welcome, as a text-book which greatly increases our knowledge of the early history of our island, which, though written with an unbiased mind, yet breathes a national and nation-loving spirit on the part of the author."—*Gwalia, 19th of April,* 1882.

Other Newspapers and Periodicals express similar views concerning this History, and commend its suitability for Colleges, Schools, and Libraries.

www.ingramcontent.com/pod-product-compliance
Lightning Source LLC
Chambersburg PA
CBHW031347020726
47499CB00005B/1431